D0481280

JACQUELINE KENNEDY

MODERN FIRST LADIES

Lewis L. Gould, Editor

JACQUELINE KENNEDY

FIRST LADY OF THE NEW FRONTIER

BARBARA A. PERRY

UNIVERSITY PRESS OF KANSAS

Song lyrics on p. 128 are from "Mona Lisa," lyrics by Jay Livingston, music by Ray Evans, Famous Music Corp., ASCAP.

© 2004 by the University Press of Kansas
All rights reserved
Published by the University Press of Kansas
(Lawrence, Kansas 66049), which was organized by
the Kansas Board of Regents and is operated and
funded by Emporia State University, Fort Hays State
University, Kansas State University, Pittsburg State
University, the University of Kansas, and Wichita
State University
Library of Congress Cataloging-in-Publication Data
Perry, Barbara A. (Barbara Ann), 1956–
Jacqueline Kennedy, first lady of the
New Frontier / Barbara A. Perry.
p. cm. — (Modern first ladies)
Includes bibliographical references (p.   ) and index.
ISBN 978-0-7006-1343-4 (cloth : alk. paper)
1. Onassis, Jacqueline Kennedy, 1929–.   2. Onassis,
Jacqueline Kennedy, 1929– —Influence.   3. Onassis,
Jacqueline Kennedy, 1929– —Public opinion.
4. Presidents' spouses—United States—Biography.
5. Presidents' spouses—United States—Political activity.
6. Popular culture—United States—History—20th
century.   7. Public opinion—United States—History—
20th century.   8. Mass media—Political aspects
—United States—History—20th century.
I. Title.   II. Series.
E843.K4P47 2004
973.922'092—dc22   2004006224
British Library Cataloguing-in-Publication Data
is available.
Printed in the United States of America
10 9 8 7 6 5 4 3
The paper used in this publication is recycled and contains
30 percent postconsumer waste. It is acid free and meets the
minimum requirements of the American National Standard for
Permanence of Paper for Printed Library Materials z39.48-1992.

To my parents,
Lillian and Louis Perry

CONTENTS

In the 1960s Jacqueline Kennedy established herself as the most glamorous and magnetic of all twentieth-century first ladies. That reputation remained intact through her death in 1994 and has continued to the present. Because of the aura of celebrity that surrounded her and the Kennedy family, her historical impact on the institution of the first lady has not received thoughtful and analytic treatment. The many biographies about her have been sensational and in some cases lurid. They have been less strong on the social and cultural background of the years in which Mrs. Kennedy grew to maturity and became the charismatic first lady of the early 1960s. Legend and gossip have been the prevailing modes of explaining why Mrs. Kennedy had such an effect on the popular imagination for the three years of her husband's presidency. Yet understanding the effect of Jacqueline Kennedy on what it means to be the wife of a president has been an urgent task for the emerging field of first ladies studies.

Barbara Perry has now written an engaging and intelligent, yet serious, examination of Jacqueline Kennedy in the White House. While admiring her subject's positive contributions to the White House and its history, Perry is also clear-eyed about Mrs. Kennedy's shortcomings. The result is a persuasive narrative of how Jacqueline Bouvier grew into the wife of John Kennedy, the assumptions she brought to the role of first lady, and the ways in which she tried to implement her vision of the proper behavior for the wife of a president. Perry has fresh and insightful ideas about why Jacqueline Kennedy captivated the American public and infused glamour into the way the presidency functioned. Her narrative blends revealing details with a mastery of the available primary sources on Mrs. Kennedy's historical importance.

Perry's fascinating book exemplifies the intentions and purposes of the Modern First Ladies series. These volumes are designed to provide accessible accounts of the way that each wife of the president has since 1900 contributed to the evolution of an American institution. Grounded in manuscript sources and the scholarly literature on each of these women, the books are intended to synthesize what is known about how each first lady performed and also to place them in the context of the women who preceded and followed them. By providing reliable, well-documented accounts of each of the eighteen presidential wives of the twentieth century, the series will enable the general reader as well as the scholarly researcher to reach conclusions about this institution from a firm factual and interpretive basis. In the second book of the series, Barbara Perry has set a high standard of excellence in her treatment of Jacqueline Kennedy. Readers will discover a complex, enigmatic woman who was far more than the stereotypes of her fame and the sum of the rumors about her life and times. Out of Perry's deft narrative appears a Jacqueline Kennedy who struggled to preserve her own identity amid the cross-pressures of an institution she changed forever.

PREFACE

My introduction to the Kennedy mystique occurred at the tender age of four. On October 5, 1960, my mother loaded me, my two brothers, and several friends into our '56 Chevy for a trip to downtown Louisville. The occasion was a personal appearance by Senator John F. Kennedy at a political rally for his presidential candidacy. Mother abhors crowds, urban traffic jams, and raucous grassroots politics. What possessed her to brave all three to take a carful of kids to a boisterous political event? The answer is simple. In the young, handsome, Catholic senator from Massachusetts, she had found a political hero. She made sure that we arrived early to stake out a spot directly in front of the podium where JFK spoke. My older brother shook hands with the future president and snagged a Kennedy poster for his scrapbook. Alas, not recognizing what the experience would mean to my future career as a political scientist, I can only dimly recall the occasion. At age four, I was too short to touch the candidate's hand as he reached out from the platform above us; but I was too old to be lifted up for a traditional "baby-kissing" political moment—not that the urbane Kennedy was prone to such displays. Mostly I remember that Mother lost an earring, which we subsequently found in a pile of confetti, slightly bent from the throng's footsteps.

Sadly, my next recollection of President Kennedy was his assassination. After the initial frantic bulletins from Dallas, my second-grade class, along with the rest of St. Albert the Great School, were led into church to recite the rosary. Our assistant pastor told us that the president had been wounded while riding in a motorcade, but Mrs. Kennedy was uninjured. Thus, my first memory of this book's subject is a painful one. I learned more about the widowed first lady when Mother bought me a children's book on John F. Kennedy shortly after his death. It was the beginning of a personal library about him and his family, a lifelong fascination with their stories, and a professional career that facilitated my scholarly interest in their contribution to American politics.

Several years ago my Sweet Briar College colleague, Steve Bragaw, asked me, "Now that you've written several books on the Supreme Court, what is your next project? What would you write about if you could choose any subject?" I knew him well enough to confess my desire to produce a book on some aspect of the Kennedy presidency. When the University Press of Kansas, a publisher I much admire for their work in history and political science, announced a new series on modern first ladies, I thought my opportunity to fulfill that wish might come true. I contacted the University Press of Kansas, which suggested I write to the series' outside editor, Professor Lewis Gould at the University of Texas. Familiar with his definitive work on Lady Bird Johnson and his reputation as a superb historian, I was naturally concerned about whether, as a political scientist with an expertise in constitutional law, I could make the grade in a new field. From the moment I contacted him, Lew Gould has been a supportive, encouraging, informative, and diplomatic guide for this project. He suggested that I submit a proposal for the volume on Jacqueline Kennedy, offered constructive criticism, shepherded me through the outside review process, shared extensive archival material from his own files, and provided timely and productive critiques of each chapter. Three years do not a historian make, but my association with Professor Gould has helped me to adapt my social science research skills to the requirements of a study that is part biography and part political history. Any shortcomings that remain in the final product are mine alone and constitute my "cross to bear," as they taught us at St. Albert the Great.

The University Press of Kansas series' goal is not to provide comprehensive biographies of modern first ladies, but rather to create studies that place their White House tenures within the context of their lives, their husbands' presidencies, and their historical eras. The handicaps in writing about Jacqueline Kennedy, however, are numerous. In light of the fact that her papers and oral history at the John F. Kennedy Library in Boston remain closed, what can one possibly say about her that has not already been written in the myriad volumes about her life? My mission was to write the first scholarly treatment of her work as first lady and filter out the extremes of previous books that range from hagiographic tributes to mean-spirited or sensationalized accounts.

Jackie Kennedy was not the first celebrity first lady. Yet her creative use of public imagery, which captured both the glamor and tragedy of the Kennedy presidency, made her an icon—one that shaped and reflected the intriguing decade of the 1960s. In addition to providing a brief biography of Jacqueline Bouvier's early life, this book focuses on her initial training in, and exposure to, the arts and culture and their impact on her future as first lady. For her White House tenure, I studied as much original material (letters, memos, interviews, schedules, oral histories, government documents, photographs, videos, and fashions) as possible and then supplemented it with secondary information when necessary. Because of her staunch devotion to privacy, and her decision to shun most interviews and a personal memoir, Jacqueline Kennedy remains an enigma. I do not pretend to have solved the riddles of her personality or her troublesome first marriage, although the book traces her political partnership with the president. Here again I credit Steve Bragaw with helping me to discover a more beneficial approach to the study. I had already evaluated another enigmatic element of American politics, the U.S. Supreme Court, not by writing an inside story of the tribunal (despite my year spent working there in 1994–95 as a judicial fellow in the Office of the Administrative Assistant to the Chief Justice), but by analyzing its image in the American mind as determined by how the court presents itself to the public, how the media cover it, and how the public responds to it. Steve suggested that Jacqueline Kennedy's first ladyship was as symbol-laden as the high court. Why not study the symbols and images she used to portray herself and her husband's presidency, and how the American people, a worldwide audience, and the media responded to them?

The book's core, therefore, examines how Mrs. Kennedy created emblems around her fashions, White House restoration, and association with the arts and culture. So much of what has been published on Jacqueline Kennedy relies on hearsay and warmed-over gossip. I specifically tried to avoid simply repeating subjective interpretations by Kennedy critics, as well as friends, relations, and associates. Instead, I focused on a systematic study of original archives, particularly Mrs. Kennedy's own words contained in correspondence with friends and professional associates. This book reexamines long-accepted generalizations (both positive and negative) about her work and life as first lady—namely, that Jackie redecorated the White House, supported the arts, and focused on her maternal duties while being an elitist fashion plate who was only a part-time White House resident and shirker of first lady duties, but who ultimately became a courageous widow.

By piecing together the historical record as it currently exists, the book delineates, in a more nuanced manner, exactly what she did as first lady and places her efforts in historical, political, and sociological contexts. She was one of a long series of White House residents who redecorated their new home. Her unique contributions to the enterprise were her meticulous attention to history and the decorative arts, her careful editing of a popular guidebook on the Executive Mansion, the establishment of the White House Historical Association and sources of funding for it, her supervisory skills in delegating duties to experts, and her use of television and state entertainment to disseminate her work to a worldwide audience, including those behind the Iron Curtain.

Jacqueline Kennedy's support of the arts was multifaceted and varied in its level of engagement. By offering the White House as a sparkling stage for the performing and fine arts and the humanities, she bolstered the artistic community's morale and President Kennedy's Cold War efforts to portray the United States as the epitome of a free society and its artistic achievements. From facilitating the Mona Lisa's loan, to her mutually admiring relationship with France's Minister of Culture André Malraux, to her persistent championing of Lafayette Square's preservation, to lending her name (if not excessive amounts of time) to fund raising for the National Cultural Center, she had a measurable impact on the artistic life of the nation. Washington's heightened cultural awareness culminated in Congressional establishment of the National Endowments for the Arts and the Humanities in 1965 as part of President Lyndon Johnson's Great Society program. Although occasional political lightening rods, they still exist as mainstays of artistic and humanistic support in the United States. Replicating their missions at the grassroots level are arts and humanities councils throughout the fifty states.

As first lady, Jackie also honed her fashion sense. Oleg Cassini, with his European pedigree and Hollywood credentials, was the perfect designer for the image-conscious president's wife. By his own admission, he created costumes for his client's starring roles on the world stage. Fresh and compelling, her clothes were an integral part of the symbolism and imagery she created for herself and her husband's administration. Her modern, sleek, stunning formal wear coordinated perfectly with her dazzling state entertaining in Washington and her goodwill visits abroad. Fashionable outfits, topped by glamorous hairdos and accessories, were in stark contrast to the drab appearances of communist leaders and their spouses.

Mrs. Kennedy and JFK often cited family obligations, especially their two young children and her problematic pregnancies, as reasons for her limited public engagements. Although the media were mesmerized by the photogenic first family, they occasionally criticized Jackie for her long vacations in New England and abroad (the latter usually without her husband and children), absences from the White House while at her home in the Virginia countryside, missteps in redecorating the Executive Mansion, and upper-class indulgences like foxhunting and shopping sprees. In general, though, the media were her best allies, fawningly reporting her activities in glossy color periodicals (from *Life* to Hollywood movie magazines), newsreels, and daily newspapers and on television. Mrs. Kennedy's reluctant hiring of a press aide, who operated to the first lady's exact specifications, was a boon to her media coverage. She doggedly controlled her exposure, and that of her children, to the media. Her selection of Letitia ("Tish") Baldrige as chief of staff and social secretary was fortuitous. As a former aide to American Ambassadors David Bruce in Paris and Clare Booth Luce in Rome, Baldrige had an unsurpassed talent for creating nearly picture-perfect public presentations. Jacqueline Kennedy's effective use of modern media imagery produced a template that subsequent first ladies could apply to their own agendas.

In addition to Lew Gould's informed editing of this project, many other friends, family, and colleagues contributed to the endeavor. As already noted, Steve Bragaw was a crucial inspiration for the book's early stages and served as a respected sounding board during the drafting process. My longtime mentor, Henry Abraham, was always prepared to bolster flagging spirits with his eternal optimism, lend an ear to my endless supply of Kennedy anecdotes, and correct stylistic barbarisms. Two research assistants, Jill Abraham and Jennifer Taylor, gathered essential materials. Friends Diana Hess, Rose Capon, Julia McDonough, Sarah Wilson, Mildred Abraham, and Tom and Jane Yarborough provided insightful advice on how to approach the subject. Betty Schulten supplied a stream of clippings on Jackie Kennedy and maintained a most welcome interest in the project, as did Betty Beckman and Jean Wieck. Doug and Gayl Perry (along with Abby and Bruno) offered respite from my Kennedy Library labors in their beautiful Marblehead home. James Giglio and an anonymous reviewer for UPK wrote useful critiques of the proposal; the former did the same for a draft of the manuscript. Sweet Briar's Dean Stephen Stahl, now dean at St. Bonaventure, could not have been more supportive in approving my sabbatical and guiding my applications for grants. The Sweet Briar College Faculty Grants Committee, led by its chairs Brent Shea and Rob Granger, and the Virginia Foundation for Independent Colleges provided financial assistance through research funding. In addition, the Newman family's generous Kenmore grant enabled me to work through the summer to conduct research and begin drafting the book. The John F. Kennedy Library's Research Archivist Stephen Plotkin assisted me in accessing the archival holdings pertinent to this study, and Sweet Briar librarian, Lisa Johnston, assisted by Thelma Jordan, acquired oral histories for me through interlibrary loan. Rosemary Switzer, special collections assistant at Princeton University's Seeley G. Mudd Manuscript Library, responded expeditiously to my request for photocopies of the Jacqueline Kennedy correspondence file in Adlai Stevenson's papers. The Library of Congress staff in the Prints and Photographs Division and in the Photoduplication Department could not have been more accommodating, as was the Kennedy Library's photo archivist, James Hill, who expertly provided the book's pictures. I also had the pleasure of talking to Tish Baldrige and Jack Warnecke, two close associates of Mrs. Kennedy. The summer 2002 exhibit on Jacqueline Kennedy at Washington's Corcoran Gallery and the simultaneous D.C. program on her were a boon to the finished product. I send my heartfelt thanks to each of these actors in my book drama.

An author could not ask for a more conscientious, gracious, or encouraging editor than Fred Woodward, director of the University Press of Kansas. He and Susan Schott, the press's assistant director and marketing manager, are the most professional, efficient, and humane members of the publishing world that I have had the good fortune to encounter. Production editor Larisa Martin is equally proficient.

This book is dedicated to two individuals who always make innumerable contributions to the successful completion of all my work, Louis and Lillian Perry, my beloved parents and genuine profiles in courage.

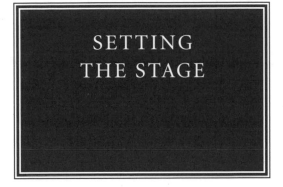

CHAPTER 1

SETTING
THE STAGE

"I want you to know that the nation will also be forever grateful for your service as First Lady. You brought to the White House charm, beauty and elegance as the official hostess of America, and the mystique of the young in heart, which was uniquely yours, made an indelible impression on the American consciousness."[1] Richard Nixon penned that tribute to Jacqueline Kennedy in a condolence note sent to her after John F. Kennedy's assassination. How unlikely that Nixon, such a socially awkward politician and her husband's bitter rival in the 1960 presidential election, should have captured so accurately, compassionately, and succinctly the essence of Mrs. Kennedy's thousand-day tenure as first lady. Indeed, she created an image of herself, her husband, and the office he served that fired the American imagination and that of admirers around the world.

One of those captivated by Jackie Kennedy's image recently recalled seeing the first lady on the world stage during her first year in the White House: "She was beautiful. Her skin was like Queen Elizabeth's. As First Lady she increased our awareness of art and culture. She and President Kennedy gave us such hope, and it was dashed when he died so tragically." The words poured from a woman I had only just met when we were seated together at a formal dinner in Washington, D.C. She had mentioned to me that her husband, a foreign service officer, was stationed in Vienna in 1961. I inquired whether she was there when the Kennedys visited the Austrian capital for the summit with Khrushchev in June of that year. My dinner partner, a contemporary of Jacqueline Kennedy, remembered the occasion as if it had just occurred. "We were in [Vienna's] St. Stephen's Cathedral to attend mass with the Kennedys," she related. "When they arrived, the congregation seemed to want to applaud, but that simply was not done in church in those days, so the Viennese took out their white handkerchiefs and waved them at the Kennedys as they walked up the aisle to their seats near the altar. It was very moving to witness this silent tribute to them."[2]

What was it about Jacqueline Kennedy that prompted these demonstrations of affection during her years as first lady—an affection that still stirs the hearts of her admirers to remember her with undiminished fondness forty years later? She was not the first first lady to capture the American imagination with stunning White House entertainment and public displays of courage. Dolley Madison was the paradigmatic presidential hostess for widowed Thomas Jefferson (1801–9) and for her husband James (1809–17). Her narrow escape from the advancing British army in 1814, and her safeguarding from the foreign marauders the massive George Washington portrait by Gilbert Stuart, are legendary. Nor was Jacqueline Kennedy the first presidential spouse to earn acclaim, and occasional criticism, for her tasteful, yet expensive, fashions. Mary Todd Lincoln's stylish wardrobe was a source of journalistic gossip, and her extravagant tastes in clothes and White House furnishings (particularly in light of national sacrifices during the Civil War) embarrassed her frugal husband. Mrs. Kennedy's White House redecoration was part of a continuing tradition of first families recreating their personal and professional spaces in the Executive Mansion. At the start of the twentieth century, Edith Roosevelt had assisted her husband Theodore in supervising a complete refurbishment of the White House and construction of its West Wing. Her successors, Grace Coolidge, Lou Henry Hoover, and Eleanor Roosevelt, all contributed to updating and documenting the White House's interiors. The Trumans guided a complete overhaul of the mansion's infrastructure and decor. Using the White House to spotlight the performing arts was another precedent traceable to Mrs. Kennedy's predecessors, especially both Roosevelt administrations. Public fascination with children of the first couple was not a new phenomenon either. Teddy Roosevelt's boisterous brood attracted the intrusive public eye, which Mrs. Kennedy would later revile for its imposition on her and her young children's lives. Previous first ladies also had been celebrated for their beauty and style. Grace Coolidge's flair for fashion and popular music was appropriate for the Jazz Age White House, although her dour husband limited her public appearances.[3]

If Jacqueline Kennedy shared numerous characteristics and conventions with her predecessors in the office of first lady, why does she seem unique? Presidential biographer Doris Kearns Goodwin has supplied a partial answer in observing that "culturally something happened between [Mrs. Kennedy] and the decade [1960s] she lived in and that is what is really interesting to try and figure out." She was more than a celebrity, not simply "a person who is known for [her] well-knownness." Unquestionably, Jackie Kennedy became a 1960s icon, a legendary figure who attracted uncritical devotion from her admirers.[4] From her emblematic pop art image, via Andy Warhol, to her creation of the "Jackie look" through her clothing, hairstyles, and accessories, to her indelible mark on history's photo album, she embodies a fascinating era, one punctuated by soaring promise and abysmal tragedy. Iconic individuals seem to fulfill the needs of, and/or epitomize, a historic period. They both reflect their era and create the lens through which we see it. Icons often suit an age's new media technology and know how to use it to their advantage.

Entertainment icons are prime examples. Who can imagine the 1950s without Elvis? His music blended soulful blues and spiritual tunes of the black South with white gospel, country, and bluegrass standards at the same moment that the nascent civil rights movement joined the races in a common social cause. The King's rockabilly rhythms, which formed part of the new world of rock and roll, initially appealed to American teens, and he captivated them at a time when a rebellious youth culture asserted itself through new prosperity and consumerism. By 1956 the U.S. population contained 13 million teenagers, who had a total income of $7 billion a year, an average of $10.55 a week for each teen. Adolescents had disposable income (unlike their parents' Depression generation) and eagerly spent it on record players, 45 rpm disks to spin on them, and new transistor radios. No longer were kids confined to parents' tastes in music. Adults were appalled at the swivel-hipped, pelvis-gyrating phenomenon from Memphis, which made him all the more attractive to his young fans. The new medium of television, with hit variety shows hosted by Steve Allen and Ed Sullivan, trans-mitted Presley directly into American living rooms, to the delight of youngsters and the dismay of their elders.[5]

Two decades earlier, one of the first American pop singers, Bing Crosby, symbolized his Depression-era fans' need for comfort and escape from the harsh economic conditions of the 1930s. His mellow baritone, such a contrast to the thin tenor voices popular in the 1920s, was a perfect match for new electronic microphones and the burgeoning medium of radio. One of his signature tunes, "Pennies from Heaven," presented a hopeful ballad, in which turning "your umbrella . . . upside-down" would reap pocket change from the raining currency. Bing's crooning of "White Christmas" consoled America through the next national trauma—World War II.[6]

Jackie not only became a pop icon, with her own recognizable symbols and images, she also created and projected emblems of American culture, the White House, and the presidency at a crucial and transformative period when television changed how the United States and the world viewed the president and his family. In 1952, the year Dwight Eisenhower was first elected president, barely one-fifth of American households had a TV; when he was reelected four years later, the percentage had reached one-half. Over 80 percent of households owned a television set by the time John Kennedy came to the White House in 1961. Although the images were only in black and white, Mrs. Kennedy's dark coloring transmitted exquisitely across the airwaves. Her thin, whispery voice was more problematic for broadcasting, but she did so few media interviews that it only became an issue for her 1962 televised tour of the White House.[7]

Mass media that published partially in color, particularly glossy magazines like *Life* and *Look,* vividly pictured the youthful first lady's fresh skin tone, shiny auburn hair, dazzling white smile, and many-hued wardrobe. Her active lifestyle provided a constant source of stories for more gossipy Hollywood magazines. By the end of 1962 ten of the previous seventeen issues of *Photoplay* had either featured a cover photo of Mrs. Kennedy or a cover blurb about her.

Periodicals discovered that placing Jackie on the cover resulted in sales of an additional 500,000 copies. Tying her celebrity status even closer to that of a movie star was the Hollywood magazines' penchant for picturing the first lady with film diva Elizabeth Taylor. In fact, *Photoplay* once featured them both on one cover with the headline "America's 2 Queens." The magazine's November 1963 edition, published before President Kennedy's assassination, carried cover photos of Jackie and JFK over the headline "Marriage & Taste," while Taylor and her husband, actor Richard Burton, appeared above the title "Passion & Waste." The subtitle read: "Why One Love [the Kennedys'] Grows Despite Fame . . . The Other [the Burtons'], Despite Shame." Mrs. Kennedy's press aide, Pamela Turnure, reported in 1962 that the White House "certainly disapprove[d] of some of the things we have seen [in the movie magazines]. They are undignified and in bad taste." Although picturing a first lady on the cover of fan magazines might have seemed disrespectful to her office, she and her family were nearly always portrayed in a positive light, despite the titillating headlines. None of the embarrassing stories about JFK's womanizing, which appeared *after* his death, ever found its way into the mainstream gossip magazines before his demise. How tame they seem now in contrast to today's vicious tabloids.[8]

Like other icons, Jackie Kennedy's image satisfied many of the needs of her time. The 1960 election revolved around alarming international tensions, unsettling demographic shifts at home, generational change in leadership, and reactions to the bland presidential style of the Eisenhower years. No wonder the victorious Kennedys struck a chord in the "greatest generation." Born in the twentieth century, deprived by years of economic depression and world conflict, stunned by new cold and hot wars, these Americans were ready for the triumph of youth, glamor, culture, sophistication, and celebrity. "[Jack] Kennedy's success was generational. It represented the coming to power of the junior officers of World War II." If the modern feminist movement had yet to raise the consciousness of American women, at least restive suburban housewives could follow, and copy if they wished, the exciting fashion trends launched by the young and vibrant first lady. For men and women alike, the Kennedys symbolized a new and promising era.[9]

Yet all American presidential administrations from Truman to Reagan had to confront constant Cold War dilemmas on the international scene and the fears they roused at home. Jackie and Jack were an effective team in portraying symbols to fight the superpowers' battle for the hearts and minds of the developing world. At the most superficial level, the first lady's sophisticated, statuesque appearance on the world stage, in shimmering gowns and colorful suits and dresses, maintained a conspicuous contrast to the dull grayness and stocky physiques of communist leaders and their wives in the 1960s. She charmed Soviet Premier Nikita Khrushchev after he had savaged her husband during their 1961 Vienna summit. She was also an incomparable asset to her husband's foreign policy overtures toward Mexico and Latin America, where she traveled with him and spoke in Spanish to admiring crowds. The first lady's semiofficial solo trip to archrivals India and Pakistan in 1962 was a tour de force of international goodwill. She beguiled both countries' leaders—India's Jawaharlal Nehru and Pakistan's Mohammed Ayub Khan. When the Kennedys arrived in foreign lands, they stepped off the new Air Force One (an impressive Boeing 707), which now displayed a large presidential seal on the doors' interiors that showed prominently when they were opened. Jackie chose the stately blue and white colors for the plane's exterior, and new furniture and art for the interior compartments.[10]

Mrs. Kennedy's restoration of the White House and its grounds, her guidebook on its furnishings and history, and her creation of the White House Historical Association drew renewed attention to this national shrine. Congress (in 1962) and the Supreme Court (in 1974) would copy her model of establishing historical societies for supporting their institutions. The first lady's televised tour of the executive mansion in February 1962 was a popular success, earned her an Emmy Award, and generated a taped version for screening abroad, even behind the Iron Curtain. JFK's cameo appearance at the end of the program served as an opportunity for him to exalt American history and the enduring republic it had produced.

As first lady (a title she initially disparaged and eschewed as sounding like the name of a saddle horse) Mrs. Kennedy effectively led the fight to preserve and restore the nineteenth-century ambiance of Lafayette Square, across from the White House, despite her concern that "the bomb" might obliterate historic preservation efforts. She advocated refurbishing Blair House, the president's official guest quarters for visiting dignitaries. Jackie explicitly resolved to make it a showplace for third world leaders who, she feared, would be more impressed by palatial digs when they visited the Kremlin.

The Kennedys wooed the developing world, as well as traditional allies, by elaborately entertaining their heads of state in Washington. The zenith of state occasions during the Kennedy era came in honor of Pakistan's President Khan. The presidential party sailed down the Potomac River to George Washington's historic Mt. Vernon, another emblem of American freedom, for an evening of military parades, dining, and orchestral music. Mrs. Kennedy suggested that the president greet most visiting heads of state with military pomp on the revitalized White House South Lawn, rather than the traditional, and rather shabby, National Airport or Union Station. At the White House President and Mrs. Kennedy hosted concerts, ballets, plays, and dramatic readings for foreign dignitaries. In addition, they honored playwrights, authors, poets, actors, musicians, painters, architects, and scientists with gala dinners in the refurbished Executive Mansion. Along with rejuvenating the stalled effort to establish a National Cultural Center, President Kennedy took these occasions to emphasize the importance of artistic accomplishment for a world power with an open society. He and the first lady facilitated the linkage between government and the arts—a relationship we now take for granted, but one that was an innovation advocated by critics of American culture in the 1950s. Mrs. Kennedy's redecoration of the White House library, and her supervision of its acquisition of American classics, bolstered the image of an intellectual presidential household.[11]

The first lady's youth resonated with the generation who came of age during World War II or just after. They remembered only grandmotherly first ladies—Eleanor Roosevelt, Bess Truman, and Mamie Eisenhower, who were age sixty, sixty-eight, and sixty-four, respectively, when they left the White House. How to assess the impact of Mrs. Kennedy's youthfulness on her husband's presidential campaign initially seemed to perplex male journalists. Fletcher Knebel wrote: "When the balance of [John] Kennedy's presidential assets and liabilities is struck, it is uncertain in which column Jacqueline belongs. She is an obvious asset to the eyes and well-being of her husband, but an old political maxim says the candidate's wife should not be too attractive. Women tend to be jealous of both. A kind of middle-aged neutrality is preferred. Whether or not this is true, if Kennedy is elected president, the First Lady will be thirty-one when she enters the White House and possessed of a supple grace and beauty. Admirers wager she will be able to go a full two terms without dieting."[12]

In contrast to her more mature predecessors, Jackie seemed like an attractive, dynamic older sister. Athleticism, reflected in her equestrian skills, waterskiing, and reports of her dancing the twist, was a sign of her youthful energy. To participate in these activities, she donned sport clothes, including bathing suits, which Americans were not used to seeing their first ladies wear in public. She even offered a hint of 1960s counterculture with her outfits of slacks, sweaters, and sunglasses. One critic labeled her "a sort of beatnik" for her choice of attire. Other traditionalists found her choice of a bandanna and sandals (worn without stockings!), for attending church in Palm Beach, a fashion faux pas. In hindsight, *Vogue*'s European editor at large wrote that Jackie "galvanized America by eschewing the hidebound, formalized elegance of the fifties."[13]

The very fact that she was of childbearing age made her unique among most twentieth-century presidential spouses, the youngest of whom (Edith Roosevelt and Edith Wilson) were already forty when they became first ladies. Mrs. Roosevelt had five children, ages four to fourteen, by the time she entered the White House; Mrs. Wilson was childless by both her first husband and her second, Woodrow Wilson.[14]

During the Great Depression, economic hardship forced young adults to forego or postpone marriage, and married couples had fewer children. World War II had the opposite effect on marriage rates, as couples accelerated courtship in response to the uncertainty of military life. At the war's end, when soldiers returned home, marriage rates continued to escalate, and the postwar baby boom followed. Birth rates rose from 18.4 per 1,000 women during the Depression to 25.3 per 1,000 in 1957. The total number of children born in the United States between 1946 and 1960 was a remarkable

59.4 million. From 1940 to 1960 birthrates for third children doubled and for fourth children tripled.[15] For the family-centered culture of the 1950s and early 1960s, Mrs. Kennedy seemed an appropriate model. Her pregnancy with John F. Kennedy Jr., just as she entered the public spotlight in her husband's presidential campaign, solidified her maternal image. The baby's birth a mere three weeks after his father's victory was a historic first for a president-elect and his spouse. Raising two adorable, photogenic, animated children while in the White House connected Jackie to the mothers of baby boomers. The press celebrated her pregnancy in 1963; the nation and the world mourned the loss of her premature infant son, Patrick, in August of that year.

America's population explosion in the aftermath of war created a massive consumer market. Suburban tract housing mushroomed to accommodate families moving from cities. In turn, they bought automobiles, every kind of household item to furnish their new homes, and food and clothing to maintain their children. The GI Bill made college affordable for veterans, and higher education qualified them for better-paying jobs. Real wages rose by half between 1947 and 1960, and the number of individuals with discretionary income doubled in the 1950s. By 1957 almost two-thirds of the population were now considered middle class, on the basis of income, compared with only 31 percent in the Roaring Twenties. Postwar prosperity unleashed an unprecedented spending spree as consumers relieved pent-up deprivation suffered during the Great Depression and subsequent war. Cars, homes, appliances, furniture, and clothing were now abundant, as they had not been during wartime rationing and military industrialization. Durable consumer goods and housing construction accounted for nearly all of the increase in the gross national product in the mid-1950s. Mrs. Kennedy's acquisitiveness, whether reflected in her designer clothing purchases, White House redecoration, or collecting antiques and objets d'art, was admittedly atypical of American middle-class consumerism. Yet nearly everyone aspired to lead "the good life"; Mrs. Kennedy just did so at a higher level. Her vacations to Italy, Greece, Morocco, and England (without her husband and, usually, her children) confirmed that fact. *Newsweek* observed in early 1962 that "millions of Americans . . . highly admired" their first lady, but

The first lady riding with her children, Caroline and John Jr.,
November 19, 1962. (Photo by Cecil Stoughton,
White House. JFK Library, Boston)

"by others who either envy her elegance or dislike her manner, she is looked upon with skepticism, and even sometimes with resentment." Family-oriented Americans least admired their first lady's jet-setting tendency, which separated her from familial responsibilities.[16]

Yet despite the obvious contrast with her two immediate predecessors, the matronly Bess Truman and the prim Mamie Eisenhower, Mrs. Kennedy was, in some ways, among the last of the traditional first ladies, those whom political scientist Robert Watson labels "supportive spouses/model wives." He groups first ladies Truman, Eisenhower, Kennedy, Johnson, and Nixon under that rubric, noting that Lady Bird Johnson is an exception for her public policy and campaign trail successes. In general, however, post–World War II first ladies before Betty Ford were a direct contrast with Eleanor Roosevelt's political activism and full partnership in her husband's presidency.[17]

Jacqueline Kennedy's hybrid first ladyship, which portrayed modern and traditional elements, typifies the "bridge" generation of women. Their lives spanned the 1950s cult of domesticity and the women's movement of the 1970s, which preached liberation from household stultification. Contrary to popular myths of the era, women increasingly entered the job market in the 1950s. By 1960 forty percent of all women over sixteen had jobs outside the home, and the female employment rate was expanding four times faster than that of males. The highest percentage of growth for women in the workforce was among those from middle-class households. They did not have to work for basic necessities, as did their counterparts from lower economic strata, but middle-class women sought employment to increase their family's standard of living in the new consumer age. A bigger house, a second car, new appliances, nice vacations, and a college education for the children were within reach of two-income households. Popular emphasis on full-time homemaking in the 1950s was not a total fabrication, however. Most mothers who joined the workforce did so only after their children started school.[18]

Mainstream media (especially magazines with female readership and television sitcoms) helped to create the stereotypic wife/mother of mid-twentieth-century America. A January 1956 edition of the *Saturday Evening Post,* for example, portrayed on its cover a woman wearing a shirtwaist dress, apron, and black pumps, standing in her basement, holding a flashlight, wondering how to change a fuse. The cover was unrelated to any story in the magazine. Presumably, it was meant to convey a Norman Rockwell–like vignette of daily life in America. The January 28, 1956, *Post* contained numerous advertisements for household appliances and furnishings (particularly washers, dryers, refrigerators, and televisions), automobiles, and convenience foods, like Chef Boy-Ar-Dee canned spaghetti and meatballs ("You're only 5 minutes away from this real Italian-style meal"), Jell-O ("It practically makes itself!"), Campbell's Soup, Swanson "TV" Dinners, and Nescafé Instant Coffee ("Tastier coffee made the modern way!"). All of the women in the ads, except one where a housewife has just painted the family living room, are dressed in the 1950s uniform of shirtwaist and heels.

The stereotype received weekly reinforcement from TV shows like *Leave It to Beaver, Father Knows Best, The Donna Reed Show*, and *The Adventures of Ozzie and Harriet*, in which mothers wore dresses, pearls, and high heels as they cheerfully performed their maternal and wifely duties in their perfect homes. (When Margaret Anderson, the mother played by Jane Wyatt on *Father Knows Best*, vacuumed, she donned a dustcoat over her dress and protected her coiffure with a bandana.) Television's nostalgic reflections on that period produced the 1970s hit television series, *Happy Days*.[19] Hollywood has also parodied 1950s domestic culture, with dark subtexts that scratch the veneer of perfection. Films like *Back to the Future* and *Pleasantville* return contemporary worldly teens to the supposedly more innocent 1950s, where they discover that the ideal is indeed flawed. *Far from Heaven*, a 2002 film, explores themes of race discrimination and homosexuality lurking just below the surface of a seemingly model household in 1957. Actress Julianne Moore, who portrays the wife of a successful (secretly gay) businessman, is a 1950s caricature in her taffeta dresses, pearls, and black pumps. She even speaks in a submissive whisper, eerily similar to Jacqueline Kennedy's sotto voce articulation.

When photographed and interviewed after her marriage to JFK in 1953, Mrs. Kennedy usually lived up to popular culture's image of the ideal housewife. She eschewed her preferred casual slacks and wore a dress and heels for a photographic essay that portrayed her daily errands around Georgetown in 1954. Foreshadowing her impact on women's fashion, however, she avoided billowy shirtwaists for more sophisticated straight-line skirts that actress Audrey Hepburn modeled in films like 1954's *Sabrina*. On the Senate and presidential campaign trails with her husband, Jackie was always properly attired in dresses, suits, pumps, and pearls or sedate costume jewelry.[20]

By the mid-twentieth century American women smoked openly. The habit among both men and women was ubiquitous in films and on television. Lucille Ball lit up on her sitcom, which was sponsored by Philip Morris. The cigarette manufacturer claimed that its product was "less irritating, definitely milder" for people who inhaled. Yet always aware of her image, Jackie, who had become a smoker in prep school, did not want to be photographed indulging her tobacco addiction. She once passed a note to friend Bill Walton during a political luncheon at the Commodore Hotel in New York City: "The boy with the crewcut, very young, three to your left, keeps taking pictures of me smoking. He just got one. Can you get it?" Long after she left the White House, she instructed the Kennedy Library not to reproduce any photographs of her smoking. While first lady, she tried to avoid smoking in public, and most photographers respected her wishes not to be pictured doing so in private. Nevertheless, she designed an ashtray for the White House state rooms and had cigarettes available at place settings for formal dinners. Chain smoker Leonard Bernstein, composer and director of the New York Philharmonic, remembered that "there were ashtrays everywhere [in the Kennedy White House] just inviting you to poison yourself with cigarettes. . . ; you were in a less querulous mood than otherwise because you ha[d] a drink and a cigarette." The antismoking movement was several years away, so Mrs. Kennedy did not violate prevailing health norms.[21] Her nicotine habit, however, may have contributed to her problematic pregnancies and the lung difficulties of her premature infants.

Although she had listed her ambition in her high school yearbook as "not to be a housewife," her self-described role as the wife of a U.S. senator was to serve as a helpmate to her husband and "not try to share the spotlight with him." After his election to the White House, she declared: "You have to do what your husband wants you to do. My life revolves around my husband. His life is my life. It is up to me to make his home a haven, a refuge, to arrange it so that he can see as much of me and his children as possible. . . . I want to take such good care of my husband that, whatever he is doing, he can do better because of me. His work is so important." In that sense, she reflected the archetypical 1950s housewife who maintained a comfortable home for her spouse and children without pursuing an independent career. Moreover, the projects that she undertook as first lady—restoring and redecorating the White House, preserving Lafayette Square, promoting the arts and a national cultural center—reflect the kind of traditional volunteer activities that have typically attracted "to the manner born" socialites. Indeed, elite Wellesley students in the 1960s aspired to pattern their lives after Mrs. Kennedy. They admiringly described her as "above all else exquisitely gracious and ornamental at her husband's side."[22] Still, by capturing headlines and camera lenses, First Lady Jacqueline Kennedy established a pattern that her successors could adopt and adapt to publicize their own less traditional policy agendas.

First ladies Ford, Carter, Reagan, Barbara Bush, and Clinton have been categorized as "modern spouses/public presidential partners," who played visible roles in the president's public and political life. Rosalynn Carter and Hillary Rodham Clinton even saw themselves as assistant presidents. Mrs. Carter asked to attend cabinet meetings so that she would be completely current on issues that faced her husband; she wanted to be prepared if the press or public asked her about President Carter's policy positions. While campaigning for president in 1992, Bill Clinton told voters that they would receive "two for one" if he was elected: his wife, an attorney, who had worked on education policy during his governorship of Arkansas, would be an equal partner in his presidency. Some of her supporters sported campaign buttons proclaiming, "I'm for Hillary's Husband." Indeed, President Clinton named his wife head of a task force on health care reform. As such, she, like other modern first ladies, testified before Congress. Since Betty Ford, who championed feminist causes, most first ladies have felt the need to associate themselves with at least one public policy issue. For Rosalynn Carter it was mental health; Nancy Reagan made famous the slogan, "Just Say No" (to drugs); Barbara and Laura Bush advocated literacy programs; Hillary Rodham Clinton worked on policies to benefit children (after her health care proposals were defeated). With presidential spouses playing such public and political roles after they arrive at the White House, they no longer have the option available to their predecessors of minimizing their campaign duties. Like their husbands, they must endure the same rigors of the marathon road to the White House.[23]

Although Mrs. Kennedy gamely campaigned with her husband, when her health allowed, she avoided the complexities and controversies of public policy debates. CBS's Charles Collingwood asked her about the role of government in the arts, during their televised White House tour, but she demurred. The topic was "too complicated," she said. Consequently, she maintained a careful division between herself and public policy when she felt the need to do so. Yet she was willing to deduce the lines of power in Washington and use them (often behind the scenes) for those political causes she supported, like creating museum status for the White House, promoting tax deductions for donations to it, establishing the White House Historical Association, and halting destruction of Lafayette Square's historic buildings. In addition, by clinging to a pre-women's movement vision of protecting home and hearth as a shelter for her husband and children, Mrs. Kennedy could maintain some semblance of a line between her private and public life. Modern feminist politics, which burst on the scene after she left the Executive Mansion, deliberately obliterated that boundary. For 1950s housewives hoping for a more complete life after reading Betty Friedan's *Feminine Mystique*, published in 1963, the personal became the political. The growth of investigative journalism in the aftermath of Watergate, and, more recently, the rise of 24/7 news coverage via cable and the Internet, have left virtually no zone of privacy for public figures.

Mrs. Kennedy, therefore, was among the last first ladies to experience some luxury of a private life. Although it was difficult to shield herself and her children from the prying eye of onlookers and cameras when they were in public, she simply drew a curtain on her private thoughts. *Newsweek* commented in 1962 that Jackie "grew expert in her role. But, as with a great actress, few people can know what study may go into the performance. An aura of remoteness plays around the public figure." At a small reception for Cuban exiles at the Kennedys' Palm Beach home, the first lady ignored reporter Robert Pierpoint when he spoke to her. Jackie would not even acknowledge his presence. He found her behavior "strange," especially since she had graciously welcomed Pierpoint and his family to a Christmas party the day before. While first lady, she granted only a handful of interviews. Unlike most of her successors, Jacqueline Kennedy left no published memoir or diary of her White

House years, and she refused to engage in public confessions so prevalent in today's American culture. Yet her very reticence only added to her mystique and enigmatic public image. Wittingly or not, she followed an intriguing adage of Walter Bagehot, the distinguished nineteenth-century British constitutional scholar. He warned that, to preserve public reverence for the monarchy, "[w]e must not let in daylight upon magic."[24]

Contrast Hillary Rodham Clinton's memoir, *Living History*, published amidst excessive media sensationalism in 2003. "I could hardly breathe. Gulping for air, I started crying and yelling at him, 'What do you mean? What are you saying? Why did you lie to me?' I was furious and getting more so by the second. He just stood there saying over and over again, 'I'm sorry. I'm so sorry. I was trying to protect you and Chelsea [President and Mrs. Clinton's daughter].' . . . I wanted to wring Bill's neck."[25] The former first lady thus describes the moment when she learned from her husband "that there had been inappropriate intimacy" with White House intern Monica Lewinsky. No mystique left here, especially since everyone already knew the nature of the euphemistic "inappropriate intimacy" from the explicit legal testimony contained in Independent Counsel Kenneth Starr's report to Congress, which had been disseminated over the Internet in the fall of 1998. Perhaps Senator Clinton felt as though she had no choice but to tell her side of the story. Whatever her motivations, the public made the memoir a runaway best seller.

If the Kennedys had similar bitter confrontations in private about JFK's infidelities, we may never know. Only rarely did Mrs. Kennedy reveal any knowledge of her husband's philandering, and certainly not to a wide public forum. Jackie reportedly chastised two of her husband's aides (in French) for including one of his paramours in a receiving line on a 1961 state trip to Canada. She was said to be furious for having to shake hands with the "blonde bimbo." Another time, as she walked past a young woman in the White House, the first lady is said to have commented *en français* to a French journalist she was touring through the mansion, "This is the girl who is supposedly sleeping with my husband."[26] It is hard to believe that she would ever have breached the self-constructed barrier around her privacy. In the early 1960s, however, she could be almost certain (as could her husband) that the mainstream press would not report problems in their marriage caused by JFK's womanizing.

By maintaining control over her public image while first lady as best she could in an increasingly intrusive media age, Mrs. Kennedy preserved the value of her political currency and the symbolism she created around it and her husband. In that sense, the reality of the Kennedy marriage or presidency is irrelevant. A political symbol "conveys a larger range of meaning, typically with emotional, moral, or psychological impact. *This larger meaning need not be independently or factually true, but will tap ideas people want to believe in as true.*" Or as presidential scholar Thomas Langston has critically observed, "presidents are icons: symbolic representations of something sacred or magical." From her first weeks as first lady, Jacqueline Kennedy set out to transform the White House, the platform of her husband's presidency, into an enchanting icon. The colorful guidebook that she produced on the White House's history, and the mansion's restoration with period antiques and decor, were intended to give Americans pride in the president's house and make it a national showplace. The Truman recreation of the White House had literally gutted the interior and placed it on a new and sturdier foundation. Mrs. Kennedy's project could, therefore, confine itself to the aesthetics of redecoration.[27]

What an intriguing coincidence that Professor Richard Neustadt's landmark book, *Presidential Power: The Politics of Leadership,* published in 1959, focused on the president's "*personal* power" as viewed from "*inside the White House.*" Previously, presidential scholars had studied the office from "outside it, looking in," emphasizing the position's formal *constitutional* powers. In contrast, Neustadt argued that the power of the president was his personal ability to persuade men in the executive branch, the other two branches of government, foreign nations, and public opinion. "The essence of a president's persuasive task is to convince such men that what *the White House* wants of them is what they ought to do for their sake and on their authority." Neustadt's study provided an owner's manual for the Kennedy administration. Mrs. Kennedy focused America's and the world's attention on the very seat of that power through her White House project.[28]

The first lady's support for the arts, another major element of her symbolic creation, bolstered the image that a new generation—to which the torch of political leadership had passed—would also spark a renaissance of cultural creativity. JFK's assassination thus represented the tragedy of truncated youth and artistic promise, as well as the perfect family shattered—all played out on television, with Mrs. Kennedy as the consummate director of funereal images. Cameras captured the horror of her bloodstained suit as she returned from Dallas with her husband's remains, followed by her stoic participation in his state funeral, with her fatherless children at her side. She prompted three-year-old John Jr.'s heart-wrenching salute of his father's casket outside St. Matthew's Cathedral. That shocking November weekend's pictures, which she helped to construct, seared themselves on the public consciousness. Her pièces de résistance of image weaving followed the tragic end of her husband's presidency. The grieving widow requested that an eternal flame, like the one at the Tomb of the Unknown Soldier under Paris's Arc de Triomphe, be placed on JFK's grave in Arlington Cemetery. And she propounded the Camelot metaphor by comparing her husband's presidency to the mythical Arthurian kingdom, popularized in Alan Jay Lerner and Frederick Loewe's Broadway musical. The enduring symbol would embody the magical quality of the Kennedy White House in the American mind. She spent the remainder of her life, a full thirty years, cementing her husband's historic legacy through the John F. Kennedy Library and Museum, the John F. Kennedy Center for the Performing Arts, and the John F. Kennedy School of Government and Institute of Politics at Harvard.

The martyrdom of President Kennedy, with his wife at his side, assured Jacqueline Kennedy's promotion from celebrity to iconic legend. Tragedy, especially premature death, can elevate the victim's public image. Mrs. Kennedy was inextricably bound to the assassination and the world's mournful response to it. The public fascination with her life in the White House, and her careful control of access to it, had already created a potent force before November 22, 1963. The very mystique that she wove around her persona allowed her admirers to shape their own image of her. Displaying both traditional and modern elements in her first ladyship reflected societal transitions from the seemingly quiescent 1950s to the turbulent 1960s. In partnership with her husband, she represented a promising guide to the uncertain future at home and abroad. New media technology captured their iconic essence while minimizing their human foibles.

Mrs. Kennedy's public image, as measured by Gallup polls, rivaled that of another heroic first lady, Eleanor Roosevelt. From 1962 to 1966, Jackie occupied the number one position in Gallup's annual list of "Most Admired Women." Neither Bess Truman nor Mamie Eisenhower achieved that spot during their tenures as first lady. Eleanor Roosevelt maintained the premier ranking from 1948 until Mrs. Kennedy displaced her in 1962. The unpopularity of her public conflict with historian William Manchester over his book, *Death of a President,* and her marriage to the unattractive and unscrupulous Greek tycoon, Aristotle Onassis, in 1968, dropped her ranking to number five throughout the late 1960s and early 1970s. After she fell from grace as "Jackie O.," the former first lady lost the number one spot to Mrs. Eisenhower, who finally ascended to it in 1969 and 1970, perhaps garnering the sympathy vote in the wake of her husband's death in 1969. Nevertheless, with only a few years' exceptions, Jackie remained in the top ten of "most admired women" polls until just before her death in 1994.[29] Yet to imply that Mrs. Kennedy's popularity rested solely on her celebrity and her creative construction of symbols unfairly devalues her essential contributions as first lady. The chapters that follow trace the substance behind the icon.

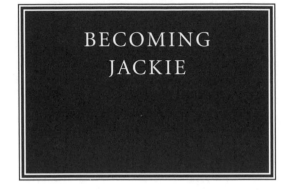

CHAPTER 2

BECOMING
JACKIE

Jacqueline Kennedy was only thirty-one years old when her husband, twelve years her senior, took the oath of office as president of the United States. Compared to other first ladies, who were forty-nine on average when they entered the White House, she had few years to prepare her for the duties of a president's wife. Nevertheless, she brought to her new position a love of art, foreign languages, literature, European history, ballet, haute couture, and antiques based on her upbringing by well-heeled parents and her education in exclusive schools at home and abroad.

Born in Long Island's Southampton Hospital on July 28, 1929, Jacqueline Lee Bouvier entered New York high society while her parents, Janet Norton Lee and John Vernou Bouvier III, summered on the East Hampton shore. Her mother, an accomplished equestrian and strict disciplinarian, was the daughter of a successful New York real estate developer. She pursued perfectionism for Jackie and her sister Caroline Lee, born in 1933, and in running the Bouviers' Manhattan household. The family regularly appeared in the New York society columns. Foreshadowing the future first lady's celebrity status, one newspaper reported in 1931, "Little Jackie Bouvier, daughter of Jack Bouvier and the former Janet Lee, will not make her bow to society for another sixteen years or more, but she was a charming hostess at her second birthday party given at the home of her parents, 'Rowdy Hall.'"[1]

With her wide-set eyes, brunette hair, and fulsome lips, young Jackie favored her father, who had earned the moniker "Black Jack" (borrowed from World War I hero, General John "Black Jack" Pershing) for his perpetual tan and pomaded black hair. His sensuous mouth and neatly trimmed mustache reminded some of the popular movie star of the era, Clark Gable. Jack was a Wall Street stock speculator whose wealth evaporated in the wake of the market crash that occurred just three months after Jackie's birth. She and her father adored each other, but Black Jack was an incorrigible womanizer who kept his marriage in constant turmoil. Jackie once told a friend that she could clearly remember one occasion when her parents came to her childhood bedroom to bid farewell before going out for an evening of dancing. The memory was so crystalline because it was one of the few times Jackie could remember her parents *not* fighting.[2]

As an adult, Mrs. Kennedy described herself as "rather a tomboy" in her youth. Writing an autobiographical essay for *Vogue* magazine's Prix de Paris contest in 1951, twenty-one-year-old Jacqueline noted: "I lived in New York City until I was thirteen and spent the summers in the country [often at her paternal grandfather's estate on Long Island]. I hated dolls, loved horses and dogs, and had skinned knees and braces on my teeth for what must have seemed an interminable length of time to my family." Photographs of young Jacqueline frequently picture her with a horse at equestrian events, where she excelled, or with one of the many family dogs, which she loved to show at competitions. She was also an avid reader, later observing in the same Prix de Paris essay, "I read a lot when I was little, much of which was too old for me. There were Chekhov and Shaw in the room where I had to take naps and I never slept but sat on the windowsill reading. . . . My heroes were Byron, Mowgli, Robin Hood, Little Lord Fauntleroy's grandfather, and Scarlett O'Hara."[3]

Perhaps the grandfather character in the Lord Fauntleroy story intrigued her because she was so close to her paternal grandfather, John V. Bouvier Jr., or "Grampy Jack," as his grandchildren called him. He had received degrees in political science and law from Columbia University and eventually became a successful trial attorney in New York City. In his opulent homes on Park Avenue and Long

Jacqueline Bouvier, with canine friend, in 1935. (JFK Library, Boston)

Island, which Jacqueline visited often, he introduced his precocious granddaughter to fine literature, antiques, and art. They delighted in memorizing poems together and writing poetry for each other. Young Jackie began illustrating her verses with whimsical drawings.[4]

Jacqueline's mother arranged for Jackie and her sister to take ballet lessons, and Jackie began to collect books on classical dance. Janet Bouvier sent Jackie for a year of preschool at Miss Yates' kindergarten before enrolling her in the elite Miss Chapin's School in New York City, where she was an A student. Her teachers there described her in glowing terms, except for her mischievous streak, which they attributed to her active, restless mind. Her homeroom teacher commented, "She was the prettiest little girl, very clever, very artistic and full of the devil. She was efficient and finished her work on time and then had nothing to do until her classmates finished theirs." The headmistress, with whom young Jackie had numerous disciplinary sessions, admitted, "I mightn't have kept Jacqueline, except that she had the most inquiring mind we'd had in the school in thirty-five years." Chapin's art teacher recalled, "She was one of the most interesting persons we ever had. I had to work hard to keep ahead of her." Years later, Mrs. Kennedy, in a handwritten note to Richard Nixon, thanking him for his condolence letter after her husband's assassination, ended her missive, "I hope your daughters love Chapin School as much as I did."[5]

Although Miss Chapin's was a posh school for socialite girls, it prided itself on the strength of its academics, taught by college-educated women, as well as its stimulating cocurricular activities. In addition to learning the standard primary school subjects of reading, writing, geography, arithmetic, and physical education, Chapin students met with authors, poets, and musicians, as well as experts on politics and foreign affairs. Jacqueline began learning French as a schoolgirl, and her mother reinforced the lessons by making a contest of speaking French at the dinner table. The person who uttered the most English words during supper lost the game. Grampy Jack asserted (in a published family history) that the Bouviers descended from French aristocrats, a myth that appeared in authorized biographies of Jacqueline Kennedy when she became first lady. In reality, her Bouvier lineage was distinctly bourgeois, and the majority of her ancestors, especially on her mother's side, were Irish.[6]

When Jackie was seven years old, the turmoil that had existed between her parents culminated in separation. The last straw for Janet had been an embarrassing photo in the New York *Daily News,* showing Black Jack holding the hand of a paramour, literally behind his wife's back, as she gazed in the opposite direction. For the remainder of their childhood, Jackie and Lee would shuttle back and forth between their parents' separate residences in New York City. While their mother was left to play her natural role of disciplinarian, their father represented the charming entertainer in their lives, treating Jackie and Lee to weekend frolics in Central Park, extravagant shopping sprees, and ice cream sundaes (just before returning them to their mother for dinner).[7]

After unsuccessful attempts at reconciliation, Janet ultimately obtained a divorce from Black Jack in 1940. In the divorce proceedings, the Bouvier household staff testified about the deleterious impact that the marital feud had on Jackie and her sister. Often they were left in the care of governesses and maids, as their mother maintained an active social life. When she was at home, they sometimes were subjected to her temper tantrums. In contrast, when the children were in his care, Jack Bouvier was a doting and attentive father. Nevertheless, as was the era's legal custom, the divorce decree placed the Bouvier girls in their mother's custody. Having endured such a tempestuous marriage and bitter divorce, particularly stigmatizing to a Roman Catholic family, the girls' parents never had a kind word to say about the other. Almost sixty years later, Lee Bouvier Radziwill, Jacqueline's younger sister, recalled that the Bouvier siblings "shared the same emotional difficulties of children with divorced parents. [But] growing up was always fun when we could see my father because he was such a joy to be with and we were the focal point of his life and so we had many wonderful times with him, but it had the difficulties . . . of being torn between two parents."[8]

In 1941 Jackie's mother took her and Lee twice to Washington, D.C., for the girls' first excursions to the nation's capital. Upon becoming first lady in 1961, Mrs. Kennedy fondly recalled on a CBS television appearance her initial visit to the National Gallery of Art twenty years previously. Jackie declared that her "love of art was born [at the Gallery]. . . . It was then that I first discovered one of my greatest delights—the deep pleasure experienced in looking at masterpieces of painting and sculpture." Young Jackie was also fascinated by trips to other D.C. tourist attractions, particularly Mount Vernon and the FBI, but she was disappointed by the tour of the White House, which she described as "rather bleak. There was nothing in the way of a booklet to take away, nothing to teach one more about the great house and the presidents who lived there."[9]

Janet Bouvier's motives for visiting Washington went beyond sightseeing. She had met a wealthy investment banker, Hugh D. ("Hughdie") Auchincloss Jr., who lived at Merrywood, his opulent estate in McLean, Virginia, high atop the Potomac River's palisades. In December 1941 she introduced her daughters to Hughdie. The exigencies of war accelerated the courtship, and Janet Bouvier became

Mrs. Auchincloss in June 1942. Actually, she was the third Mrs. Hugh D. Auchincloss Jr., and the marriage presented Jackie and Lee with two stepbrothers, a stepsister, and, eventually, a half-sister and half-brother. In addition to their new palatial Merrywood home, Jackie and her sister would spend time at the equally impressive Auchincloss summer estate, Hammersmith Farm, in Newport, Rhode Island. Their mother was now financially stable, and the stolid "Uncle Hughdie," as Jackie and Lee called him, provided some emotional balance as well. Jackie would later write to her stepbrother, Yusha, "I always love it so at Merrywood—so peaceful—with the river and the dogs—and listening to the Victrola. I will never know which I love best—Hammersmith with its green fields and summer winds—or Merrywood in the snow—with the river and those great steep hills. . . . all the places and feelings and happiness that bind you to a family you love."10

In fall 1942 Jacqueline enrolled in her new school, Holton-Arms, which was then located in nearby D.C. Following her stepfather's advice to take classes taught by the best instructors, even if she was not immediately drawn to the subject, she studied Latin with an exacting teacher. She learned to adore the language. Proficient in French, she also added Spanish to her curriculum and reported to Grampy Jack that she had learned the mildly epithetical *caramba*.11

At age fifteen Jackie was sent to board at Miss Porter's School in Farmington, Connecticut, to complete her college preparatory courses. There she discovered other wealthy East Coast Establishment girls, with upper-class customs and lifestyles similar to hers. The school had begun to concentrate on academics, rather than "finishing" young women, but the norms at Miss Porter's continued to emphasize elite manners. Tish Baldrige, who was three years ahead of Jackie at Miss Porter's, and would later become her social secretary and chief of staff in the White House, notes that the school's homogeneity even extended to the girls' accents. Baldrige calls it "Locust Valley Lockjaw," or "affected English," spoken by refined women along the East Coast. She remembers that "the entire Bouvier-Auchincloss tribe of women spoke the same way. Certainly Jackie's mother, sister, half-sister, and cousins did."12

Jackie maintained her strong academic record with an A-minus average over her three years at the school. Her favorite courses and teachers were in the disciplines of art history, French, and literature. Access to the extensive scholarly library of her stepaunt and uncle in Farmington expanded her horizons to include political philosophy. Black Jack Bouvier continued to play a role in his daughter's life. He provided her with an allowance and visited on weekends, when he would take Jackie and her friends for sumptuous lunches. She convinced him that she should be allowed to stable her favorite horse, Danseuse, on campus, and she spent a good portion of each day riding and grooming her equine companion.[13]

As a high school student, Jackie sustained her interest in writing poetry and drawing. Like her early childhood poems, those from this era often portray her contemplations on solitude and experiencing a favorite season, location, or pastime. In addition to contributing humorous cartoons to the student newspaper, Jackie also wrote serious essays on World War II and the history of American political theory, especially its inspiration from the French Enlightenment. She was interested in current events, and, when President Franklin Roosevelt died during the spring of her first year at Miss Porter's, she expressed concern over the post-FDR presidency and empathy for the grieving Roosevelt family. She admitted that she had been influenced by her Republican father's disparaging remarks about Roosevelt's impact on the stock market, but she now deemed FDR "great."[14]

When Jacqueline graduated in 1947, her yearbook entry declared that she was "most known for [her] wit," which she had frequently displayed in improvisational stage productions at the school. Her oft-quoted yearbook "ambition" was "not to be a housewife." On a more serious note, she received the Maria McKinney Memorial Award for Excellence in Literature. The prize was a volume of Edna St. Vincent Millay's poetry, a fitting gift for the amateur poet. Jackie left Miss Porter's with another lifelong habit: despite the institution's formal ban on smoking among its refined student body and Janet's vociferous opposition to demon tobacco (although she herself smoked), Jackie acquired the vice there.[15]

The summer after Jacqueline's graduation, she celebrated her eighteenth birthday and her debut into Newport society with a tea and, later, a dance, both sponsored by the Auchinclosses. By footing the bill for the festivities, Uncle Hughdie assured the exclusion of Black Jack Bouvier. Nonetheless, Jackie already evinced the coquettish mannerisms that her father had encouraged. A photo taken at Hammersmith Farm, just before the coming-out dance, pictures Jacqueline glancing over her shoulder with a hint of flirtation. "Daddy" had advised her and her teenage friends to "play the game" with members of the opposite sex. "You can't be so eager, you must make them wait!" Perhaps recollecting his own notorious record with women, Black Jack, according to Lee Bouvier, warned her and Jackie that "all men are rats." One of Jacqueline's schoolmates recalled that part of the "game" was modulating one's voice to a breathy, cooing tone, which the future first lady affected, apparently sometime after leaving Miss Porter's. As a young man, author George Plimpton witnessed the Jackie persona in Newport: "I remember that talking with her was very different. She sort of enveloped you—rare for someone of that age to be able to learn how to. She had a wonderful way of looking at you and enveloping you with this gaze."[16] With her dark features and magnetic personality, she was undoubtedly remarkable among her peers. Not surprisingly, Cholly Knickerbocker, the nom de plume of Hearst columnist Igor Cassini, named her 1947's "Deb of the Year."

Her excellent grades at Miss Porter's, along with aptitude test scores in the ninetieth percentile, assured her acceptance at Vassar College, where she enrolled in the fall of 1947. Although she continued the extracurricular activities she had pursued at prep school (drama, student newspaper, riding), by most accounts, including her own, she was not a full participant in the social life there. Her cousin, John Davis, claims that her "Queen Deb" distinction "distanced her from her freshman classmates." In her 1951 autobiographical essay, she frankly observed: "I spent two years at Vassar and cannot quite decide whether I liked it or not. I wish I had worked harder and gone away less on weekends." In the classroom, where she intended to major in literature, she maintained high grades and was particularly inspired by two professors, one who taught the history of religion and one who offered a Shakespeare class. She later remarked that "[a]ll my greatest interests—in literature and art, Shakespeare and poetry—were formed because I was fortunate enough to find superb teachers in these fields."[17]

In the middle of her freshman year, Jackie's beloved Grampy Jack died, leaving a depleted estate. The future Mrs. Kennedy must have realized that she would inherit no wealth from the Bouvier family, nor would her Auchincloss ties assure her a posh lifestyle, as Uncle Hughdie did not establish trust funds for her or Lee. (He did so for his own offspring, however.) During this period, Black Jack attempted to reassert his influence over Jackie, perhaps because he saw her drifting away from him toward adulthood. Periodically, he would threaten to cut off her $50-per-month allowance if she did not follow his advice on her education and future career.[18]

During the summer between her freshman and sophomore years at Vassar, Jacqueline made her first trip to Europe, along with three friends and a teacher from Holton-Arms as their chaperone. Jackie was entirely smitten by her Grand Tour of the Old Country. Her travel companions' connections garnered invitations for the group to a Buckingham Palace garden party, where the girls glimpsed King George VI and Queen Elizabeth and shook hands with Winston Churchill.

"Junior year abroad" was a typical experience for wealthy coeds in the late 1940s, and Jackie returned to the States determined to find a program that would enable her to study in Europe. Vassar did not offer such a curriculum, but when she discovered that Smith College sponsored study trips abroad, she convinced her parents and the Vassar administration that she should be allowed to spend her junior year in France. Jackie set sail for her next foreign adventure in August 1949 and began an intensive French course at the University of Grenoble, from which she took side trips to the Riviera and Italy. That fall she enrolled in the Sorbonne, lived with a French family (instead of inhabiting a dormitory for American students), and took courses in French history and art history. To her academic program she added an art course at the École Louvre and one in diplomatic history at the École de Science Politique. She giddily wrote her stepbrother that she had "an absolute mania now about learning to speak French perfectly. . . . The most wonderful thing here is all the operas and theatres and ballets and how easy they are to get to and how cheap. . . . I do love Paris." The sophisticated French parties and salons that Jackie attended found an echo in her White House entertaining a decade later.[19]

During the winter break, Jackie's mother and stepfather accompanied her on a vacation trip to Germany and Austria. Over the

Easter holiday she and a new friend, a young French-Argentinian comte, visited Spain. After her courses ended that spring, she toured the south of France with her French landlady's daughter, Claude De Renty, soaking up yet more culture and ambience. De Renty later commented, "Once she was in Paris . . . she realized that nothing was comparable to what she would see there, in French museums, or French homes. She realized that France was the place where she could see the best of the arts she loved—even of Italian, and German, and Dutch. And some French homes were like museums, where you could find the best quality of things. France did not mean just French culture but the best of European art and culture. I think she took the best from everywhere. Good paintings, good architecture, good wallpaper, good furnishings." That summer, before returning to the states, she and Yusha toured Ireland and Scotland, where Jackie exhibited just as much interest in the colorful history of the British Isles as she had in French history. The European experience convinced her that the United States needed greater exposure to the best of European art and culture.[20]

With such a year of constant intellectual, cultural, artistic, and social stimulation behind her, rural Poughkeepsie and staid Vassar, about which she was already dubious, did not hold any charm for her. Though Black Jack insisted that she should return to Vassar to complete her senior year, earn a degree from one of the respected "Seven Sisters," and live just seventy miles from his apartment in New York City, Jackie decided to finish her undergraduate work at George Washington University. She would commute from Merrywood in Northern Virginia to the GW campus in downtown Washington.[21]

At GW she majored in French literature, minored in art, and took courses in journalism and creative writing. Years later her former English professor remembered: "She was an extremely intelligent young woman, but she also possessed a brilliant imagination. This was coupled with a genuine talent for the craft of writing. She had a gift as a writer and might have become prominent in her own right as a writer had she followed another path. She covered many different subjects—the beauty and peace of her family's home in Virginia, the night of faint romance in Florence, a festival in Italy, the purpose and excitement of art to the soul. She was beautiful, and she could write like a million. She didn't need to take my classes."[22]

In spring 1951, with graduation near, Jacqueline Bouvier faced the dilemma common to all college seniors: what to do with the rest of her life. She had already set herself apart from most women of her generation by earning a university degree. Among those women who did complete undergraduate training in the 1950s, a sizable proportion tended to marry within a year of leaving college (known as earning one's "MRS Degree"). During her senior year, Jackie had pursued a long-distance courtship with John Husted Jr., a Wall Street investment banker whose family knew both Hughdie and Black Jack; but her romance with this to-the-manner-born junior executive had not yet led to a marriage proposal.[23]

Vogue's 1951 Prix de Paris competition seemed like the perfect answer to the professional aspect of her dilemma. The prize was a year's stint with the fashion magazine—six months each in its Paris and New York offices. She could combine her interests in couture, drawing, writing, and travel while receiving valuable training from the premier fashion publication of the day. Throughout the spring term of her senior year, she worked diligently on the competition's requirements, including an autobiography; technical papers on modeling, fashions for coeds, beauty treatments, and the marketing of perfume; a plan for how to teach women about men's clothing; a proposal for a complete issue of *Vogue;* and an essay on "People I Wish I Had Known." Her responses to each of the assignments contain the most information that the future first lady would ever reveal about herself in a public setting. The autobiography described the chronology of her young life (omitting references to her parents' painful divorce) with characteristic self-effacement. Her essay revealed a skillfully light touch of sarcasm and irony, particularly when portraying her relationship with Janet Auchincloss. The application's technical portions demonstrated her knowledge of, and creativity in, the fashion world that would become a hallmark of her tenure as first lady. Jackie's essay on historical figures, which specifically asked contestants to focus on "the world of art, literature, and other milieu," prompted her to select French poet Charles Baudelaire, Irish writer Oscar Wilde, and Russian ballet impresario Serge Diaghileff for their edifying contributions to artistic theories.[24]

Vogue named Jacqueline Bouvier a finalist in the competition, and, after her interview with the award's director, informed her that she had won first prize. Jackie had bested 1,280 contestants from 225 women's colleges. In August 1951 the magazine published her portrait with an announcement of her achievement. Accounts differ on why she eventually declined the impressive and coveted offer. Perhaps her mother and stepfather feared that she would fall back under the spell of Black Jack during the prize's six-month stint in New York. Or they may have been concerned that she would become an expatriate if she moved to Paris for another long stay. Janet might have believed that her daughter was unqualified for such a sophisticated position and that she was falling behind in the "race" to find a suitable mate. *Vogue*'s managing editor reportedly told Jackie to "go to Washington . . . where all the boys are." Jackie may have feared that the gay men in *Vogue*'s New York office could not possibly expand her circle of marriageable males. Apparently, Jackie informed *Vogue*'s editors that her parents wanted to keep her close to home. That was the explanation Mrs. Kennedy allowed Mary Thayer to report in the first lady's 1961 authorized biography.[25]

Ironically, if indeed Janet and Hughdie wanted to keep Jackie close to Merrywood, the Auchinclosses sent her and Lee on a summer-long European tour in 1951 as a graduation gift for both daughters. (Lee had just received her diploma from Miss Porter's.) Perhaps inspired by her Prix de Paris application, Jackie designed her own clothes for the trip. A few days before the journey commenced, she accepted a long-standing invitation from journalist Charles Bartlett and his wife to attend a dinner party in order to meet their friend, Democratic Congressman John F. Kennedy of Massachusetts. Jackie realized that she had chatted with the young congressman briefly two years before on a train. After dinner he "shyly" asked if "they could go someplace and have a drink," but his suggestion was cut short when Jackie discovered that a male friend was waiting for her outside the Bartletts' house.[26]

Soon Jackie was off to Europe again. Her itinerary with Lee included London, Paris, Venice, Rome, and Florence. As a thank-you gift to their parents for sponsoring the trip, the two young women produced a book entitled *One Special Summer,* which included photographs and commentary on their travels, along with Jackie's poetry and drawings. One biographer captures the essence of Jackie's sketches. They "reveal not only her artistic gifts but also her delicious sense of satire. In its bold exaggeration, the style is partly that of cartoonist William Steig; in deadpan humor, it resembles the wonderfully lunatic world of James Thurber; and perhaps most of all, there is the whimsical influence of Ludwig Bemelmans and his fanciful Madeline. . . . [Jackie's] original artwork suggests Grandma Moses reworked by Raoul Dufy."[27]

A highlight for both women on the trip was a visit with renowned art critic Bernard Berenson at his villa near Florence. From prep school, young Lee, enamored of Italian Renaissance art, had written a fan letter to Berenson, who issued an invitation to meet with him. According to their record of the visit, both sisters were captivated by Berenson's joie de vivre, especially his admonition to spend one's days with "life-affirming" rather than with "life-diminishing" people. Jackie later attributed her appreciation for art to Berenson's seemingly simple, yet demanding, practice of "focusing your whole attention on a work of art, to try to understand the message the artist wants to convey."[28]

After her third sojourn to Europe in four years, and with her declination of the Prix de Paris behind her, Jacqueline Bouvier returned to the Auchincloss Merrywood estate with still no direction for her personal or professional life by fall 1951. Jackie's courtship with John Husted continued, however. Thinking she might like to pursue journalism, through her stepfather's contacts, she acquired a job as a girl Friday at the Washington *Times-Herald*. Shortly thereafter she approached the paper's editor in chief to talk about upgrading her position to something more substantive. The editor, displaying a typical perspective in that era, admonished her not to bother if she was simply marking time until she married. Jacqueline assured him that she was serious about a writing career. He suggested that she assume the job of "Inquiring Photografer" [*sic*] at the paper. In January 1952, after getting up to speed on how to use a professional-quality camera, she tackled the job of posing provocative questions to, and snapping photographs of, selected respondents, everyone from persons in the street to members of Congress. Her starting weekly salary was $42.50.[29]

With Jacqueline's professional life coming into focus, she turned to the nagging question of her matrimonial plans. She had accepted John Husted's proposal over the Christmas holidays, and her engagement was announced on January 21, 1952, with a June wedding planned. The engagement was short-lived. After a visit with John at Merrywood, Jackie slipped the engagement ring into his pocket as they said their goodbyes at the airport. Husted later remembered, "She didn't say much and neither did I. There wasn't much you could say." A combination of factors probably led to the broken engagement. Husted's junior-executive salary (reportedly $17,000 a year) was not enough to support the Bouvier-Auchincloss lifestyle, though accounts differ on whether this fact more upset Janet or Jackie. Life as the spouse of an investment banker might be dull, and Jackie was enjoying her newfound independence. She had also renewed her Kennedy connection while visiting the family's Palm Beach retreat during a winter vacation with Lee.[30]

Not long after Jackie ended her betrothal to Husted, the Bartletts convened another dinner party, almost a year to the date when they had first tried to play matchmaker with Jackie Bouvier and Jack Kennedy. Charles Bartlett thought "[Jackie] always had these sort of English beaus, and I must say they were not up to her. She was an enormously attractive girl." He and his wife encouraged her to bring the Massachusetts congressman to their May 8, 1952, soirée. She did, and this time, at least some spark of interest was kindled.

JFK, a candidate for the U.S. Senate, was still boyishly handsome, even at almost thirty-five years of age. A war hero from his service as a PT-boat skipper in the South Pacific, he stood just over six feet tall and appeared lanky for a man approaching middle age. (His thin frame, which sometimes bordered on the gaunt, resulted from chronic ill health that included digestive ailments, a degenerative back condition, and Addison's disease, an adrenal deficiency. Historian Robert Dallek, the first biographer granted access, along with a physician, to JFK's secret medical records, concluded that steroid treatments for Kennedy's gastroenterological condition may have actually triggered his Addison's disease, and ultimately contributed to osteoporosis in his spine.) The young congressman's shock of auburn hair, twinkling eyes, and dazzling smile were unquestionably attractive. Photos of his early congressional campaigns show eager women of all ages huddled around him, attempting to shake his hand and have a word with him. "Every woman who met Kennedy wanted to mother him or to marry him."[31]

Jack and Jackie had enough in common at least to start a relationship. They were from the same socioeconomic class (Jack had been a multimillionaire since the age of majority, thanks to a trust fund established by his tycoon father, Joseph P. Kennedy, the former ambassador to Great Britain), were Roman Catholic (if not entirely devout), were well educated at the finest schools (JFK was the product of Choate and Harvard), were avid readers who loved history and poetry, were well traveled, and were drawn to athletic competition and soulful walks along the seashore. They both possessed a ready sense of humor and a sparkling wit that could be endearingly self-effacing.

Yet Kennedy and Bouvier had divergent lifestyles. More than just a dozen years in their ages separated them. Although not naturally gregarious, partly the result of his sickly childhood, Jack had acclimated to the rough-and-tumble of public life and was surrounded by hard-bitten Irish pols and a large, boisterous family; Jackie preferred solitude in a contemplative atmosphere and had virtually no experience in politics. She had never even voted. His taste in history ran to English political sagas and the U.S. Civil War; she adored all things Continental. He had no facility for foreign languages; she was multilingual. He loved epic poets, she the romantics. He cared not a whit for fashion, including his own; she was the queen of couture. He loved sailing and those now-legendary Kennedy family touch football games; she was a talented equestrian. He was allergic to horses and dogs; she had grown up surrounded by equine and canine pets. He had never owned a home and had no interest in or taste for decorating; she had a natural eye for the finest decorative arts. His idea of the perfect night out was to see a movie Western and grab a hamburger and malt; she loved the ballet, opera, and symphony and maintained her taste for French cuisine and wine. He would have been hard-pressed to distinguish Manet from Monet; she was a connoisseur of art and talented amateur sketch artist. He was an infamous ladies' man (to put it quaintly); at only twenty-two years of age, her romantic experiences were far narrower. Many years later Charles Bartlett admitted that he had been aware of Jack's "running around," but he claimed not to know that JFK "was as much of a romancer as he turned out to be. . . . I'm not sure I'd have pushed it [the Kennedy-

Bouvier match] if I had realized that he was." To the extent that Bartlett recognized Kennedy's womanizing, he thought that the relationship with the "extraordinary" Jackie "would settle Jack" and offer her a fascinating partner.[32]

Writing in 1960, Mary Thayer, Mrs. Kennedy's authorized biographer, reported Jackie's feelings upon meeting her future husband: "Jacqueline looked into Jack's laughingly aroused, intelligently inquisitive face and knew instantly that he would have a profound, perhaps a disturbing influence on her life. In a flash of inner perception she realized that here was a man who did not want to marry. She was frightened. Jacqueline, in this revealing moment, envisaged heartbreak, but just as swiftly determined such a heartbreak would be worth the pain."[33]

The courtship consisted of private evenings spent playing parlor games with the Bartletts or Jack's brother Bobby and his wife Ethel, or double-dating with them to see a movie. Their first formal date was to attend a dance at the Blue Room of Washington's Shoreham Hotel, but one of JFK's political cronies tagged along. Jackie would find this pattern particularly tiresome after her marriage. Her new beau spent considerable time in his home state of Massachusetts, campaigning throughout the Bay State to defeat the incumbent Senator Henry Cabot Lodge. Yet Kennedy kept in touch with Jackie. As she later remembered, "He'd call me from some oyster bar up on the Cape with a great clinking of coins, to ask me out to the movies the following Wednesday." That summer he took her to the Kennedy family's summer home at Hyannis Port on Cape Cod, where she charmed the congressman's formidable parents and made an effort to get along with Jack's rowdy, competitive trio of sisters, who were none too impressed by Jackie's demure demeanor and girlish voice. Jack's youngest sibling, Ted, later recalled Jackie's visit more charitably: "My brother really was smitten with her right from the very beginning when he first met her at dinner. Members of the [Kennedy] family knew right away that she was very special to him, and saw the developing of their relationship. I remember her coming up to Cape Cod at that time and involving herself in the life of the family. He was fascinated by her intelligence: they read together, painted together, enjoyed good conversation together and walks together." Jackie also joined JFK for a political rally or two in Boston and its environs.[34]

In November 1952, despite the Republican landslide that elected Dwight Eisenhower president, Kennedy upset Lodge to capture his Senate seat. The following January Jack invited Jackie to attend the Inaugural Ball with him. Shortly thereafter, she began to translate French books on Southeast Asia so that he could use the material for a foreign policy paper that he planned as his maiden speech on the floor of the U.S. Senate. Jackie continued her work with the *Times-Herald* and acquired her own byline for the newspaper's "Inquiring Camera Girl" feature. The questions she posed to the subjects of her column seemed to reflect her own concerns about her relationship with "the Senate's Gay Young Bachelor," as the *Saturday Evening Post* would label him later that year: Can you give me any reason why a contented bachelor should get married? Should couples reveal their pasts? Do you agree with Irish author Sean O'Faolain that the Irish are deficient in the art of love? What is your candid opinion of marriage? She even included Kennedy and his office neighbor, Senator Richard Nixon, in one of her columns, asking the senators and Senate pages what they thought of each other. Typically wry and self-deprecating, JFK responded, "I've often thought that the country might be better off if we Senators and pages traded jobs."[35]

If not for his aspirations to attain higher office, Jack Kennedy might have remained a confirmed bachelor. Yet the family-centered culture of the 1950s placed a premium on married political candidates. A man who had never been married might even prompt whispers about the nature of his sexuality. Accounts differ on exactly when Kennedy asked Jackie to marry him, but most seem to agree that while she was in London covering the coronation of Queen Elizabeth II in spring 1953, he determined to make Miss Bouvier his bride. While Jackie filed stories, photographs, and sketches portraying the colorful pageantry surrounding her and searched bookshops to find presents for her suitor, he cabled her: "Articles Excellent But You Are Missed. Love, Jack." His use of the passive voice may have signaled a dearth of romance on his part, but he made sure to meet Jackie's plane when it arrived from England. Upon her return, JFK presented Jackie with a two-carat diamond-and-emerald engagement ring. She accepted but asked her family to delay their announcement of the news until after the *Saturday Evening Post* published its story on Kennedy's bachelor status. With the article's publication, the Kennedys and Bouviers revealed their exciting news in June 1953. The *New York Times* trumpeted, "Senator Kennedy to Marry in Fall: Son of Former Envoy Is Fiancé of Miss Jacqueline Bouvier, Newport Society Girl."[36]

Later that summer *Life* magazine featured the prospective bride and groom in a story reporting their engagement. The cover photo captured a smiling Jack and Jackie sailing off the Hyannis Port shore. The couple thus unleashed the media's fascination with every aspect of their photogenic lives. Even Jackie, who was far warier of the camera's intruding eye than her fiancé, consented to a variety of poses during *Life*'s photo shoot at the Kennedy compound in the summer of 1953. Dressed in shorts and a sleeveless blouse, she duly joined in the family's athletic contests, sat adoringly at her fiancé's feet (while he casually sprawled in a chair), tousled his hair at the breakfast table, and balanced herself on the front porch rail in a 1950s-style pinup pose.[37]

The groom's father, Ambassador Joe Kennedy, saw to it that the nuptials would garner maximum publicity for JFK and fuel his increasingly ambitious political aspirations. The wedding was scheduled for September 12, 1953, at St. Mary's Catholic Church, Newport, Rhode Island. Although the church held no more than 750 people, Joe supervised invitations to 1,400 guests for the reception to be held at the Auchincloss's Hammersmith Farm. The former ambassador arranged for his friend, Archbishop Richard Cushing of Boston, to concelebrate, with other prominent clerics, the wedding mass, which would receive a special papal blessing. The groom's father could not have been happier when a crowd of 3,000 surrounded the church to catch a glimpse of America's newest celebrity couple. The bride's dress, with a tight bodice, cinched waist, and frilly taffeta skirt, was typical of 1950s women's fashion and its post–World War II emphasis on excess. Jacqueline had already begun to prefer simpler designs that would hint at the body's form without tightly defining it. Nevertheless, her preferences were apparently overruled by her mother and future father-in-law, whose meticulous attention to image making even extended to the bridal dress. Joe reportedly was particularly pleased at the potential political capital to be earned by Janet Auchincloss's commissioning of her African American seamstress, Ann Lowe, to create the gown.[38]

Postcard of Senator and Mrs. John F. Kennedy on their wedding day,
September 12, 1953. (author's collection)

Although most of the photographs and newsreels of the day do
not portray anything but serenity and delight in the bride's expression, Jacqueline's last day as Miss Bouvier was marred by the fact
that her father did not escort her down the aisle, as they both had
planned. Stepfather Hugh Auchincloss performed the paternal duty
when Black Jack Bouvier was deemed too inebriated to do so, at

least by his grudge-bearing ex-wife. By ostracizing him from pre-wedding events, she virtually guaranteed that he would turn to the bottle. Janet also barred Black Jack from the reception.[39]

After a honeymoon trip to Acapulco, Mexico, Jack and Jackie returned to the Kennedy family compound at Hyannis Port, where they would commute from Washington on the weekends. During the week, the newlyweds lived at Merrywood. For a considerable portion of their early married years, the Kennedys would rely on their parents' estates (at Hyannis Port, Palm Beach, Merrywood, and Hammersmith Farm) for bed and board. Jackie captured her husband's restless and ambitious spirit in a poem that she wrote for him one month after their marriage. Inspired by Stephen Vincent Benét's "John Brown's Body," the poem, which Jackie entitled "Meanwhile in Massachusetts," reveals her romanticized view of JFK:

> Meanwhile in Massachusetts Jack Kennedy dreamed
> Walking the shore of the Cape Cod Sea
> Of all of the things he was going to be. . . .
> Part he must serve, a part he must lead
> Both were his calling, both were his need. . . .
> He would build empires
> And he would have sons
> Others would fall
> Where the current runs
> IIe would find love
> He would never find peace
> For he must go seeking
> The Golden Fleece.[40]

For the new Mrs. John F. Kennedy, the first months of her marriage presented difficult challenges. Living with parents and in-laws, commuting on the weekends, is not exactly how a bride wishes to start married life. JFK wanted to settle eventually in the Georgetown section of D.C. to be close to his work and to brother Bobby, who had successfully managed Jack's first Senate campaign. In January 1954 Senator Kennedy and his wife signed a six-months lease on a Georgetown home and began what would pass for routine in their married life. They rented the house furnished, but Jackie had the bedroom furniture painted, which caused a problem with the home's owners when they moved back after the lease ended. They had stipulated that the Kennedys could repaint the furniture, but the agreed-upon color was green, not black![41]

Jackie frequently found herself alone as her husband attended to Senate duties, traveled around the country in an effort to gain national recognition, and, unfortunately, continued the womanizing habits of his bachelor days. An old JFK Navy buddy reported that Jack claimed Jackie was unsuspecting of his infidelity, but the friend thought otherwise. When JFK was home in Georgetown, he often brought his political friends with him, and Jackie was shocked by their raucous and slovenly behavior. The tension made her moody and sometimes uncommunicative, traits for which JFK, like most spouses, had little patience. Apparently, Jackie let Mary Thayer make reference to these mood swings in the latter's report that JFK once drew a straight line to symbolize his steadiness, with an undulating line over it representing his wife's "ups and downs." Jackie observed that her husband was "a rock . . . never irritable or sulky."[42]

During the 1960 presidential campaign, an ad for JFK featured his wife in an interview with actress Myrna Loy, who asked Mrs. Kennedy if she ever wished "her husband wasn't a busy candidate." Jackie admitted: "In the beginning I wished that. When I was first married, our life was almost as hectic as it is now, and I found it rather hard to adjust."[43]

As a newlywed, Mrs. Kennedy attempted to busy herself by taking classes at nearby Georgetown University's School of Foreign Service (the only section of the university that enrolled women) to brush up on American history. She earned Bs on her essays and final exam. She also learned housekeeping tips from the live-in maid, coordinated her husband's wardrobe, and supervised his menus to see that he ate nutritious meals both at home and the office, although she discovered that she was not a skilled cook. Jackie tried socializing and doing charitable work with other Senate wives, but at only twenty-four years of age and childless, she felt detached from their conversations about children and grandchildren. Still, she made an effort to join in with observations about her six-year-old half-brother, Jamie Auchincloss.[44]

Those who worked with Senator Kennedy noticed a change in his appearance and routine after Jackie came into his life. His longtime secretary, Evelyn Lincoln, observed, "After their marriage his suits fit perfectly, were conservatively cut and perfectly pressed. . . . From a fumbling person who couldn't tie his own tie, and it was always too long, to an immaculate dresser." A former Senate page from that time recalled that Mrs. Kennedy would bring picnic lunches to Senator Kennedy and that she would encourage him to get away from the Senate floor briefly so they could sit on the Capitol steps or enjoy the beautiful grounds around the building. She would also assist in his office, helping with correspondence from ethnic constituents or translating French documents.[45]

Although Jackie herself admitted that she had not been very interested in politics before her marriage, she believed that she learned it "by osmosis . . . just being around politicians." She attended committee hearings and floor debates involving her husband and developed several pet issues, including immigration policy, relief for Korea, and student exchange programs with Cuba. She would sometimes substitute for her husband at receptions honoring foreign dignitaries. Kennedy aide Ted Sorensen remembered of this period,

I don't think she herself regarded herself as a political savant or counselor. She had judgments of political figures as people, as individuals, but usually unrelated to their political positions. . . . Offhand, I don't recall hearing about her being his political sounding board. In a meeting, or even to me in private, he never said, "I was discussing this with Jackie and it occurred to her that we should do this, or, in her opinion so and so is unreliable." However, their personal relationship was totally private and kept very private. She could have played such a role without anyone knowing about it. And, secondly, it was certainly my impression that he shared a great many things with her and told her a great many things in his life and what was on his mind, so in a sense, her reactions may have had some help or influence.[46]

Jackie seemingly agreed with Sorensen's impression of her role in Senator Kennedy's professional life: "I thought the best thing I could do was to be a distraction. Jack lived and breathed politics all day long. If he came home to more table thumping, how could he ever relax?" Besides, Jack was surrounded by talented aides, political cronies, and shrewd relatives (like his father and brother Bobby), with whom he could discuss both policy and political strategy. Even if he had viewed women as professional equals, and nothing in the record indicates that he did, why would he need yet another political adviser on the home front? Katharine Graham, the late *Washington Post* publisher, observed in her Pulitzer Prize–winning memoir, "The Kennedy men were . . . unabashed chauvinists, as were the great majority of men at the time, including Phil [Graham, her husband]. They liked other bright men, and they liked girls, but they didn't really know how to relate to middle-aged women, in whom they didn't have a whole lot of interest. . . . Though the men were polite, we somehow knew we had no place in their spectrum."[47]

A portion of the Kennedys' first year of marriage comes to life in a unique photo essay created for *McCall's* magazine in May 1954. Orlando Suero, a staff photographer for a New York picture agency, spent an entire week with the newlyweds, recording their personal and professional activities. Obviously, the couple dictated the conditions of the photo shoot, but Suero's published collection from that assignment reflects a certain intimate (if not exactly candid) quality. As a women's magazine, *McCall's* wanted to focus on the life of a new Senate wife, yet Suero noticed that "John Kennedy kept sneaking himself into the pictures."[48]

Jackie, sporting her 1950s short "poodle" haircut, looks chicly studious on the Georgetown University campus in a simple sweater top and straight-line skirt with wedge pumps (while her fellow female students wear shirtwaist dresses, loafers, and bobby socks). Even to run errands around Georgetown shops, she wore a sophisticated black day dress with a white beaded necklace and black heels. When photographers were not present, she flitted around Georgetown in capri pants, much to her mother's horror. Many of the Suero photos are of Jackie and her husband together in casual, business, or formal attire in a variety of settings that represented the parts of their life they did share together (at least for the camera). Senator Kennedy had just returned from a trip to California before the photo shoot and would leave for New York as soon as it ended the next week. During the photographed week, they entertained Bobby Kennedy and his wife Ethel for an informal supper, held a formal dinner party for ten, strolled around Georgetown and the Capitol grounds, spent time working in JFK's Senate office, attended a seventieth birthday party for former President Harry Truman, lounged in their back garden (while the senator, clad in a white T-shirt and khaki trousers, read the Sunday paper and painted seascapes), and scattered a boxful of wedding photos on the floor as they rummaged through them and reminisced with Bobby and Ethel.[49]

The photos also depict Jack's ubiquitous prep-school friend, K. LeMoyne ("Lem") Billings, who was the proverbial "man who came to dinner." He was a nearly permanent houseguest, along with his large poodle. Although posed pictures of Jack, Jackie, and Lem portray them as a congenial threesome, his constant presence, during which he often let Jackie dogsit, must have been yet another annoyance during the early months of the Kennedy marriage.[50]

One photograph stands out among all the others for its stunning beauty and, in retrospect, predictive elements. It features young Jacqueline Kennedy in a strapless evening gown and what would be become her signature set of three-strand pearls, lighting the candles on her exquisitely set table in preparation for a formal dinner party on May 7, 1954. Many years later, Suero easily recalled the photo of Mrs. Kennedy preparing the table for her guests' arrival: "She was falling-down beautiful—gorgeous. When she started to light the candles I said to myself 'Oh, my God!' It was one of those moments when a photographer can see that he has a marvelous shot. . . . I kept thinking 'She's a princess!'"[51]

Of course, the Kennedys' real life was not the fairy tale represented in the photos. In addition to the difficulties of adjusting to her husband's schedule and peccadilloes, Jackie had to face JFK's deteriorating health in mid-1954. Jack's chronically painful back, the product of college football and war injuries, and osteoporosis, possibly caused by steroid treatment for colitis and malfunctioning adrenal glands, worsened to the point of requiring him to walk with crutches and be carried up and down stairs. Once their lease ended on the Georgetown home, they decided to abandon house hunting until Jack's health improved. They spent the summer of 1954 in Hyannis Port, while Jack consulted with doctors in Boston about his prognosis. The medical experts agreed that only another lumbar fusion, which he had undergone unsuccessfully in 1945, could possibly repair his back. Without the operation he might eventually be confined to a wheelchair. His Addison's disease, however, made the already risky procedure even more dangerous by increasing the chance of severe postoperative infection. Giving him only a fifty-fifty chance of surviving the surgery, the doctors advised against it. Yet Jack insisted on having the operation and found compliant physicians at the New York Hospital for Special Surgery, who performed the procedure on October 21, 1954.[52]

As predicted, a life-threatening infection ensued. Kennedy slipped into a coma, doctors summoned the Kennedys to his bedside, and a priest administered the last rites of the Catholic Church. Defying the odds, JFK regained consciousness to survive the initial crisis, yet recuperation was as painful as it was unproductive. He spent the next two months in the New York hospital, with Jackie at his side providing nurturing and morale-boosting assistance. Caring for a hospitalized loved one virtually around the clock is physically and emotionally exhausting, but Jackie remained remarkably strong throughout the ordeal.

Two months after the operation, the physicians reluctantly agreed to release Kennedy so that he could be flown to his parents' Palm Beach home for Christmas and a change of scene. Still barely able to sit, stand, or walk, he spent much of his time confined to bed. His gaping surgical wound, around a steel plate that doctors had implanted in his back, would simply not heal. Again, Jackie steadfastly attended to her husband's needs, from changing the dressing on his gruesome wound to updating him on Washington news and gossip.[53]

She also contributed inspiration and research assistance for her husband's new writing projects: first, an article for the *New York Times Magazine* and then a book, both on political courage in the United States Senate. The topic of political valor had been one of the themes in the American history course that she had taken at Georgetown with Professor Jules Davids. He and Kennedy aide Ted Sorensen provided chapter drafts for the ailing senator, who contributed dictated passages and written notes to the project. Jackie helped with editing along the way. JFK also relied on a team of academicians to provide scholarly guidance. Kennedy dedicated *Profiles in Courage,* the Pulitzer Prize–winning book resulting from this corporate effort, to his wife and expressed his gratitude to her in the preface: "This book would not have been possible without the encouragement, assistance and criticisms offered from the very beginning by my wife, Jacqueline, whose help during all the days of my convalescence I cannot ever adequately acknowledge." This was effusive praise indeed from a man who was not given to public displays of spousal affection.[54]

By February 1955 so little progress had been made in Jack's condition that he decided to try yet another surgical procedure by the New York doctors—this time a spinal bone graft and removal of the troublesome metal plate in his back. The third operation on his back in a decade healed successfully and provided some relief. After another round of convalescence in Palm Beach, Jack was referred to Dr. Janet Travell in New York, who was able to diminish his chronic back spasms with localized novocaine injections and a shoe lift to correct his slightly shorter left leg, which then evened his gait. Although he was now mobile and able to return to the Senate in May 1955, he would suffer from periodic back pain for the rest of his life.

Thayer's biography of Jackie asserted that "[t]hese shared troubles helped knit them [Jackie and her husband] together." Yet during the 1955 summer congressional recess, when the Kennedys traveled in Europe, they followed separate itineraries several times, sparking rumors among their friends about the precarious state of the Kennedy marriage. Divorce would not have been an option, however, for an aspiring presidential candidate in the 1950s, especially a Roman Catholic one. Democratic presidential candidate Adlai Stevenson had lost support from Roman Catholic voters in 1952 in part because of his divorced status. Not until Ronald Reagan in 1980 would a divorced candidate be elected president. By then, his 1949 split from actress Jane Wyman was in his distant Hollywood past, and he had a solid marriage of nearly thirty years to Nancy Reagan.[55]

Returning to Washington in fall 1955, the Kennedys still had no home to call their own. They stayed at Merrywood or in a Capitol Hill hotel when the Senate was in session. Jackie's discovery of her first pregnancy spurred her to start house hunting again. For a time she considered building a home on the Auchincloss's Merrywood estate. The cost of running utilities to the house would have been prohibitive, however, so she rejected that idea. Soon after, her mother and stepfather alerted her and Jack to a nearby property for sale in McLean, Virginia: Hickory Hill, a large estate previously owned by U.S. Supreme Court Justice Robert Jackson, was on the market in the wake of his death. The fifteen-room, white brick, Georgian-Colonial house, surrounded by acres of wooded property, with a pool and stable, appealed to the country-style living that Jackie so appreciated at Merrywood. The home's historic lineage as the Civil War headquarters of Union General George B. McClellan captured Jack's imagination. In October the Kennedys closed on the property for a selling price of $125,000. Jackie began the first major redecorating and remodeling project she had ever undertaken and created a template for her future work on White House interiors. She was meticulous in planning the home that she intended to inhabit with her husband and their much-anticipated children. She even made sure that shelving and drawers in her husband's bath- and dressing rooms were high enough so that he would not have to strain his back in bending over to reach them. The delight in planning her marital home, with a nursery for her first child, was dampened when she miscarried in the fall of 1955. That November she broke her ankle while gamely trying to keep up with the Kennedy clan in a football scrimmage at Hyannis Port. Now she was back at Merrywood while her foot healed and work was completed on Hickory Hill.[56]

When she and Jack finally settled in their own estate, Jackie found herself alone once more as her husband continued his hectic schedule. At least from their Georgetown home she could easily take a taxi to the Hill for lunch with him or to work in his office. From their country estate in McLean, however, the commute to Capitol Hill could take nearly an hour. Perhaps in retaliation for JFK's neglect and continued philandering, she started to spend time and money buying designer clothes, whose high price tags irked her husband. Coming to the marriage with virtually no money of her own, Jackie could offer nothing toward paying household bills, both for decorating her home and herself. Despite JFK's vast financial resources, these expenditures rankled him and added another source of friction to the marriage. At least the new year, 1956, brought good news; Jackie was again pregnant.[57]

That summer Jack would burst onto the national political scene with a respectable showing in the contest for the vice presidential nomination held at the Democratic Party's August convention in Chicago. Although he would lose the delegate tally to Tennessee's Senator Estes Kefauver, JFK had already secured a place for himself as a leading voice of the party. In his distinctive Boston brogue, he effectively narrated the convention's PR film on the Democratic Party's history, and he delivered an inspiring nomination speech for the party's presidential nominee, Adlai Stevenson. The *New York Times* captured Kennedy's charismatic essence: "Senator Kennedy came before the convention tonight as a photogenic movie star."[58]

By the convention, Jackie was well into the third trimester of her pregnancy. Against her better judgment, in light of her recent miscarriage, she decided to join Jack in Chicago to provide moral support. The Windy City was experiencing a heat wave, combined with the political frenzy surrounding the convention. Jackie later recalled that she avoided most of the commotion in the heart of the city by staying with Jack's sister and brother-in-law, Eunice and Sargent Shriver, in their Lake Shore Drive apartment, while JFK had accommodations in one of the convention hotels downtown. Jackie took her place in the convention arena's viewing box during the vice presidential balloting and attracted considerable press attention. At age twenty-seven, she now wore her hair longer, in a softer, more sophisticated cut. Her convention dress was a black V-neck with sheer sleeves. The look, accessorized with pearl-drop earrings and three-strand pearl necklace, was simply elegant, especially for maternity garb. Although she was not eager to have her husband on the Democratic ticket that year, despite her admiration for the urbane Stevenson, she described how the Kennedy family felt "a letdown" as they headed back east after JFK's first and, what would be the only, political defeat of his career.[59]

Kennedy's loss was the classic blessing in disguise, in light of the drubbing the Democratic ticket would receive in the fall election by the Republican incumbents, President Dwight Eisenhower and Vice President Richard Nixon. The worst of 1956 for the Kennedys, however, was just ahead. While Jack sailed in the Mediterranean, rendezvousing with women in ports of call, Jackie stayed at Hammersmith Farm during the last stages of her pregnancy. Less than two weeks after the convention, she began hemorrhaging and delivered a stillborn baby girl by cesarean section. Still on his sailing holiday, JFK was initially incommunicado, and his brother Bobby had to break the devastating news of the baby's loss to Jackie when she awoke from the anesthetic. One can imagine how she felt to lose a second baby, which she desperately wanted, and not have her husband by her side. Only when his travel companion, Senator George Smathers, convinced Jack that returning to his wife might avoid negative publicity did he truncate his vacation. Their relationship had reached its nadir. Jackie was so disconsolate that she could not face living in the cavernous Hickory Hill house, her planned familial home, especially with its nursery, which she had so lovingly prepared for her firstborn. Jack sold the estate to Bobby and Ethel, who had just welcomed their fifth child (of an eventual eleven, the last born after RFK's 1968 assassination).[60]

After Jackie recovered her health at Hammersmith and visited her sister Lee in London, Jack and Jackie moved back to Georgetown to another rented house in early 1957. Jack's reelection campaign for his U.S. Senate seat was on the horizon, and he was already gearing up for a serious run at the 1960 presidential nomination. Jackie's morale improved with news in March that she was again pregnant, which set off another round of house hunting. Nearly four years after their marriage, the Kennedys finally bought their first home together, at 3307 N Street NW in Georgetown. They paid $82,000 for a three-story, red-brick, Federal-era house, built in 1812, with a charming garden in the back. This time, for the task of decorating, Jackie hired well-known New York decorator Dorothy ("Sister") Parish, who had perfected a classic country style, emphasizing chintz fabrics, that softened her client's more formal Francophilic tastes. Jackie happily immersed herself in every detail of the $18,000 remodeling project, from paint colors to carpets to antiques to flower arrangements. The summer of 1957 brought more sadness, however. Her beloved father, Black Jack Bouvier, died of cancer in August. With her mother estranged from Bouvier and her sister abroad, Jackie meticulously planned the funeral and arranged for his burial in the cemetery of the church where he had married her mother in East Hampton on Long Island. In his coffin, she placed a bracelet that he had given to her as a graduation gift from Miss Porter's. Jackie received an inheritance of nearly $80,000 from her father's estate.[61]

While Jack was frequently on the road, fulfilling some of the thousands of speaking invitations he received that year, Jackie decided to remain in New York. There she was near the best doctors for the birth of her baby, due in late fall. On November 27, 1957, a day Jackie Kennedy would later describe as the happiest of her life, Caroline Bouvier Kennedy (named for Jackie's sister) was born by cesarean section. This time Jack Kennedy was close by, keeping watch in the waiting room with Jackie's mother and stepfather. Janet Auchincloss recalled JFK's speechless reaction to the news that mother and baby were fine: "I will always remember the sweet expression on his face and the way he smiled. . . . He just looked radiant when he heard that all was well." The senator arranged to take the baby to his wife when she awakened, and Janet noted how comfortable he was in holding his newborn daughter. His old friend Lem Billings thought that Jack "was more emotional about Caroline's birth than he was about anything else, and I had seen him respond to a hell of a lot of emotional occasions over the years. I remember how his voice cracked when he called to tell the news, and when he showed me the baby he looked happier than I had seen him look in a long time. With this child, he finally had a family of his own."[62]

The new Kennedy family threesome, plus nanny Maud Shaw, moved into the N Street house when Caroline was three weeks old. They would soon add a butler, maid, and cook to the household staff, which freed Jackie to continue her decorating jag. The living room was double-sized, with an archway separating each half. Jackie added new mantels to the room's two fireplaces and had the hardwood floors painted white with a diamond pattern overlay in pale green. In the dining and living rooms she used eighteenth-century-style French chairs combined with more comfortable furniture. She loved displaying French porcelain and fine woven carpets, and she would rearrange rooms on a whim, including repainting and rewallpapering them. Janet Auchincloss remembered "that when [Jackie] got the N Street house, it was going to be just right. It was a house with a lot of feeling about it and a lot of charm, but she did that living room . . . over at least three times within the first four months they were there. . . . Rugs, curtains, upholstery, everything, was suddenly turned lovely different shades of beige. . . . I can remember Jack just saying to me, 'Mrs. Auchincloss, do you think we're prisoners of beige?'" The house proved the perfect backdrop for compelling photo essays on the Kennedy trio: Jack, the handsome husband and father, Jackie, the beautiful mother and wife, and Caroline, the darling baby.[63]

Jack not only had his own photogenic family; he had produced a celebrity trio. Posed family portraits became centerpieces of media profiles in JFK's 1958 Senate reelection race. One Boston newspaper declared Jackie "the youngest and prettiest" campaign wife. "Up early each morning, the team of Jack and Jackie is criss-crossing the state by auto, pumping hands of thousands of voters, and appearing on public platforms 10 or 15 times a day," the paper reported.

With her talent for languages, Jackie was most effective at ethnic political rallies. In Worcester, Massachusetts, she spoke to the Cercle Français in French and concluded, "It was not as frightening [to speak] as it would have been in English." Jack told a reporter, "She is simply invaluable. In French-speaking areas of the state, she is able to converse easily with them, and everyone seems to like her. She never complains about the rugged schedule, but seems to enjoy it." To an audience of almost 1,000 Italian Americans in her husband's home state, she made remarks in their native language. An Italian ward heeler in Boston commented: "When [Jackie] opened her mouth and introduced herself in Italian, fluent Italian, . . . all pandemonium broke loose. All the people went over and started to kiss her, and the old women spoke to her as if she were a native of the North End [Boston's Italian section]. And I think her talk is actually what cemented the relationship between Senator Kennedy and the Italian-Americans of the district." Jackie also appeared on television during the campaign, introducing nearly one-year-old Caroline to the viewing audience. In the 1958 November election, JFK won with 73.2 percent of the ballots cast, or 874,608 more votes than his Republican opponent.[64]

Jackie also began to accompany Jack on some of his numerous political forays beyond Massachusetts, traveling with him to Nebraska, Iowa, Louisiana, Florida, New York, New Jersey, and Ohio. By the time she curtailed her travels in mid-1960 because of pregnancy, she had visited forty-six states with her husband. Her powers of political observation particularly impressed Kennedy adviser, Professor Arthur Schlesinger Jr., who recalled, "I realized that, underneath a veil of lovely inconsequence, she concealed tremendous awareness, an all-seeing eye and a ruthless judgment." Economist John Kenneth Galbraith was equally struck by this trait: "[Jackie] had a very shrewd view of people and who the real people were and who the phonies were. She also had a clear distinction as between those who were bright and those who were stupid."65 Her keen discernment proved a valuable asset on the presidential campaign trail.

CHAPTER 3

BEING FIRST LADY

Jacqueline Kennedy's journey to the White House began before her husband's official announcement of his candidacy for president of the United States on January 2, 1960. She had joined JFK on the political circuit long before his declaration. Jackie's youthful appearance at age thirty was an attractive novelty when compared with the wives of other prominent candidates, who were nearly twenty years her senior. Her vitality contributed to the vigorous image JFK fostered as a counter to stories about his painful back ailment. *Look* magazine reported in late 1959 that "[Jack] Kennedy's nonstop campaigning has silenced talk about his ill health." The article included glossy photos of the active couple and toddler Caroline sailing and swimming at Hyannis. Their suntans and glowing smiles radiated youth and well-being.[1]

Between campaign stops Jackie was apt to read trendy Beat poet Jack Kerouac's memoir *On the Road*. Yet despite her soft-spoken, bookish nature, she had a knack for charming audiences. Her husband knew the value of such grace on the hustings, especially in states that would be crucial to his victory. In spring 1959 Mrs. Kennedy accompanied JFK to electoral-vote-rich New York State for an appearance in Buffalo. Later that year the couple traveled to West Virginia, a predominantly Protestant state, where Senator Kennedy hoped to capture a 1960 primary election victory as a sign that his

Roman Catholicism was not a disqualifying handicap. In a follow-up letter to several West Virginia supporters, Senator Kennedy specifically mentioned his wife: "Jackie and I certainly enjoyed our recent visit to West Virginia. We appreciated your interest in our activities and Jackie especially wants to be remembered to you because of the pleasant meeting at the Chernenko [presumably a pro-Kennedy constituent] home."[2]

In the first half of 1960 Jackie traveled with her husband to a dozen states. Three weeks after Kennedy announced his presidential candidacy in the Old Senate Caucus Room, with his wife in attendance, they kicked off his campaign in New Hampshire, which by tradition holds the first primary contest of each quadrennial cycle. The *Washington Post*/UPI pictured the couple chatting with residents and supporters in Nashua, and the *Post* reported that Senator Kennedy's "attractive wife, Jacqueline, wearing a flaming red coat and dark fur hat, accompanied him" as he stumped for votes in the upcoming March 8 primary.[3]

In February 1960, with JFK battling regional favorite Senator Hubert H. Humphrey in the Wisconsin primary, Jackie joined in a three-day swing through the Dairy State. Each evening she attended receptions for her husband in one of a trio of eastern Wisconsin cities: Kenosha, Fond du Lac, and Green Bay. Even in the bitterly cold winter weather, she and her husband would each take a side of the main street in small towns, chatting with pedestrians as they ran their errands. Occasionally, the candidate remarked to his aides, "Jackie's drawing more people than I am, as usual." Despite her innate shyness, she would sometimes surprise the Kennedy campaign staff with her assertiveness, as when she commandeered the public address system in a Kenosha supermarket and urged the shoppers to vote for her husband. Her campaign instincts were not always in tune with the rank-and-file Wisconsin voter, however. Attempting to entertain Kennedy supporters waiting for her husband's arrival at a rally, she suggested that they all join in singing an Irish tune. Unfortunately, she merely perplexed the Midwesterners with a melody popular only in South Boston.[4]

Jackie's paradoxical personality, which could be both aloof and engaging, was an unusual asset in grassroots politics. She exuded charisma that captivated audiences, and she simultaneously maintained an emotional distance that created a seductive aura around her. John Kenneth Galbraith, whom President Kennedy would name U.S. ambassador to India, captured one important element of her campaign persona: "Jacqueline Kennedy did not talk politics; she celebrated her detachment therefrom. . . . [D]uring the campaign of 1960 JFK and Jackie were leaving for a day of vote-getting in Pennsylvania. He had a briefcase full of speech drafts, political memoranda, biographical material on the politicians he would meet. She had the *Mémoirs du Duc de Saint-Simon* in French. She would take no part in the day's political persuasion. It was only important that she be there; she, as much as the candidate, was the one the crowds wanted to see. But she had a deeper purpose: it was she, not the more trusting JFK, who would observe, hear and render judgment on the politicians they would encounter."[5]

A few days before Wisconsin's April 5, 1960, primary election date, Jackie appeared with her husband at a boisterous campaign rally in Milwaukee's Fourth Congressional District. Robert Drew, an innovative documentarian, captured their appearance on tape for his film, *Primary,* released in 1960. The work, which was the first to acquire such candid visual and audio records of the political process, followed Kennedy and Humphrey as they campaigned through Wisconsin. Drew's film displays a typical campaign rally appearance for Mrs. Kennedy. Dressed in a stylish but simple dark suit, topped by an orchid corsage and costume necklace, she makes her way through the crowd, waiting in the wings, to the stage of a packed auditorium. There she takes her place behind the podium, smiling radiantly and joining supporters in singing the Kennedy campaign song, to the tune of Frank Sinatra's 1959 hit, "High Hopes":

> Everyone is voting for Jack.
> 'Cause he's got what all the rest lack.
> Everyone wants to back Jack.
> Jack is on the right track.
> 'Cause he's got high hopes!
> He's got hiiiigh hopes! . . .[6]

Jackie looks slightly embarrassed by the inane lyrics, as does her husband, who stands next to her on stage. (They could console themselves that at least they had borrowed the hip Sinatra's anthem, as opposed to Humphrey's folksy campaign ditty, "Hubert, Hubert Humphrey, the president for you and me," accompanied by a twangy rendition of the theme from Walt Disney's popular 1955 film, *Davy Crockett, King of the Wild Frontier.*) Mrs. Kennedy approaches the microphone, nervously knits her white-gloved fingers behind her back, and speaks a few words (unintelligible on the film's primitive soundtrack) in Polish to the predominantly ethnic crowd, which roars its approval. After JFK exhorts them to vote for him on election day, the Kennedys form a receiving line. Jackie maintains her warm smile but says little as she shakes hands with audience members, who press in from all sides. JFK manages a quick "thank you" and the glad-handing politician's mainstay, "good to see you," for each of the voters as they greet him. The documentary cameras were also with Senator and Mrs. Kennedy, and his campaign staff, as they anxiously awaited the election returns in a Milwaukee hotel suite. Winning six out of ten congressional districts was not the knockout punch that JFK had hoped to deliver against Humphrey, who vowed to continue his fight for the nomination against his Senate colleague in the May 10 West Virginia primary.[7]

By early spring Mrs. Kennedy was again pregnant, with a due date in December, but she insisted on campaigning for her husband over a three-week period in the critical Mountain State. After she took time to visit an elderly man who could not leave his invalid wife alone, he gushed, "Now I believe in Santa Claus. [Jackie] looks like a real queen." Despite her elite roots and upbringing, she once more surprised Kennedy staffers by her willingness to communicate with the wives of West Virginia's poverty-stricken coal miners, as well as with railroad workers she spotted along the back roads. Not even her most ardent admirers claim that she did so with the ease of Eleanor Roosevelt, but when Mrs. Kennedy, as first lady, was procuring new glassware for the White House, she insisted on ordering from glassworks in West Virginia to boost the state's economy.[8]

JFK scored a major symbolic victory over Humphrey in West Virginia, proving that a Catholic could carry an overwhelmingly Protestant state, and eliminating one of his key opponents for the nomination. Ample Kennedy funds, generously distributed throughout the state, and a campaign blitz by Franklin Roosevelt Jr. undoubtedly contributed to the win. Ben Bradlee, *Newsweek*'s

Washington bureau chief and Kennedy friend in the 1960s, noted in his 1975 memoir that the victorious candidate ignored Jackie at the celebratory rally in Charleston. Whether the crowd even noticed is another question. In that era, most candidates (and certainly the aloof Jack Kennedy) simply did not gush over their spouses in public. Today, "family values" constituencies virtually demand such public displays.[9]

The Kennedy campaign's strategy and tactics were beginning to bear fruit. In the race for the 1960 Democratic presidential nomination, only sixteen states held primary elections, choosing just over a third of the convention delegates (in contrast with forty states selecting over four-fifths of the Democratic delegates in 2000). Nevertheless, as a forty-two-year-old Catholic with only seven years' experience in the U.S. Senate, JFK had to prove that he could win in varied regions of the country and among constituencies different from those in his native Massachusetts. He strategically chose to concentrate on the following seven primary election contests: New Hampshire, Wisconsin, Indiana, West Virginia, Nebraska, Maryland, and Oregon. He could not sew up the nomination in those states, but by compiling wins in each (sometimes without opposition), he could demonstrate his electability.[10]

It seems more than coincidental that his wife would overcome her aversion to grassroots politics, and, later, jitters over her nascent pregnancy, to follow JFK on the campaign trail in the key states of New Hampshire, Wisconsin, and West Virginia. To the extent that she did not always accompany him, Senator Kennedy could rely on a bevy of family members (his mother, sisters, brothers, and in-laws) to join in the effort. Jackie's campaign absences were not negatively reported in the press because of the perfectly legitimate medical reason for excusing herself. Until relatively recently, American society viewed pregnancy as a private and delicate condition, often necessitating "confinement" of the mother-to-be. For example, network censors forbade writers of *I Love Lucy,* the popular 1950s sitcom, from using the word *pregnant* to describe Lucille Ball's obvious impending "blessed events" when she was expecting her real-life children. Only in the 1970s did public policy, as defined by courts and legislatures, take a realistic approach to pregnancy. Moreover, even Eleanor Roosevelt had once questioned the propriety of women campaigning for their husbands, although she did so for her less mobile spouse. Bess Truman left most of the public campaigning to her husband, but she was a steadfast helpmate in his private decision making and speech writing. Mamie Eisenhower lacked a sturdy constitution and eschewed the rigors of presidential campaigns whenever possible. She did not even want Ike to run for reelection in 1956 after his heart attack the previous year. In fact, candidates' spouses in the 1960 election (including Mesdames Kennedy, Johnson, Humphrey, Nixon, and Lodge) set precedents for active participation in their husbands' campaigns, which helped define the prominent political role of modern first ladies in the late twentieth century. *Look* magazine briefly profiled four wives of presidential candidates in midsummer 1960. The publication reported that Mrs. Kennedy "owns a lithe model's figure, went to fashionable schools, speaks French. She is gay, friendly and a little eggheadish and has a daughter, 2½."[11]

Given her problematic obstetric history, Jackie reduced her campaign participation in the second trimester of her pregnancy. In light of the disastrous end to her 1956 pregnancy, just after she had traveled to that year's Democratic Convention, she stayed at the Kennedy summer home in Hyannis Port with Caroline while her husband attended the 1960 Democratic Convention in Los Angeles. Interviewed on TV the day after her husband's nomination victory, Mrs. Kennedy was asked when she heard the good news. With her characteristically coy smile, she replied, "Well, I was watching television, so I suppose at the same time everyone else did." The interviewer wanted to know if her baby was due before Inauguration Day; "Uh," she paused with a twinkle in her eye, "when's Inauguration Day?" Her insouciance struck the right balance between the enigmatic and charming facets of her personality. Despite her expressed ignorance of the inaugural calendar, she phoned her old friend Tish Baldrige and asked her to "head up my staff" in the event JFK landed in the White House.[12]

By September 1960 Mrs. Kennedy had scaled back personal appearances on her husband's behalf. Yet JFK only once mentioned his wife's pregnancy on the campaign trail, even though his staff told him that "housewives would disapprove of Jacqueline's absence." On a trip through California, he said of his spouse, "She's home having a boy." The press wanted to know how he already knew the baby's sex, to which he replied, "She [Jackie] told me—you would have to ask her." In mid-September Jackie noted that her doctor had allowed her to travel to New York for two days of campaigning. She appeared on *Today* for a televised interview with host Dave Garroway. The next day she attended a full round of luncheons, rallies, and receptions with JFK. About the luncheon at the Commodore Hotel she commented, "Everyone seemed so enthusiastic about Jack that I loved every minute of it." For three of his four landmark TV debates with Vice President Richard Nixon, she tuned in at her Georgetown home and hosted listening parties for the first two contests. The gatherings included women leaders from the Democratic Party who promised to host similar events in their hometowns for the remainder of the Nixon-Kennedy debates. On October 13 Mrs. Kennedy managed to attend the third debate with her husband in New York City.[13]

Despite the limits on her travel, the Democratic candidate's wife did not disappear from the public eye. Her European taste in clothes generated a controversy in the American fashion trade and among labor unions in the garment business. The Associated Press published a story from *Women's Wear Daily* that criticized Mrs. Kennedy's (and her mother-in-law's) preferences for French designers. The AP estimated that Jackie spent $30,000 annually on her wardrobe. When a *New York Times* reporter questioned her about the reported expenditure, Jackie flippantly replied, "I couldn't spend that much unless I wore sable underwear." The Republican candidate's wife, Pat Nixon, attempted to distinguish her tastes by commenting that she liked "American designers" and that she usually chose clothes "off the rack in different stores around Washington." The International Ladies' Garment Workers' Union contributed $300,000 to JFK's campaign and lobbied the future president to encourage his wife to "buy American."[14]

Anna Roosevelt, FDR's only daughter and a Kennedy supporter, worried about the negative press that Jackie was generating. When Anna came upon a more favorable piece, authored by Bess Furman in the *New York Times* on September 20, 1960, she clipped it and sent it along to Arthur Schlesinger Jr., commenting, "This is the first good 'Jackie story,' and it's excellent. Bess is good at getting the 'folksy stuff' with all the necessary dignity. Too bad this couldn't have been sent to the [Louisville, Kentucky] *Courier-Journal.* I hope that it went to other papers in doubtful states." Perhaps Furman recalled the enthusiastic and deferential handwritten thank-you note that a young Jacqueline Bouvier had sent to her eight years previously. Furman, who had authored a history of the White House, encouraged Jackie to write a children's book on the executive mansion as a follow-up to her 1952 "Inquiring Camera Girl" story of President and Mrs. Eisenhower's nieces.[15]

Furman's September 1960 article on Mrs. Kennedy emphasized her foreign-language political ads that she would tape that fall in Italian, French, and Spanish for ethnic voters. Much of the Furman story contained comments Jackie offered during a tea for reporters at her Georgetown home. The reporters' questions ranged from whether she was prepared for large-scale entertaining in the White House, to whether she would hold press conferences and/or write a daily column. With her experience in running "three houses" for her husband, "one of the busiest men in the country," and entertaining "large and small groups on long and short notice," she felt up to the task of White House hostess. She would preside over press conferences and pen a column "if Jack wanted me to." (She did neither.) When questioned whether being first lady would change her, she responded honestly and prophetically, "I wouldn't pretend to be anything that I wasn't." The fashion scandal resurfaced at the tea, and Mrs. Kennedy diplomatically sidestepped the query, "whose clothes [hers or Mrs. Nixon's] cost more?" She cited former President Truman's response: "The wives of these candidates are both wonderful ladies and that's the way they ought to be treated." No more fresh references to fur undergarments! She spoke about the impending birth of her baby, Caroline's reaction to a new sibling, and Dr. Spock's suggestions for preparing a toddler for a new baby brother or sister, which gave Jackie the opportunity to report that the famous pediatrician had announced his support for JFK. (She met with him later in the fall to discuss education and medical care for the elderly—two of his pet issues.) The article ended with an interview of Margaret Price, vice chairman of the Democratic National Committee, who had just completed a thirteen-state tour that included the West Coast, Texas, and New Jersey, with the Kennedy campaign. She remarked, "I have not had one question on Mrs. Kennedy's wardrobe." Rather, the women she had talked to were more interested in a strong economy and world peace, Price observed.[16]

A constant stream of stories about her efforts on JFK's behalf appeared in the press during the last seven weeks of the campaign. Mrs. Kennedy's friend, Joan Braden, pointing out to Bobby Kennedy that Jack had failed to mention Jackie in his convention speech, urged the campaign to "bring in Jackie." Braden, whose husband was in the newspaper business, suggested that Jackie write a column expressing her opinions and sharing stories of her family. Modeled on Eleanor Roosevelt's famous commentaries, "My Day," Mrs. Kennedy's column, entitled "Campaign Wife," was distributed weekly by the Democratic National Committee on a syndicated basis to newspapers. The DNC offered to furnish, on request, a photo of the Kennedys and their daughter for newspapers to run with the piece. The former "Inquiring Camera Girl" was back in journalism.[17]

The first "Campaign Wife" column, released on September 16, 1960, was filled with Mrs. Kennedy's comments about not being on the stump with her husband "[f]or the first time since Jack and I have been married." She reminisced about "the few weeks of being with Jack in Wisconsin and West Virginia [where] I met so many people whom I would still like to be in touch with. The worst part was not being in Los Angeles for the nomination . . . but my obstetrician firmly disagreed [with my desire to attend]." She told stories of spending time with Caroline and shopping for "maternity clothes," which gave her a chance to broach the fashion controversy that had broken in that week's press. "All the talk over what I wear and how I fix my hair has amused me and puzzled me. What does my hairdo have to do with my husband's ability to be President? Actually I've always loved clothes, and when I've had the time I've enjoyed the universal feminine sport of shopping from store to store and looking for new styles in the women's magazines." She concluded her first column, "I hope soon to be able to go along with Jack as much as possible, particularly on trips not too far away from Washington."[18]

Two weeks later she was again waxing nostalgic about previous travels with her husband. She listed his campaign visits that September 1960 to Tennessee, Wyoming, Colorado, Utah, and Ohio, and recalled trips with JFK to those states in 1959. "All the parts of this great and beautiful country I have seen with my husband—all the people I have met, I will always be grateful to politics for showing me America," she wrote wistfully.[19]

The "Campaign Wife" column also addressed policy issues, particularly those of interest to women. Expressing her concern over where Caroline would go to nursery school, Jackie discussed the need for adequate classroom space and qualified teachers around the country, both of which she said her husband supported through federal aid programs. Very clearly, Mrs. Kennedy's weekly column targeted female voters. She announced the "Calling for Kennedy" week, October 17–24, "during which women all over the country will call on other women to find out what they feel are the important issues today and to answer any questions they may have about my husband." Reported the *Washington Post*'s women's section, "The sparkling-eyed, eager young wife whose pregnancy keeps her from participating in the strenuous campaign tactics of her husband launched the national program" with two hundred other women in Arlington, Virginia. Pictured in the newspaper with a phone to her ear, she conducted a conference call with a dozen women volunteers throughout the country. Mrs. Kennedy reported that "thousands of 'Calling for Kennedy' forms telling what women believe to be the most important issues facing the country" came pouring in. "Without exception the issue uppermost in every woman's mind is peace—not a single person put the budget first. Next came education, medical care for the aged, and the cost of living," she explained. Although the initiative was to gather women's opinions on public policy, Kennedy volunteers would also use the contacts for a get-out-the-vote push just before election day.[20]

Another issues-oriented initiative for female voters, labeled "Women's Committee for the New Frontiers," featured twenty-seven women experts in economics, health care, education, civil rights, and foreign policy who met three times at the Kennedys' Georgetown home for panel discussions. "[W]e lay the groundwork for a major source of information for my husband," Mrs. Kennedy told the press, which reported that the format might continue to be used if JFK were elected president. (President Kennedy established the President's Commission on the Status of Women in late 1961, with Eleanor Roosevelt as its chairman. Mrs. Kennedy did not participate.) Frances Perkins, labor secretary in Franklin Roosevelt's administration, summarized the preelection committee's findings for the press. Just before November 1960, the Women's Committee released a report, "Medical Care for the Aged," which called for "increased medical care through the social security system," a precursor to Medicare, passed in 1965 under the Johnson administration.[21]

In the final two weeks of the campaign, Mrs. Kennedy admitted her mounting excitement over the outcome. In late October her doctor ordered her not to add any more campaign appearances to her schedule. She wrote in her column that she was glad to spend more time with Caroline, who, "seeing her father's picture on lapel pins and bumpers . . . [is] wondering why so many people are talking about him and why he isn't home more often." Nonetheless, she fulfilled a previously scheduled appearance with JFK for a rally in Spanish Harlem, where she spoke in Spanish to the crowd, and for a ticker-tape parade through New York City on October 19. Perched on the back seat of a convertible, the couple was cheered by throngs of an estimated two million people, some of whom broke through the lines and pressed against the car to shake hands with them. Despite her pregnancy, Jackie looked glamorous in a Givenchy coat and sported what would become her trademark pillbox hat.[22]

Mrs. Kennedy continued working for her husband's election, even after returning from New York. She conducted a tea/press conference at her Georgetown home for nearly fifty women journalists and two of their male colleagues. She received nothing but praise from her authorized biographer, Mary V. R. Thayer, who reported in the *Washington Post* of Mrs. Kennedy's "polished dignity" and "strength of character revealed in restraint." Thayer claimed that the journalists in attendance "were spellbound" by the Democratic candidate's wife. "They just seemed to like listening to and looking at Mrs. Kennedy," Thayer enthused. She defended Jackie's neat bouffant hairstyle, "often criticized by those who couldn't get away with a fashionable hairdo."[23]

In the final week of the campaign, Jack, Jackie, and Caroline participated in a television interview by actor Henry Fonda, complicated by the fact that JFK and Fonda were in California and she and her daughter in Washington. While trying to keep Caroline from fidgeting, Jackie posed questions to Jack from the "Calling for Kennedy" forms. She concluded her final "Campaign Wife" column, "I've missed terribly campaigning with Jack and meeting all of you, but at least since I had campaigned with him so often before I could pretend I was there." With that, she and Caroline left for Hyannis Port to rendezvous with her husband and await the election returns.[24]

At about 10:30 on election night, votes mounted for JFK from the industrial states, and Jackie, calling the candidate by her pet name for him, declared, "Oh, Bunny, you're president now!" But he responded that it was "too early" to predict victory. In fact, when he finally retired to bed around 4:00 AM, he still did not know the outcome of one of the closest presidential races in U.S. history. A seesaw battle for popular and electoral votes between Kennedy and Nixon kept the result unclear until midmorning of the day after the election. Ultimately, JFK's margin of victory was just over 118,000 of the nearly 70 million popular votes cast. Yet Kennedy racked up wins in states with large numbers of electoral votes, giving him a 303–219 edge (33 more votes than the 270 needed to be elected president). Rehearsed by her nanny, three-year-old Caroline awakened her father with a sunny "Good morning, Mr. President," to his delight. His faithful aide, Ted Sorensen, confirmed the victory, leaving the new president-elect to have a quiet breakfast with his wife and daughter. Jackie later disappeared for a solitary walk on the beach, like those she described in her poem, "Sea Joy," twenty years earlier. JFK caught up with her and reported that it was time to change from her faded raincoat, beach shoes, and scarf for a historic family portrait. In contrast to her walking attire, her red dress, pearls, and black pumps made her appear utterly dazzling, seated on a couch, surrounded by her husband, his parents, siblings, and in-laws, all smiling joyously over their good fortune. Later that day, at a victory rally in Hyannis, Jackie took center stage with her husband as he concluded, "My wife and I look forward to a new administration and a new baby!"[25]

Just two weeks later, and almost a month prematurely, John F. Kennedy Jr. entered the world, the first child born to a president-elect. Unfortunately for Jackie, the labor began traumatically, with sharp pains, hemorrhaging, and a frantic ambulance ride to Georgetown Hospital, without her husband, who was on his way to

Palm Beach that night. By the time JFK returned to Washington, his wife had undergone another cesarean delivery, and the baby, who weighed barely six pounds, had been placed in an incubator to alleviate breathing difficulties. Although mother and baby were hospitalized nearly two weeks, they were finally well enough to fly to the Kennedy home at Palm Beach in early December. There the future first lady stayed until just before the inauguration, attempting to regain her strength, studying the history of White House redecorations, and issuing lengthy memos to her Chief of Staff Tish Baldrige. Many years later Baldrige wrote that Mrs. Kennedy designed her mission as first lady along the following lines: "preservation of her family, entertaining with style and grace in the number one house in the world, the makeover of the White House itself as a focus of American history and accomplishment, and the raising of the cultural stature of this country."[26]

Another of Mrs. Kennedy's concerns in the aftermath of her husband's victory centered around her wardrobe and choice of an "official" designer. She knew well that her fashion decisions could become a source of controversy in JFK's presidency, as they had during the campaign. While still in Georgetown Hospital, convalescing from John Jr.'s birth, she invited Kennedy family friend and fashion designer Oleg Cassini to visit and bring suggestions for how he would attire the future first lady. His background and couturier philosophy were a perfect match for Jackie. Parisian-born Cassini had settled in the United States, married actress Gene Tierney, and designed wardrobe for Hollywood films after World War II. He had both a European flair and dramatic sense, blended with fresh American tastes, that appealed to Mrs. Kennedy. He later admitted that he "talked to her like a movie star, and told her that she needed a story, a scenario as First Lady," one that would make her "the most elegant woman in the world." He explained his view of "fashion [as] a mirror of history; . . . the message that her clothes would send—simple, youthful, elegant—. . . would reinforce the image of her husband's administration." Cassini struck just the right chord with the Francophilic first-lady-to-be when he announced, "You have an opportunity here for an American Versailles." Mrs. Kennedy chose him as her primary designer on the spot and followed up with a long letter to him once she reached Palm Beach, in which she categorized "PUBLICITY" as one of her concerns: "One reason I am so happy to be working with you is that I have some control over my fashion publicity which has gotten so vulgarly out of hand. . . . BUT—you realize I know that I am so much more of fashion interest than other First Ladies—I refuse to have Jack's administration plagued by fashion stories of a sensational nature—& to be the Marie Antoinette or Josephine [Bonaparte] of the 1960's—So I will have to go over it with you before we release future things—because I don't want to be seen as buying too much—You can make the stories available—but with my approval first—There just may be a few things we won't tell them about!"[27]

In an attempt to diminish gossip about her wardrobe, Mrs. Kennedy drafted a letter that she ultimately sent over Tish Baldrige's signature to the editor of *Women's Wear Daily*, which Jackie considered one of the worst offenders in publishing "erroneous articles about her clothes." The letter attempted to craft the public image of her clothing that she desired: "Mrs Kennedy realizes that the clothes she wears are of interest to the public, but she is distressed by the implications of extravagance, of over-emphasis of fashion in relation to her life, and of the misuse of her name by firms from which she has not bought clothes." The letter reported that Cassini would be the first lady's official designer and that the wardrobe would be "made in America." She would purchase only necessary items, "without extravagance," and would even wear the same outfit more than once.[28]

Just after noon on January 20, 1961, thirty-one-year-old Jacqueline Kennedy assumed the role of first lady when her husband was sworn in as president of the United States. She had already dazzled Washington and the media the evening before, with her appearance at a preinaugural concert and gala, wearing diamond and emerald jewelry and dressed in a Cassini ivory satin evening gown. Bereft of ornamentation, except for a French-inspired rosette made from the same ivory fabric as the dress and worn to the side at the waist, the gown, with its overskirt that fell into a simple train, could not have been more elegant. The president-elect was captivated by the image, instructing his friend, Bill Walton, to turn on the limousine's interior light so revelers could "see Jackie." A snowfall that blanketed the nation's capital that night made her debut even more magical, if inconvenient for motorists stranded in clogged streets.[29]

The next day Mrs. Kennedy again stood out from the crowd by wearing another Cassini creation, a sleek fawn-colored wool coat with matching pillbox hat, positioned to the back of her bouffant hairdo. A sable muff that matched the hint of fur trim around her collar was a charming and warm accessory. She appeared in contrast to the other women who wore dowdy hats and brightly colored cloth coats or bulky furs that made them look "like a bunch of bears." She was so overwhelmed by the soaring rhetoric of her husband's inaugural address that all she could think to do afterward, back in the Capitol building, was touch his cheek and exclaim, "Jack, you were wonderful!" (In 1961 the tradition at presidential swearing-in ceremonies was to have the clerk of the U.S. Supreme Court hold the Bible as the new president took the oath of office from the chief justice. Subsequent inaugurations began a new tradition of having the president-elect's wife hold the Bible. The Clintons included their daughter Chelsea at the podium for her father's 1993 and 1997 swearing-in ceremonies. Likewise, George W. Bush invited his twin daughters Jenna and Barbara to join their mother Laura for the administration of the oath of office in 2001.)[30]

After the postceremony luncheon in the Old Supreme Court Chamber at the Capitol, the motorcade down Pennsylvania Avenue with her husband in an open car, and nearly an hour on the inaugural parade viewing stand, Jackie could bear the excitement and frigid temperatures no longer. Still weakened from the previous month's difficult childbirth, she made her way back to her new home in the White House and collapsed into bed for an afternoon nap. The first lady overcame her exhaustion to accompany her husband to two of the five inaugural balls that night. (He attended all five, plus a postball party at columnist Joe Alsop's Georgetown home.) Her luminous presence, in a self-designed, shimmering, beaded, chiffon and silk gown, topped with a stunning ivory silk cape (created at Bergdorf Goodman in New York), belied the fact that her health was not yet fully restored. Mrs. Kennedy had released to the press a description of her inaugural ball costume. Ultimately, she would donate the dress and cape to the Smithsonian Institution for its First Ladies collection, although she actually preferred the Cassini preinaugural gala gown. The Smithsonian collection dates to the early twentieth century, indicating a long public interest in first ladies' fashion.[31]

The new president and first lady arrive at an inaugural ball, January 20, 1961.
(Photo by Abbie Rowe, White House. JFK Library, Boston)

The Associated Press wired photos around the country of the stunning Mrs. Kennedy in each of her inaugural outfits, and local papers printed them prominently in their publications. The Louisville *Courier-Journal,* the newspaper that Anna Roosevelt had wanted to publish a "good 'Jackie story'" during the campaign, pictured JFK and the new first lady in their inaugural finery. Although Louisville only had two television stations at the time (NBC and CBS affiliates), each broadcast the inaugural balls live in their late-night programming on January 20, 1961. The televised presidency, and its accouterments, had arrived. In the nation's capital, the *Washington Post,* whose owners and publishers, Phil and Katherine

Graham, hosted a dinner for the Kennedys the night before the inauguration, reported that "Mrs. Kennedy was [as] sparkling as the
diamonds she wore with the white gown and coat she designed" for
the inaugural balls. "Everyone agreed that Jacqueline Kennedy's career as a major fashion influence was beginning impressively," the
paper trumpeted. The *Post* also ran a serialization of the Mary
Thayer biography of Jackie, which was advertised in the *Post* by the
Ladies' Home Journal, where it would appear in February 1961. In
addition, a Washington department store, Hecht's, sponsored a full-
page photo of Mrs. Kennedy and Caroline with the following copy:
"We speak for all America when we say: Our hearts belong to daddy!
Today, the most famous family in world-news will have a new address: The White House . . . To our young First Lady and her children—to Caroline and her little brother, John F. Kennedy, Jr.—we
echo the sentiments of millions of American families when we say:
as with you . . . our hearts belong to Daddy . . . As he takes the oath
to the highest office in the land, we are proud to honor him as the
35th president of the United States. Here is a national concept alive
before our eyes: the American family personified . . . working for
youth, for the future . . . striving for the peaceful prosperity of our
country and the world." *Newsweek* proclaimed in a postinaugural
story on Oleg Cassini, "Jacqueline Kennedy had sparked a revolution
in fashion." The Kennedy image, furbished by the White House aura,
was now a bona fide commercial, as well as political, commodity.[32]

To give the first lady time to get settled and redecorate the family
quarters, Caroline and John Jr. remained in Palm Beach, with their
nanny, Maud Shaw, a pediatric nurse, and their paternal grandpar-
ents, until the first week in February. Their return to Washington
sparked headlines, photos of the children sitting on their parents'
laps for the drive from National Airport to their new home, and an
AP portrait of Caroline mesmerized by a giant snowman built to
greet her by one of the White House gardeners. Once ensconced in
their new home, the children were established in a routine that must
have been reassuring to them and their parents. Miss Shaw, the epitome of a British nanny, saw to all of the quotidian matters of child
raising—bathing, dressing, feeding, playing, reading, teaching, disci-
plining. Like the well-to-do parents of other nanny-reared children,
President and Mrs. Kennedy could enjoy the limited time that they

had with their offspring, knowing that they were comfortable and happy with their expert and loving caretaker.[33]

When their parents were on the road, the children and Miss Shaw would often spend time at the Kennedy homes in Palm Beach, Hyannis Port, and northern Virginia, or at the estate of their maternal grandmother in Newport. For all of the controversy that has swirled around the Kennedys' marriage in the revisionist studies of Camelot, no one has ever accused them of incompetent parenting. The accounts of those who saw the family in private, and certainly the public record, indicate that Jack and Jackie genuinely delighted in their adorable son and daughter, who, again by all accounts, were mannerly, unspoiled, and well-disciplined children. Mrs. Kennedy took pride in that fact, for, as she told correspondent Sander Vanocur in an interview after JFK's election, "It doesn't matter what else you do if you don't do that [attend to your family] well. If you fail your husband and your children—That really is the role [wife and mother] that means the most to me, though obviously I have a sense of obligation for others. But that's the one that comes first."[34]

Unlike her kids, Mrs. Kennedy had a less predictable schedule, at least in the morning. According to J. B. West, the White House's chief usher, she awoke anytime between 8:00 AM and noon, depending on whether her duties had kept her up late the night before. After having breakfast on a tray in her room, she would see her children briefly, then spend an hour exercising with a walk around the sixteen-acre White House grounds, sometimes pushing baby John in his pram. Initially, she would stop by Mr. West's office to apprise him of her needs for the day, but eventually, she began writing memos to him. Some were short and others lengthy. All reflected her astute attention to detail. Her preferred style was to draft them in her own hand on legal-size yellow tablet paper while sitting in the second-floor family quarters at a desk once owned by her father. Later she moved her work to the Treaty Room, also on the second floor, after it had been redecorated. She would meet with West in unscheduled conferences to go over her memos. The chief White House usher supervises the domestic staff and administration of the mansion. West worked tirelessly with Mrs. Kennedy on two of her most important concerns, redecorating the White House (first the private quarters and then the remainder of the home) and state entertaining. She spent innumerable hours on the White House restoration project, as Chapter 4 documents.[35]

Mrs. Kennedy frequently joined her children while they lunched and then took her own midday meal in her room before napping in the afternoon. If her husband was free for lunch, he might join her, and they would spend a quiet hour or so together. She attempted to leave time in the afternoon to play with the children and read to Caroline in the evening. When her own evenings were not filled with state entertainment obligations, she often organized private dinner parties with friends and relations to give the president opportunities to relax.

In an April 1961 NBC television interview, along with her husband, Jackie discussed her concerns for Caroline and John's privacy: "She [Caroline] is going to have to go to school, and if she is in the papers all the time, that will affect her little classmates, and they will treat her differently." The first lady addressed the problem by organizing a play group for her daughter and her friends, and then a nursery school and kindergarten for them, in the White House. The "school" functioned as a cooperative, with the children's parents paying for all the expenses related to teachers' salaries, equipment, and supplies. Mrs. Kennedy was determined to preserve as much privacy and normalcy as possible for her two youngsters. By forming a "pre-K" and kindergarten class for Caroline in the White House's third floor solarium, the first lady avoided the glare of media attention that would have followed her child to school outside the Executive Mansion. In addition to designing the play- and schoolroom and selecting books for the children, Mrs. Kennedy took her turn with the other parents in serving as a teacher's aide and even wrote memos on organizing the car pool.[36]

The school was controversial. From its inception, the children's group attracted questions from Americans who wanted to know whether it was racially integrated—a major issue in the turbulent years after the U.S. Supreme Court's 1954 desegregation ruling in *Brown v. Board of Education*. The White House received telegrams and mail, sometimes addressed to President Kennedy, sometimes to his wife, urging the addition of "a few children from some of the embassies, plus children of White House servants and staff members, plus a few non-white children from the families of professional people in Washington." This forerunner of an affirmative action plan was suggested by Ada Rose, the retired editor of the children's magazine *Jack and Jill*. She argued that such an example "would do more for the cause of integration than all the Supreme Court rulings." Initially, Tish Baldrige replied to these letters with the admission that "there are no negro children" in the group. She noted, however, that this fact "is certainly not a point of discrimination" because the children in the play group were friends of Caroline's who had lived in her Georgetown neighborhood. Absolving the group from the legal ramifications of a governmental entity, Baldrige declared that "there is no Government expenditure whatsoever." A few months later, Baldrige was responding to inquiries about the "White House Special Class" with the declaration that "the President and Mrs. Kennedy certainly espouse the principles of integrated schools. However, Caroline's playgroup is not a school nor a special class. It is simply a group of friends with supervised play." By the fall of 1962 the play group had evolved into a nursery school–kindergarten with approximately twenty four- and five-year-old students, who met five days a week in their unique setting. Mrs. Kennedy's press secretary issued a media release describing the "White House School," including its schedule, activities, funding, and two teachers' biographies. A year later Nancy Tuckerman, Baldrige's replacement, wrote on behalf of the first lady that "the kindergarten is integrated [with one black child in attendance]," but no information on the children could be released "as it is a private school with no government expenditures involved." (The African American student was the son of Andrew Hatcher, President Kennedy's assistant press secretary.)[37]

Jackie Kennedy also attempted to preserve her children's privacy by trying to thwart press photographs of them. JFK's press secretary, Pierre Salinger, remembers, "She was always in touch with me because she didn't want the press to do photography of the kids. And I said, 'If they're outside the White House I can't do anything about it.' . . . But . . . John Kennedy had another mentality. Every time that Jackie went on a trip somewhere, he'd say, 'Well, now's the time to get good pictures of the kids.' And that was something he wanted to have done." Obviously, the president was attuned to the public relations benefits of releasing pictures of his beguiling children. Not since the presidency of Theodore Roosevelt had such a vigorous young family occupied the White House. Newspapers and magazines simply could not get their fill of the photogenic Kennedys.[38]

Stanley Tretick, a photojournalist hired by *Look* magazine to cover JFK and his family, created lasting iconic images of the era. The cover of *Look*'s January 2, 1962, issue on "The New Frontier: Kennedy One Year Later" carried a glossy color portrait of Jack Kennedy piloting a speeding golf cart filled with his nieces and nephews at Hyannis Port. Although Mrs. Kennedy had nixed a proposed Tretick photo story on Caroline and her friendship with the president's longtime secretary, Evelyn Lincoln, JFK had told Tretick, "John [Jr.] is OK [to photograph]," and he allowed Tretick to snap pictures for a *Look* story entitled "The President and His Son." Taken while Mrs. Kennedy was on her October 1963 holiday in Greece, the photos included the indelible image of John Jr. peeking out from under his father's desk in the Oval Office while his bemused dad pretended not to notice. "That was a complete surprise," Tretick said about the photo. "John just was in the office running around and the President's desk [door] flew open and there he was. . . . I almost fainted. But you know instinctively that that's a hell of a picture." Just four days before JFK's assassination, papers around the country published what would be become the achingly poignant photo of the president and his son sharing a playful moment. The complete Tretick spread appeared in *Look* on December 3, 1963, as a tribute to the slain president.[39]

Atypically, Jackie approved a book featuring Caroline's photo on the cover, entitled "The Caroline Kennedy First Lady Dress-Up Book." The thin volume contained poems and cartoon drawings of Caroline dressed as historic first ladies. Compiled by Arlene Dalton, a friend of Mrs. Kennedy, the book was to be introduced in late November 1963 but never made it to stores in the wake of the assassination. Perhaps the book recalled for Jackie the illustrated story she was urged to write by Bess Furman, which would have contained Kennedy-penned cartoons of President Eisenhower's young nieces in the White House.[40]

Jacqueline Kennedy's efforts to draw the line between her personal and public life were fierce. Although she had held press conferences when her husband was running for president, she refused to do so once she was in the White House, explaining, "The press always covers my official engagements and is kept abreast of my projects and I prefer not to answer personal questions, so that leaves little for a press conference." Occasionally, she participated in televised interviews (one with her husband on NBC in April 1961, another *en français* for the French Television Network before her Paris trip in June 1961, her famous tour of the White House with CBS's Charles Collingwood in February 1962, and an interview with NBC's Sander Vanocur on the National Cultural Center in October 1962).[41]

When asked in early 1963 which presidential wife from the past was her favorite, Mrs. Kennedy responded, "Bess Truman, because she brought her daughter to the White House at a most difficult age—managed to keep her from being spoiled so that she found a happy life married with children. Mrs. Truman kept her family close together in spite of White House demands and that is the hardest thing to do—and in my opinion the most important." The response is a bit odd, given that Margaret Truman was an adult (twenty-one years of age and soon to be a college graduate) when her father assumed the presidency upon Franklin Roosevelt's death in 1945. Moreover, as President Truman's biographer, David McCullough, has so vividly portrayed, Bess Truman shunned Washington life during her husband's presidency and spent weeks at a time in their Independence, Missouri, home, despite Harry's upset over her absence.[42] In that sense, Mrs. Truman was an apt role model for Jackie Kennedy; from the beginning of her tenure as first lady, she spent many days away from Washington. She and the president, much to his chagrin because of the cost and his own preference for beach retreats, rented a house in the rolling hunt country of Virginia, where she indulged her passion for "riding to hounds" (foxhunting). She ultimately convinced her husband to build a house in the Virginia countryside, which was completed in the autumn of 1963. Before its completion, the Kennedys spent some weekends at Camp David in the Maryland mountains; Jackie was surprised at how comfortable she was there. Most fall and winter weekends, Mrs. Kennedy could be found in northern Virginia. In March 1961 the press reported that the first lady had canceled her Washington engagements on the pretense of having a cold, only to be seen foxhunting with the Orange County Hunt in the Old Dominion. In trying to schedule Mrs. Kennedy's appearances before groups visiting the White

House, Tish Baldrige had to be prepared for a last-minute change in plans. "If she had one failing—not actually a failing, but let's call it a lack of enthusiasm—it was a reluctance to spend a lot of time with women's groups," remembers Baldrige. Virtually every women's organization at home and abroad tried to obtain an audience with the first lady. After much urging from Baldrige, Jackie might agree to receive the ladies but then cancel at the last minute "because of sudden ill health." Baldrige could always rely on Vice President Lyndon Johnson's wife Lady Bird (Baldrige's office called her "Saint Bird" for her reliability) to substitute, along with Rose Kennedy, the president's mother, and Eunice Kennedy Shriver, the president's sister. Four days after her husband's assassination Mrs. Kennedy wrote to the new president, Lyndon Johnson, praising his wife Lady Bird and "her willingness to assume every burden. She assumed so many for me and I love her very much." Jackie admitted, "I always thought . . . that Lady Bird should be First Lady."[43]

The *Saturday Evening Post* published a lengthy feature story in February 1963 on the sport of foxhunting and Mrs. Kennedy's penchant for participating in the upper-class pastime. The article, which read like an exposé, noted that critics objected to

> her passion for a sport they think both indecorous and cruel. On occasion she has neglected ceremonious luncheons in favor of a day's sport in the field. Throughout the long winter season she rides to hounds at least twice a week, which is often enough to provoke indignant remarks from congressional wives who fear that their company and conversation is less interesting than the sight of a small and rather nasty animal. The standard textbooks on American government recommend that the President's wife remain above any hint of controversy, that she be a gracious hostess, elegantly dressed, whom schoolchildren should imagine as a fine lady, like the paintings in a museum, forever pouring tea. The newspaper photographs of Mrs. Kennedy astride a horse, however, have dispelled that particular illusion and have embroiled the Administration in yet another welter of gossip. The White House every week receives a swarm of letters from outraged citizens who, judging from the nature of their complaints, think of fox hunting either as an unnecessary cruelty to animals or a trifling indulgence of the very rich. . . . Certainly it is alien to

a world of supermarkets, suburbs and bowling alleys. It is a sport as inseparably identified with the civilization of the 18th century as is the "New Frontier" with the 20th century.

Despite that snide reflection, the article reported that critics of the first lady did not appreciate the finer points of the "art" of fox-hunting, which requires "impeccable manners . . . and a hell of a lot of guts." Fellow hunters observed that the first lady had demonstrated both.[44]

In a rare response to press questions, Mrs. Kennedy wrote answers to typed queries submitted by United Press International's White House correspondent, Helen Thomas, in early 1963, including one that asked the first lady to name her "favorite sport." Mrs. Kennedy sidestepped the direct question, but took the opportunity to relate that she liked "to be out in the air away from details—that is why I like to ride—not for fox hunting—just be with nature." Thomas, perhaps miffed that the first lady was obfuscating, omitted Kennedy's response from her article on the interview. Mrs. Kennedy had told the press in September 1960 that if she moved to the White House "she wouldn't pretend to be anything that I wasn't." She kept her word in continuing to pursue the activities from which she derived the most pleasure.[45]

Following the Kennedy family tradition of spending summers in Hyannis Port and Thanksgiving, Christmas, and Easter at Joseph P. Kennedy's Palm Beach winter retreat, the first lady took such opportunities to leave Washington behind. To these absences she added several vacations abroad without the president (nearly a week in Greece after their visits to Paris, Vienna, and London in 1961; three weeks in Italy with Caroline in 1962; and over two weeks in Greece and Turkey, with her sister and Aristotle Onassis, and Morocco in 1963); combined with her semiofficial trip to the Vatican and South Asia with a private stop in England (nearly three weeks in 1962); plus her extended stays at Hammersmith Farm with her mother and stepfather in Newport. In summer 1962, just after Mrs. Kennedy returned from her extended Italian holiday, respondents surveyed by the Gallup Poll most frequently listed "travels too much, away from family" as the characteristic they least liked about the first lady.[46] She did not shirk all duties while away from the White House, however. In fact, she continued to correspond with her staff via her famous handwritten memos, which allowed her to keep up to date on the White House's restoration project and up-coming state occasions that required her input.

Unfortunately, her absences enabled JFK's womanizing, which did not abate with his presidency. Secret Service logs reveal that the president entertained various female companions (including Mafia moll Judith Campbell and Ben Bradlee's sister-in-law, Mary Meyer) at the White House when his wife was traveling. Most recently, once-secret material from an oral history at the Kennedy Library revealed that President Kennedy had a sexual relationship with a college-age intern in the White House press office. The woman, now sixty years old, admitted that the dalliance lasted from June 1962 to the pre-sident's death in November 1963. One biographer suggests that Jackie simply could not bear to be confronted with her husband's philandering in her own home, and thus chose to remove herself from the venue. Or perhaps her absenteeism was a form of punish-ment for her husband, especially when she garnered headlines for her jet-setting lifestyle. Because Mrs. Kennedy left no record of her motivations, all such theories remain speculative.[47]

Jackie offered a public explanation for why she did not accom-pany her husband on routine political trips around the country (giving him even more opportunities to be unfaithful, including his infamous affair with Marilyn Monroe), especially because crowds were known to shout at him, "Where's Jackie?" She told re-porter Helen Thomas, "The official side of my life takes me away from my children enough. If I were to add political duties—I would have practically no time with them. They are my first re-sponsibility. My husband agrees with this. If he wanted me to come I would."[48]

The White House's published lists of Mrs. Kennedy's official en-gagements and social schedule for 1961 and 1962 (her two full years as first lady) indicate that she participated in a total of 136 events, divided nearly evenly between each year. The figure includes her official and semiofficial trips to eleven countries (Canada, France, Austria, England, Greece, Venezuela, Columbia, the Vatican, India, Pakistan, and Mexico) and Puerto Rico, but not the total number of events she attended in each. The "high" months of the social cal-endar—April, May, October, and November—were her busiest.

Typically, she would attend ten events in these months, but in May 1962 she appeared at seventeen. The events ranged from the relatively brief (taking a publicity photo for a charitable cause, like Christmas Seals) to the prolonged visits with heads of state that started with welcoming ceremonies and ended late in the evening with elaborate dinners. In April 1963 the White House announced that Mrs. Kennedy was pregnant and would curtail her official duties until the after the baby's birth in late summer, under orders from her obstetrician.[49]

In addition to the Executive Mansion's supportive household personnel and a personal secretary, Mrs. Kennedy was aided in her work by a competent, diligent, and loyal East Wing staff, which was often at odds with the president's advisers in the West Wing. Tish Baldrige, the first lady's chief of staff, recalls that in the "war of the sexes" between the White House's two wings, she sometimes had to rely upon her diplomatic training to smooth the conflicts presented by the differing personalities and agendas of the president and his wife. For example, JFK's advisers would attempt to add political donors to the guest lists for state dinners, bumping art patrons Baldrige knew Mrs. Kennedy would prefer for support of her cultural projects. "We were always fighting with Pierre Salinger and [presidential aide] Kenny O'Donnell about our rights and privileges because the men in the West Wing would just simply go ahead and plan things including our functions and walk all over us," remembers Baldrige. She reports that she usually prevailed, especially if she went directly to the president with her complaint on the first lady's behalf.[50]

In her East Wing province, Baldrige supervised two secretaries (along with several assistants she borrowed from other government agencies) and four departments: Social Entertainments, which included Calligraphy, Protocol, and Social Records, with at least five holdovers from the previous administration, who were calligraphers and typists for printing invitations, lists, menus, and place cards; Press; Correspondence, with fifteen workers (almost double from the Eisenhower years) that wrestled with the thousands of letters addressed to the first lady (she received four thousand per week), her children, and even their pets; and Social Files. A "Gifts Room" required a staffer to sort the mountain of presents sent by the public to the first family, especially the children.[51]

In an unprecedented move for the East Wing, Mrs. Kennedy appointed a press secretary, although her initial title was assistant social secretary for the press, who had her own clerical secretary. After Baldrige had made several flippant remarks at her first press conference, Jackie decided that Tish should be chief of staff and social secretary but not her liaison to journalists. That duty fell to Pamela Turnure, only twenty-three at the time of her appointment, and a former member of JFK's Senate staff. Before the inauguration Turnure received a confidential memo from her new boss. Mrs. Kennedy, in typical stream-of-consciousness style, candidly expressed her attitude toward the press and her plan for handling the fourth estate, as follows:

> I hate that tub-thumping-everything-is-great-about-my-boss kind of press relations—. . . [E]veryone is trying to get at us—but you will be there as a buffer—to shield our privacy—not get us in the papers—. . . I feel so strongly that publicity in this era has gotten so completely out of hand—& you must really protect the privacy of me and my children—
>
> 1. You can invent some ladylike title for yourself—. . . but I don't think it should be Press Secretary as I don't think a First Lady should have a Press Secretary—maybe Assistant Social Secretary in charge of Press, etc. [By December 1962 the title had become press secretary to Mrs. Kennedy.]
>
> 2. Pierre [Salinger] will be your boss (I will be really—as you & I will decide everything together)—but all releases & things will come from him—But you must work in my offices—. . . in the W. House.
>
> 3. I hope you will be fairly anonymous—. . . You are speaking for me—and one misstep & I get a million letters. . . . Perhaps magazines & papers will want to do interviews on you—Please check with me before you accept—if you want to do it and it looks OK—just know that you can't discuss us—JFK, me & infants.
>
> 4. . . . [I]n your own private life . . . you mustn't answer their questions about what it is like working for us—just smile and look evasive! As everyone exaggerates so—& some tiny insignificant thing you say goes from one person to another & ends up horribly in some gossip column a week later—

None of this is meant to sound reproachful—it is just that I have suddenly realized what it means to completely lose one's privacy—everyone is so interested in us—SO BE DISCREET.

5. My press relations will be minimum information given with maximum politeness—. . . .

6. In the beginning when I first move in [to the White House]—answer all questions saying Mrs. K's biggest desire right now is to reunite her family—bring her children back from Fla. & have everything arranged for them—She is busy moving (so busy) that I can't really give you exact details—but will later. Then you can tell me what they ask & we'll decide what to answer.

I won't give any interviews—pose for any photographs, etc. for next four years—don't say it that categorically but check with Pierre on a policy statement—a polite way to turn down all requests for interviews—also fotos [*sic*]—Pierre will bring in *Life* & *Look* or Stan Tretwick [*sic*] a couple of times a year & we'll have an ok on it—so find out from him how to turn down everyone who wants to photograph me giving the baby a bottle, etc.

I did say I'd have a press conference but tell them it won't be for a while—until I have something to tell them—& then it won't be a press conference—just having them to tea—When they ask when is [the] press conference say Mrs. K. Looks forward to having you all to tea—once she's settled—[52]

Three months into her husband's presidency, Mrs. Kennedy hosted a luncheon for two hundred women journalists, whom *Time* condescendingly referred to as "newshens." Allowed access to the White House grounds through the southwest gate, usually reserved for state visitors, the women were treated to a gourmet lunch, prepared by the first lady's new French chef. Jackie welcomed the ladies to the grand setting of the East Room and thanked them for the positive stories they had reported on her announced efforts to restore the White House.[53]

With the Kennedys' private life sealed from public view, the press was left to focus on the first lady's public activities: redecorating the Executive Mansion, collecting antiques and art for its refurbished rooms, entertaining state visitors in grand style, and traveling to foreign countries. The occasional negative report, involving her fashions, foxhunting and waterskiing, vacations without her husband, or White House furnishings, seem tame by today's standards. The pre-Watergate, pre–Monica Lewinsky ethos of journalists, who did not have to feed a 24/7 appetite for tabloid-style news (so prevalent in the era of cable television, talk radio, and Internet Web sites and Web logs), undoubtedly protected the Kennedys from unseemly stories.

Maxine Cheshire, society and women's page reporter for the *Washington Post* during the Kennedy administration, admitted in her 1978 memoir that

> [c]ontemporary readers must feel that the Washington press corps was guilty of covering up JFK's extramarital affairs; we were. Social and journalistic customs were different then. That simply was not the way one covered the presidency at that time. Even if we had written about the [president's] girl friends, our editors would never have published the information. . . . Many of the men who covered Kennedy were hardly in a position to cast stones at a president who was playing around. They, too, got lonely with so much traveling away from home. I always felt that one reason so many of them resented having women reporters aboard presidential aircraft during the Kennedy years was that they felt we might tell their wives about their activities on the road. As for getting the sexual escapades of the Camelot days into print, the only way would have been to write a novel.[54]

White House correspondent Robert Pierpoint agreed: "I decided I was not going to get into it [Kennedy's womanizing or the personal misdeeds of other presidents and their families] because I didn't want to be . . . a gossip columnist. That's not why I got into this business."[55]

Mrs. Kennedy's enforced dichotomy between her private and public life thus meshed perfectly with the media's standards in the early 1960s. Consequently, the press coverage of Jacqueline Kennedy usually emphasized the fairy-tale elements of the Kennedy White House. In that sense, she made it easy for the press by genuinely revolutionizing how the president and the first lady presented themselves to the world, at home and abroad. Her exquisite taste in ambiance, menu, entertainment, and dress ensured a revitalized

White House social scene. From staff Christmas parties, to receptions for members of Congress and the Supreme Court, to the high drama of state dinners, she "changed the White House completely." Tish Baldrige, whose father had been a member of Congress, was familiar with the Executive Mansion going back to the Hoover administration. She found the house "stuffy, pedestrian, boring, stiff." Parties had been cold affairs, resulting from the dearth of liquor, formal receiving lines, drab decor, harsh lighting, and uninspiring entertainment and food. In contrast, "the Kennedys ran the White House like an intimate, very attractive, luxurious, private house. And so the parties were so delightful, like going to a great party in someone's private house," remembered Marion Cannon Schlesinger. At the less formal occasions, Mrs. Schlesinger recalled, "Jackie would often greet the guests for cocktails before dinner and the president would come in, informal but still so charismatic. Of course, they were both good actors, maybe they were putting on a show, but the impression was one of good natured relaxation and high spirits and friendliness." The Kennedys' youth, especially in contrast to the elderly Eisenhowers, became a symbol for opening the White House to fresh ideas. Indeed, President and Mrs. Kennedy made their home a frequent venue for welcoming leaders from around the world, particularly those from what was then called the Third World. In the bipolar Cold War atmosphere of the early 1960s, courting such countries was simply good geopolitics, and it complemented more tangible efforts like JFK's Peace Corps. In their first two years in office, the Kennedys held *ten* state dinners—for leaders from four African countries (Tunisia, Sudan, Saudi Arabia, and Ivory Coast) and one each from South America (Peru), the Middle East (Iran), two from South Asia (Pakistan and India), and Europe (France's cultural affairs minister), plus Puerto Rico's governor. (In 1963, when pregnancy and childbirth limited the first lady's official schedule, the White House still held *six* state dinners: for the president of Venezuela; the king of Morocco; the grand duchess of Luxembourg; the president of India; the emperor of Ethiopia; and the king and queen of Afghanistan.) President George W. Bush and his wife Laura offered *two* such evenings in the first half of their term in the White House. The somber aftermath of the terrorist attacks of September 11, 2001, combined with resulting security concerns, may have precluded such lavish entertaining, but Bush, who prefers the simple life of his remote Texas ranch, shuns most presidential pomp.[56]

Before the Kennedys entered the White House, dinners in the dull green State Dining Room were held around a U- or E-shaped table decorated with massive flower arrangements that blocked conversation. Before dinner, guests had to mill about in the East Room, sipping punch and waiting for the presidential party to appear so that the music could start and the receiving line could begin. Only after shuffling through the line could diners take their place at the table. The Eisenhowers enjoyed state functions but preferred a more formal atmosphere for them, perhaps owing to their military background. Ike's illnesses during his presidency, however, forced him and Mamie to curtail their entertaining. The Kennedy White House, in contrast, was marked by an elegant informality. Guests listened to Broadway show tunes from a Marine Corps orchestra while being offered champagne, cocktails, or juice before dinner and waiting for the first couple to appear. Dispensing with the receiving line, except for state occasions, the Kennedys often mingled with their guests and chatted more casually. The State Dining Room, repainted a bright shade of white in the White House restoration, seemed gayer. Mrs. Kennedy suggested a series of round tables hung with pastel table cloths and decorated with smaller flowered centerpieces. Seating eight to ten guests, the table arrangements were more conducive to relaxing conversation. The first lady ordered the White House fireplaces reopened, and they added warmth to the festivities. Indulging her own habit, she repealed the mansion's ban on smoking at state events and even designed new ashtrays for the public areas. Mrs. Kennedy hired a French chef, René Verdon, who provided fewer courses, at the first lady's request, but of excellent quality. The public clamored for his recipes. President Kennedy, however, grew concerned over the increasing Francophilic tone of the White House ambience, complaining "that he had heard from several congressmen that we were getting too Frenchy and too international, and why weren't we more American, and nobody could read or understand the [state dinner] menus." JFK challenged Baldrige to translate the dinner selections into English, but he relented when she convincingly argued that not all descriptions of the dishes sounded very appetizing when converted from the original French.[57]

"Jackie is at home with the two great assets of the White House— its social facilities and its history," commented one of the first lady's friends in the *Saturday Evening Post*. "The history dignifies her entertainment, and her hospitality makes the history really human." *Look* magazine exclaimed, "White House parties have never been gayer." "Since President John F. Kennedy and his beautiful wife, Jacqueline, moved into the White House. . . , the rustle of haute couture, the fizz of bubbling champagne, and the social exuberance of the New Frontier are just as likely to wind up on page one as in the society columns," reported *Newsweek*. As Maxine Cheshire remembered, "[S]uddenly, the whole world wanted to read about [the Kennedys]. The average housewife and her husband began to care more about what was happening in Washington than in Hollywood. So, with the Kennedys as star material, I became the Hedda Hopper of the Potomac."[58]

Although the White House stopped releasing details of Mrs. Kennedy's wardrobe after the inauguration, the media always reported the particulars of her evening gowns, hairstyles, jewelry, designers, and hairdressers. The White House continued to issue press releases on the menus and entertainment provided at state dinners. Accompanying the reports were stunning portraits of the first lady, President Kennedy, and their distinguished guests. Cliched though it sounds, current *Vogue* editor at large Hamish Bowles describes Jacqueline Kennedy as "the physical embodiment of the New Frontier." Bernadine Morris, who reported on fashion for *Women's Wear Daily* and the *New York Times* during the Kennedy administration, explains: "At a time when clothes were fancy and obtrusive, she developed what later would be call minimalism—simple, undecorated shapes that looked to the future." When pictured next to 1950s celebrities Mamie Eisenhower and Queen Elizabeth II, dressed in their brightly colored fitted bodices and wide crinoline skirts, Jacqueline Kennedy represented a new decade with her narrow, straight-cut gowns, whose fabric seemed to float over her figure. The design complemented her felicitous physical attributes, described by Cassini as reminiscent of "an Egyptian princess, very geometric, even hieroglyphic, with the sphinx-like quality of her eyes, her long neck, slim torso, broad shoulders, narrow hips, and regal carriage."[59]

Jackie often chose her evening wear to highlight the context of a dinner's setting or theme. For the dinner honoring Pakistani President Mohammed Ayub Khan on the lawn at Mount Vernon, she selected a full-length sleeveless gown with lateral rows of white lace over white organza. The first lady had discussed with Cassini "how the dress should have a romantic antebellum look, in keeping with the pillared elegance and historical setting of Mount Vernon." The evening at George Washington's home, the first state dinner to be held outside the White House, still represents the epitome of presidential entertainment. Guests arrived by boat on the Potomac River, were transported to the home past a double row of U.S. Marines performing their "Rippling Salute," partook of mint juleps served in silver cups, witnessed a presentation of the Fife and Drum Corps dressed in Revolutionary War uniforms, feasted in Tiffany-decorated tents, and listened to an after-dinner concert by the National Symphony Orchestra. The evening's planners perfectly negotiated the logistical pitfalls and created a memorable event for all in attendance. Nonetheless, journalists, even those who had been invited to the soirée, urged Pierre Salinger to reveal the cost of such an extravaganza. He maintained that most of the function's elements were donated and that only the food required government expenditure, which fell "within the normal State Department allocation for such entertainment."[60]

In addition to sixteen state occasions for heads of state, the Kennedys also hosted a trio of official dinners during their administration: a nostalgic evening for former President and Mrs. Harry Truman, their first visit to the White House since he left office in 1953; a dinner honoring the vice president, chief justice, and speaker of the House; and a celebration of Nobel Prize winners of the Western Hemisphere. The Nobel dinner was one of the most stellar of the Kennedy era for the sheer intellectual brilliance of the forty-nine laureates in attendance. Once more the first lady graced the event, swathed in a Cassini celadon silk jersey creation, a "liquid, columnar dress . . . suggestive of ancient statuary." In the admittedly inflated description of *Vogue*'s Bowles, "Jacqueline Kennedy cast herself as the dynamic modern embodiment of an ancient muse."

Author William Styron wrote of the Kennedys' entrance that evening, "Jack and Jackie actually *shimmered.* . . . [E]ven Republicans
were gaga." JFK, rarely captured on film displaying affection toward
his wife, that evening was photographed with his hand resting on
her bare shoulder, as they chatted with writer Pearl Buck.[61]

On the world stage Jacqueline Kennedy expanded her charismatic triumphs. From her first state trip, to Canada with her husband in May 1961, she established herself as a compelling symbol of
her country and John Kennedy's presidency. United Press International reported that in Canada she "shared equal billing with her
husband." All of the Canadian leaders noted her French heritage, a
point in common with one-third of Canadians. The American press
exalted that among the cheering throngs in Ottawa who greeted her
were heard such comments as, "Isn't she lovely!" and "Is she ever a
doll!" The speaker of the Canadian Senate declared that Mrs. Kennedy "has conquered our hearts," and the director of Canada's National Gallery remarked that he was especially impressed by her artistic knowledge. Each of her daytime and evening outfits was
described in vivid detail, particularly the Pierre Cardin "martial-cut"
red wool twill suit that she chose for her visit with the scarlet-clad
Royal Canadian Mounted Police. For its cover story, "The Kennedys
in Canada," *Life* magazine featured a dazzling color photo of the
first lady and a Mountie in their bright red regalia. The president
failed to make the cover. On the day they returned to Washington,
the *Post* reported that President Kennedy would probably meet with
Soviet Premier Nikita Khrushchev in Vienna the next month. The
same article noted, "The Kennedy trip to Ottawa appears to have
been a success, in some considerable part because of the extremely
favorable impression made by Mrs. Kennedy."[62]

JFK did meet in Vienna with Khrushchev in June 1961, but the
Kennedys made a state visit to Paris beforehand. Of all the trips
abroad with her husband, this event would represent the quintes-
sence of Jacqueline Kennedy's place on the world scene. *Time* magazine seemed to take special delight in noting that the president had
to play second fiddle to his "*ravissante*," "*charmante*" wife. "There
was also that fellow who came with her," *Time* chortled. Even JFK
had to admit, self-deprecatingly, "I am the man who accompanied
Jacqueline Kennedy to Paris—and I have enjoyed it!" Contained in a

reported two truckloads of White House luggage was a complete fashion show of primarily Cassini-styled suits, coats, and gowns. The day wear sparkled with colors of "jonquil yellow" and "Watteau pink." For the state dinner at Elysee Palace, where the first lady charmed the dour president of France, Charles de Gaulle, with her fluent command of the French language, she modeled a pink-and-white straw-lace straight-line dress. During the dinner toasts, President Kennedy paid tribute to his wife: "My preparation for the presidency did not include acquiring first-hand knowledge of France through diplomatic experience. I acquired it through marriage instead." Thousands of the first lady's French admirers lined the streets of Paris, shouting, "Vive Jacqui!" wherever she appeared. While she attempted to dampen the controversy over her wardrobe at home by wearing American-designed outfits to all of the official events, to flatter her hosts, she donned a Paris-designed Hubert de Givenchy evening gown and coat for the "private" dinner hosted by the de Gaulles at Versailles. Her ivory silk *manteau* matched the gown's skirt, which was slightly gathered at the waist. Pastel flowers embroidered in silk floss, ribbon, and seed pearls decorated the bodice. In another compliment to Parisians, Mrs. Kennedy chose the leading French hairdresser to style her hair for each of the events. A tiara crowned her coiffure for the evening at Versailles. Parisians called her "*La Présidente,*" but, more accurately, she appeared as "*La Reine*" (the queen).[63]

The Kennedys' next stop was Vienna, and the president's meeting with Khrushchev. During their official discussions, President Kennedy was stunned by the Russian Cold Warrior's ferocity, which seemed immune to JFK's urbane charm. Yet photos taken at the state dinner held in opulent Schönbrunn Palace show Khrushchev smiling broadly at Mrs. Kennedy, who was dressed, as Cassini described her, like a "mermaid" in her shimmering pink-silver gown. The narrow sheath highlighted her figure and added another facet to her image: a sparkling American sophistication in stark contrast to the dull grayness and stocky physiques of communist leaders and their wives in the 1960s. As the *Washington Post* gushed in its international news section—not the women's page—"Jackie Kennedy waltzed through Vienna today in an elegant triumph that included Soviet Premier Nikita S. Khrushchev. Meeting her for the first time,

First Lady Jacqueline Kennedy, fluent in French, charms
President Charles De Gaulle at Versailles, June 1961. (JFK Library, Boston)

the tough and often belligerent Communist leader looked like a smitten schoolboy when the ice thaws along the Volga in springtime. 'I'd like to shake her hand first,' he told a photographer who asked him to shake hands with President Kennedy for a picture. . . . At one point during the evening, he pointed to her long sparkling dress and said, 'It's beautiful.'" As Kenneth Galbraith described Jackie's hold over political leaders, "No one ever paid more evident

Jackie dazzles Soviet Premier Nikita Khrushchev after his
Vienna summit meeting with JFK, June 1961. (JFK Library, Boston)

attention to what they wanted to tell of their own achievements, and nothing so attracts a public figure as a genuinely receptive audience. Of this, Jackie was well aware." Perhaps it was those long-ago lessons from her father Black Jack Bouvier on how to attract a man. Or maybe it was a natural skill refined over time. Whichever, Jackie Kennedy had perfected the art of flirtatious behavior that men, especially older ones, found so intriguing: drawing close to them, speaking softly as if just the two of them were part of an *intime* dialog, laughing gaily at their attempted witticisms. Even hard-boiled statesmen were not immune to the "Jackie treatment."[64]

On their two trips south of the U.S. border, first to Puerto Rico, Colombia, and Venezuela in December 1961, and then to Mexico in

June 1962, the first lady played a more substantive role, according to Arthur Schlesinger Jr. He maintains that Mrs. Kennedy's "interest was considerable" in the social, economic, and cultural aspects of the Alliance for Progress, the Kennedy administration's major policy toward Latin America, and that she "was a great asset in organizing support" for it. As with her European travels, she garnered adulation from crowds who welcomed her and her husband. Outside Caracas she particularly charmed farmers and their families, who were awarded tracts of land with affordable long-term mortgages by the Agrarian Housing Development. After JFK's speech there, he proudly introduced the first lady, noting, "One of the Kennedys does not need an interpreter—my wife, who would like to say a few words." Drawing on her college-level Spanish, rehearsed on the flight to South America, she delighted the crowd (even if some heard a slight French accent), with her brief message: "I've been very happy to be able to accompany my husband here. I have been greatly impressed by the efforts made here to improve the life of the people. . . . [T]he possibility of jobs and education . . . must be for all not for just a fortunate few." Her gaily colored suits and dresses, chosen for the warm climate in the Southern Hemisphere, dazzled the crowds all the more.[65]

The same would be true of her "semiofficial" trip to India and Pakistan in March 1962, where, for daytime events, she wore apricot, fuchsia, yellow, and ice blue dresses and shifts in sleeveless patterns to account for the heat. The fact that she made the trip without her husband (her sister Lee accompanied her) meant that the press focused—in even more detail—on the first lady. Her journey began with a stop at the Vatican for an audience with Pope John XXIII, with whom the first lady, in a dramatic floor-length black dress and lace mantilla, spoke French during their half-hour meeting. Every move, every comment, every event, every outfit on her 16,000 mile voyage appeared in journalistic photographs and narratives. The United States Information Agency paid a Hollywood producer and cameraman to record the visit, the first ever to these two fractious South Asian countries by an incumbent first lady. The film's $45,000 price tag prompted criticism from a member of Congress, who thought that regular newsreel footage, as usually taken of presidential trips, should have sufficed. The first lady, who had already met

Mrs. Kennedy speaks in Spanish at a luncheon with
President Adolfo Lopez Mateos (to her right) in Mexico City,
June 1962. (Photo by Robert Knudsen, White House. JFK Library, Boston)

and entertained the leader of each country (President Ayub Khan at
Mount Vernon and Prime Minister Jawaharlal Nehru at a private
dinner in Newport and a state dinner at the White House), charmed
each man, and his countrymen and -women, equally. John Kenneth
Galbraith, the American ambassador to India during Mrs. Kennedy's
trip, years later described Nehru's response to her visit: He "insisted
on moving her and her sister . . . from the rather commonplace
house we had borrowed for her visit . . . to a more spacious and de-
cidedly more attractive apartment that opened on the great lawn of
his official residence. He told her that these were rooms once occupied by Edwina Mountbatten (the wife of Louis Mountbatten, the
last Viceroy of India), with whom Nehru had an association the nature of which has been long . . . debated."[66]

Not to be outdone, Ayub Khan presented her with a magnificent horse named Sardar (Chief), which the first lady took through its paces in a ride captured by Associated Press photographers. She shipped the gelding back to the United States, where she happily rode the exquisitely trained animal. In India she met with Peace Corps volunteers, giving her an opportunity to speak of her husband's goals for the program. As was typical of her preparation for new experiences, she read voraciously before the trip about the history of the region, its people, and its natural and historical sites. She proved a superb goodwill ambassador as she maintained her poise and graciousness throughout the grueling schedule of events. JFK lauded her performance in the spotlight. From the White House, he cabled his wife via the American Embassy in New Delhi, "The stories and pictures on your trip have been wonderful. The reports and pictures seem to confirm that you are well and happy. Galbraith is looking a little tired. Caroline and John came home [from Palm Beach] yesterday and are very well and brown. We all miss you very much. All love. Jack"[67]

Interviewed on the flight back to the States by her friend, Joan Braden, for a *Saturday Evening Post* feature story on the visit, Jackie mused, "I just pray I was all right and that the trip did some good. I'm glad I went, but I'd never take a trip like this again without Jack. There were moments like that time in Lahore at the governor's house, when I sat at the window and looked at the fantastic lighted trees reflected in moonlight pools, and wondered what I was doing so far away alone, without Jack or the children to see them. Jack's always so proud of me when I do something like this, but I can't stand being out in front. I know it sounds trite, but what I really want is to be behind him and to be a good wife and mother." Nevertheless, she spent another week away from her immediate family, in London recuperating from her travels. To cheer her children while she was abroad, Jackie had written postcards to them before she left and instructed J. B. West to give them one each day, complete with stamps so Caroline would think they really arrived by mail. When the first lady landed at Washington National Airport, the president "hurried aboard," according to the *Washington Post*, to welcome her back. Beaming as they disembarked, they made a quick departure for the White House and a reunion with their children.[68]

Jackie's articulated preference for not traveling without her husband apparently applied only to state trips, for she took a long private vacation that summer in Italy. What started as a two-week visit to Italy's Mediterranean Coast with four-year-old Caroline, sister Lee, her husband, and two children, stretched into nearly a month. The press had a field day with stories and pictures of the first lady boating, swimming, waterskiing (balancing Caroline on the front of the skis), and dancing at nightclubs. A London tabloid begged the first lady to stop the "madness" and hazards of waterskiing with her young daughter. Paparazzi photographed her strolling with Fiat mogul and playboy Gianni Agnelli, in whose yacht she sailed along the Amalfi coast and to the Isle of Capri, prompting JFK allegedly to cable, "More Caroline. Less Agnelli." A Baptist minister in Colorado chastised Jackie for appearing in public wearing a bathing suit, which he considered inappropriate for "a First Lady of our great U.S. We believe she should honor the position to which the public has elected her husband." He did not escape criticism either. The minister noted that JFK had been photographed on a California beach in his swimsuit surrounded by women. The minister blustered, "Has a former President of the U.S. ever been caught in shorts with a group of women hanging on him as he made a public splash, such as our President did recently on the Western Coast?" In a more wholesome vein, JFK used Jackie's absence as an opportunity to invite the press to photograph him and John Jr. swimming together in Newport.[69]

When Jackie and Caroline returned from their Italian holiday in late August, they each grasped the president's arms tightly as he accompanied them along the tarmac. Whether absence had made the couple's hearts grow fonder, they remained in close proximity during the fearful days of the Cuban missile crisis that fall. He asked Jackie and the children to return from northern Virginia to join him at the White House in the initial days of the emergency. As the threat of war escalated, he cautioned her to take the children and move closer to the government's underground shelter, in case of a nuclear strike on Washington. She refused to leave him. After the trauma of October 1962 ended peacefully, President and Mrs. Kennedy looked forward to a joint trip to Europe for the summer of 1963, but her pregnancy that year forced her to remain behind in Hyannis Port.

Thus, she missed her husband's triumphal speech at the Berlin Wall and his nostalgic visit to Ireland.[70]

Well into her third year as first lady, Jacqueline Kennedy seemed to have found a comfortable accommodation with her duties as presidential spouse. Kenneth Galbraith has observed that "with acute self-knowledge she had chosen her own role carefully." Her East Wing staff was in the expert hands of Tish Baldrige (followed by Nancy Tuckerman), and the mansion ran smoothly under the capable guidance of J. B. West. She knew her wishes would be fulfilled while she remained aloof from facilitating mundane details. Her press secretary, Pam Turnure, enacted Mrs. Kennedy's initial directive of "minimum information given with maximum politeness." Despite occasional mildly critical stories, the press burnished the first lady's public image and that of her husband. She had taken her strengths as a campaigner to new levels on the international stage with her impeccable flair for fashion and state entertainment. When Jackie decided to sidestep ceremonial or political duties, she could always use the excuse that her children, or pregnancy, were priorities. Yet the first lady had public and private resources, as well as a professional child care, at her command when she wished to disappear from Washington and travel on her own. For her special projects as first lady she chose to concentrate on "restoring" the White House and promoting the arts and culture. Once more, she approached these ventures on her own terms, with results that enhanced the symbolism surrounding the modern presidency.

CHAPTER 4

RESTORING
THE WHITE HOUSE

Jacqueline Kennedy, looking slightly pale and managing only a wan smile, stands stiffly in the White House's Red Room. Wearing a somber black dress, she is shaking hands with a line of statesmen. The scene, recorded by a photographer on November 25, 1963, depicts Mrs. Kennedy accepting the condolences of foreign dignitaries after her husband's funeral. What a poignant tableau. Set in one of the first lady's favorite White House parlors, the first of the state rooms to be totally redecorated during the Kennedy administration, the Red Room displayed her Franco-American tastes in furniture, wall and window treatments, and lighting. Mrs. Kennedy was so delighted with the room's new look that she chose a watercolor painting of it for the front of her and the president's 1962 Christmas cards. Sadly, one of her last official duties in the White House, undertaken amidst such unimaginable tragedy, occurred in refurbished surroundings that had given her such joy.[1]

Years later, Kennedy Social Secretary Tish Baldrige recalled that "the make-over of the White House . . . as the focus of American history and accomplishment" was one of her boss's missions, delineated in an avalanche of memos immediately after JFK's election to the presidency. In March 1963, when much of the work was nearing completion, Mrs. Kennedy admitted that the White House restoration idea "did not spring full blown from my forehead at any special

Jackie and her brother-in-law, Senator Edward M. Kennedy,
greet foreign dignitaries in the White House's restored Red Room,
November 1963. (Photo by Robert Knudsen, White House. JFK Library, Boston)

moment—I have always cared about old houses—about preserving
the past. . . . When I learned we would be living in the White House
how could I help but think of restoring as much of its past as possible. It would have seemed criminal to me not to—and I cared terribly about it. Here is a house that all Americans love and almost re-
vere—and practically nothing in it earlier than 1948 [when President
Truman ordered the demolition and replacement of the building's
interior and infrastructure]."[2]

Certainly Mrs. Kennedy was accurate in her description of the
symbolic importance that Americans have attached to their
president's official home, though its iconic status has evolved through
U.S. and presidential history. White House curator Betty Monkman
traces the birth of this national symbol to its opening in 1802. Others

focus on the building's partial destruction by the British during the War of 1812, which marked an emotional milestone in American views of "The President's House," as it was then called. Historian Robert Remini surmises that, after the British ransacked and burned the Executive Mansion, as well as the Capitol, in 1814, "perhaps unconsciously, the press, and probably the American people, started to view the White House and the Capitol as national symbols." President James Monroe, faced with refurnishing the restored and repainted "White House" in 1818, asserted in a message to Congress that the home represented all Americans and should be held in "trust" for future generations. Yet architectural historian William Seale observes that the White House's "image was not clear in the public mind until after Lincoln's presidency," forever etched in the public consciousness by the outpouring of grief over his assassination.[3]

The next major symbolic turning point for the president's home coincided with the turn of the twentieth century, when President Theodore Roosevelt supervised a complete interior remodeling, demolition of the mansion's attached conservatories and greenhouses, and construction of the West Wing, thus creating a national stage for performing his activist presidential role. Seale credits the salutary outcome of the Roosevelt renovation to the efforts of renowned architect, Charles McKim, who masterfully led the project. "A sharp, crisp image against the sky, a Georgian mansion of stone unique in its painted whiteness, the house seemed to be at last in architectural focus. . . . [McKim] had re-created the enduring symbol of the presidency. The White House inevitably took on a more widespread and powerful meaning for the American people." The simultaneous rise of mass media and expanded presidential agendas in the twentieth century provided a potent mix for projecting the architectural symbolism of the Executive Mansion. Franklin Roosevelt's radio Fireside Chats forged a link between the president's home and the hearths of his listeners, and President Harry Truman opened the Executive Mansion to the visual medium of television with a broadcast tour of the reconstructed White House interior in 1952.[4]

Ironically, the symbolic potential of the White House proved a two-edged sword for any occupant eager to modify it, as Truman discovered in his controversial addition of a second-story balcony to the building's South Portico. In 1963 Mrs. Kennedy recalled a similar dilemma: "I was warned and begged and practically threatened! (not by my husband) but by people who had been in government a long time [Clark Clifford, for example]—not to dream of touching the White House. They said it was such a symbol of the American people that anyone who had the audacity to tamper with it could only bring down the wrath of a nation on their head and it would hurt my husband politically and turn into a cause célèbre like the Truman Balcony (which by the way Latrobe included in his plans for the South Portico for Thomas Jefferson!)."[5]

Mrs. Kennedy recollected the project's initial controversy, and her determination to overcome it: "But I said . . . I would do it the right way—I couldn't believe if people saw you wanted to save something for them and their children that our country could be proud of—they would be irate. My husband knew all these objections—He said if I cared that much to do it—and he cared too and knew of every new step along the way."[6]

The new first lady was not the first White House tenant to launch a refurbishing project. In fact, her enterprise was one in a long line of Executive Mansion makeovers. The three most extensive were the post-1814 restructuring (necessitated by the ravages of war), the 1901–2 remodeling (required to update the building and render it livable for the large and boisterous family of Theodore Roosevelt), and the 1949–52 gutting of the interior to prevent its collapse and modernize its systems. Aside from these major structural revampings, presidents and their spouses have been as prone to recreate the home's interior decoration as any inhabitant of a new abode. As Seale puts it, "[I]mprovements [to the White House] have entered as a constant flow. In this way the place is sort of Everyhouse . . . a cultural artifact." Some presidential couples have focused on remaking the family living quarters, others on remodeling the public state rooms, and some on both.[7]

Dolley Madison worked closely with architect Benjamin Latrobe to furnish public rooms in the Executive Mansion. With her finely tuned political sense, she carefully created an image of the president's home that bridged the gap between the populist sentiments of Democratic-Republicans and the elitist tastes of Federalists. The invading British army destroyed her scrupulous attention to detail when it set the mansion ablaze, reducing it to a burned-out shell.[8] President James Monroe was the first chief executive to initiate a complete refurnishing and redecorating project in the aftermath of the 1814 destruction at the hands of the British invaders. With his extensive European experience, having served as U.S. minister to France, England, and Spain, and his fondness for French decorative arts, the house took on a "dignity and grandeur" that Mrs. Kennedy would imitate a century and a half later. Presidents and/or their spouses often faced political and journalistic criticism for what were perceived as lavish tastes. President Martin Van Buren, a widower by the time he was elected to the White House in 1836, eagerly spent the $20,000 Congress appropriated for refurbishing his new home, which bore the wear and tear of Andrew Jackson's eight-year tenure. In contrast to Jackson's frontier heritage and democratic bent, New Yorker Van Buren's lifestyle was more sophisticated, even regal. As a Kentucky congressman who visited the Van Buren White House commented, the president had taken on the trappings of the "prince of Democracy."[9]

Mary Todd Lincoln undertook the next major refurnishing of the White House, which was a precursor to Jacqueline Kennedy's. In many ways Mrs. Lincoln foreshadowed the Kennedy first ladyship. Both earned praise, as well as disapproval, for their sophisticated and expensive tastes in clothes and furnishings, both suffered with frequently inattentive husbands (some would even argue that their extravagant shopping sprees were attempts to dull the pain of difficult marriages), each bore the grief of losing a child while first lady, and, of course, each left the White House a widow, having witnessed the horrific assassination of her husband.

As it had for Van Buren, Congress again appropriated $20,000 for refurbishing the White House in the new Lincoln administration, but after only six months in her new home, Mrs. Lincoln had exhausted the initial allotment (which was intended to last four years). Unquestionably, the White House's interior decorations were in a sorry state when the Lincolns arrived, but Mary simply had no budgetary discipline in choosing replacement furniture, window, wall, and floor treatments, and china. She ordered the most extravagant items, infuriating and embarrassing her husband when he discovered the bills. Scrupulous, as always, he wanted to pay for his wife's indiscreet purchases out of his private funds, but two more congressional allocations ultimately covered the costs. Admittedly, the White House had never looked more exquisite than it did under Mrs. Lincoln's supervision, but she had a political tin ear when it came to presenting the elegant Executive Mansion, and its Victorian excesses, to the public during a bloody Civil War.[10]

In the first four years of the postbellum period (1865–69), however, another $135,000 was spent on the White House interiors. President Ulysses S. Grant and his wife Julia labored to make the White House a symbol of prosperity, and they completely refurbished the East Room, site of their daughter's 1874 wedding, in the bold, glittery New Grecian style that was fashionable in the Gilded Age. (Mrs. Kennedy would reinstall Grant's Cabinet Room furniture in the second-floor chamber that she renamed the Treaty Room.) While engravings and daguerreotypes of the White House had been available before the Civil War, during the Grant administration, mass-produced stereographic slides of the Blue and Red Rooms were sold to tourists in Washington hotels and at newsstands around the city as souvenirs of the public tours offered of the mansion. First Lady Jacqueline Kennedy would offer a book-length history of the White House for visitors, filling a deficiency she had noticed on her first trip to the mansion as a sightseeing adolescent.[11]

President Rutherford Hayes and his spouse Lucy were among the first residents who wanted to preserve a sense of presidential history in their decorations; they hung portraits of George and Martha Washington in the mansion. Nostalgia for the White House did not guide Chester Arthur, who ascended to the presidency after the assassination of James Garfield in 1881. Arthur wanted an entirely new home constructed for the chief executive on the White House site, but the House of Representatives nixed his proposal. Instead, he spent well over the $30,000 appropriated by Congress on refurbishing in the colorful style of Louis Tiffany. Lacking sentimental attachment to the White House itself, he certainly had no interest in maintaining broken, worn, or outdated furnishings, so he simply auctioned them off for $3,000—an event that would later appall Mrs. Kennedy. In a reversal of his cavalier approach to old furniture, she was able to reacquire from a donor a Japanese-style ebony sofa that Arthur had purchased for the East Room. The White House had sold the sofa in 1903 to a furniture dealer after renovations during Theodore Roosevelt's administration.[12]

With the advent of Benjamin Harrison's one-term presidency in 1889, a series of first ladies took a keen interest in the historical elements of White House accouterments. Caroline Harrison collected pieces of White House porcelain used by previous administrations on state occasions, which eventually culminated in the China Room display, inaugurated in 1917 under the direction of Woodrow Wilson's second wife, Edith.[13]

Mrs. Theodore Roosevelt was a powerful force in the 1902 remodeling of the White House. As Mrs. Kennedy would sixty years later, Edith Roosevelt saw the Executive Mansion as a "patriotic showcase" as well as a commodious home for her family and a professional space for the president. She and her husband loved Victorian furniture. They ultimately agreed to architect McKim's preference for Beaux Arts, but Edith Roosevelt insisted that the famous Lincoln bed and other nineteenth-century furnishings be spared from the auction block.[14]

It was Grace Coolidge, however, who created a modern precedent for Mrs. Kennedy to follow. President Calvin Coolidge's wife was a stylish beauty, pursued by a burgeoning press in the Roaring Twenties. In addition to being celebrated for her fashionable entertainment at the White House, she hoped to restore historical furniture to the president's home, but her search for such pieces was futile. Grace then attempted to encourage donations of furniture from the early 1800s, so that she would not have to rely on appropriations from Congress. She thus began the "antiques movement" that Mrs. Kennedy perfected in the 1960s and that continues to guide White House acquisitions. Mrs. Coolidge thereby launched the concept of the White House as a museum of presidential history. She even foreshadowed Mrs. Kennedy's establishment of an advisory committee on, complete with controversy over, decorating the White House. The differences of opinion on how to furnish the Executive Mansion began to garner publicity, and President Coolidge consequently banned the advisory committee from the president's house.[15]

President Herbert Hoover and his wife Lou were sophisticated devotees of history, and they strove to inject the spirit of past White House occupants into their decorative efforts. They were especially enamored of Monroe and Lincoln furniture and memorabilia and collected them at every opportunity. Always the scholar, Lou Hoover planned, supervised, and subsidized the first cataloging of White House furnishings, which included recording possessions and acquisitions, oral histories of the mansion's staff, and documentary photos of state, as well as private, room settings.[16] Jacqueline Kennedy would routinize and formalize the recording of presidential furniture and decor.

Despite the Franklin Roosevelts' record length of White House occupancy (twelve years), the Great Depression, World War II, and the first lady's extensive public policy concerns gave them little time for considering more mundane matters of decoration. Eleanor established an advisory committee for refurbishment of the Red Room, and several years later another for the Blue Room, but she ignored its advice in decorating the latter. FDR wanted to create a formal presidential museum in a portion of the White House's East Wing, constructed in 1942, but the war disrupted his plans. He did, however, supervise the creation of the White House library; Jacqueline Kennedy ultimately redecorated it and reconstructed its bibliographic collection.[17]

The extensive and expensive Truman renovation continues to draw controversy from architectural historians over the authenticity of its style, but the press and public generally gave it high marks at the time. Because the process of gutting and reconstructing the White House interior was so expensive ($5.76 million), period antiques were beyond the government's budget. In any case, Truman was not a connoisseur of antique furnishings and thought them impractical for the high-traffic state rooms, despite the opposite views of the White House furnishings advisory committee. He ordered furniture reproductions of English and New England neoclassical pieces for the private residence. As Seale notes, "[M]ost of the magic of the White House is in the mystique it carries. . . . [T]he past . . . gives the symbolic place its luster." To the extent that Truman preserved the historical "look" of the home, he maintained its aura.[18]

Yet the combination of Truman's pragmatism, the Eisenhowers' frugality, and the 1950's knotty-pine craze, in Jacqueline Kennedy's eyes, created a lowbrow, faux colonial ambiance, evident when she toured the White House with Mamie Eisenhower a month after

JFK's election to the presidency. Before Inauguration Day Jackie acquainted herself with the White House's complex decorative history by reading everything she could find on the mansion from the Library of Congress. As she admitted, her familiarity with the showplaces of Europe colored her thinking: "Perhaps it was a bit chauvinistic—I had seen palaces or official residences abroad—Why should not the residence of the President of the United States show all that is finest—(pictures—portraits of great men in our history—furniture—books) in our heritage—our frontier past too—Therefore all the portraits of the [George] Catlin Indians," which she borrowed from the Smithsonian, reframed, and displayed in the second floor center hall.[19]

Time magazine, in its inauguration week cover story on Mrs. Kennedy, reported that she was preparing for her new role by learning every detail of the White House, including the inadequacy of its budget. "It's stone broke," *Time* quoted her as saying. A slip of the tongue by her new chief of staff, Tish Baldrige, at a press conference had caused a stir that Jackie was going to display modern art in the White House. Mrs. Kennedy countered with a foreshadowing of her approach to decorating this national icon, "The White House is an 18th and 19th century house. Whatever one does, one does gradually, to make a house a more lived-in house, with beautiful things of its period. I would write 50 letters to 50 museum curators if I could bring Andrew Jackson's inkwell home."[20]

Jacqueline Kennedy's White House project became the primary official focus of her tenure as first lady. She managed to complete the successful enterprise in the fewer than three years of her husband's presidency. She also played a major role in redecorating Blair House, the president's guest quarters on Pennsylvania Avenue. She insisted on referring to her White House project as a restoration, rather than decoration. To *Life* magazine correspondent, Hugh Sidey, whom she allowed access for a cover story on her in September 1961, she emphasized, "It would be a sacrilege merely to *redecorate* [the White House]—a word I hate. It must be *restored,* and that has nothing to do with decoration. . . . That is a question of scholarship."[21]

The restoration/redecoration distinction splits semantic hairs. Unlike her predecessor, Mary Todd Lincoln, however, Jacqueline Kennedy had a finely tuned political ear. Certainly in the long history of White House makeovers, with which she was so acquainted, *restoration* sounded much worthier of support than mere *redecoration*. Restoring the White House on the basis of historical records was a more scholarly enterprise than simply repainting or changing the wallpaper. Without question, she redecorated all of the White House rooms, and some she restored to particular historical eras through furniture, wall, floor, and window treatments, and lighting. The Blue Room took on the air of its Monroe-period, Francophilic incarnation; the Red Room depicted early nineteenth-century Franco-American Empire; the Green Room displayed Federal-era furniture; the Treaty Room and the Lincoln Bedroom exhibited Victorian decor (Mrs. Kennedy's least favorite style but one she felt compelled to represent); the East Room and State Dining Room preserved many of the 1902 McKim elements. Betty Monkman accurately summarizes this segment of Mrs. Kennedy's contributions: Her "efforts at recapturing a sense of the nation's history . . . led to a revival of interest in and new appreciation of American neoclassical furnishings. . . . She set a standard for refurbishing the White House."[22]

The project's overall success illustrates Mrs. Kennedy's abundant energy and managerial talents. As an admiring Arthur Schlesinger Jr. put it, she was "tireless" in her search for White House treasures from bygone eras, "spelunking" and "ransacking" her way through dusty government warehouses and White House storerooms. She was a "great manager" who had a "capacious memory," a "quiet, deft, subtle" way of accomplishing her goals, and was "skilled at coordinating antagonistic temperaments" of the decorators and collectors she employed to serve her.[23]

The first lady methodically tackled her monumental venture. In addition to reading about past White House restoration plans, she pored over a binder of photographs of the mansion's private rooms taken during the Truman and Eisenhower administrations, annotating it for Sister Parish, who had decorated her Georgetown home. Mrs. Kennedy encouraged her to add "your touches . . . [including] getting rid of plants and hotel furniture," a reference to the reproductions acquired by President Truman. Thus prepared, Jackie presided over a complete refurbishment of the Kennedy family's rooms within two weeks after the inauguration. Gone were the Eisenhower's preferences for green (Ike's bedroom) and pink (Mamie's boudoir,

though three-year-old Caroline Kennedy's new bedroom was decorated in pink and white), replaced with neutral yet bright off-white
walls, light blue chintz fabrics, tasteful furniture, and artwork borrowed from museums. In a fortnight the first lady spent $50,000 of
congressionally appropriated funds for the White House on redecorating the private living quarters alone.[24]

Looking back from 1963, the first lady described her next step: "I
knew funds would be needed and that one could not possibly ask
Congress for them. So the obvious solution was a committee—It had
to be fairly small to start with as we had to work hard and together
and the task seemed Herculean—if not impossible." She continued:

> The logical chairman of such a committee—never for a mo-
> ment did anyone else cross my mind—was Henry F. du Pont
> [highly recommended by Jackie's friend, Jayne Wrightsman].
> Just go and see Winterthur [du Pont's home and museum of
> American decorative arts in Wilmington, Delaware] and you will
> see why! His life has been devoted to the study and collection of
> Americana—He has a collection that is equaled no where else in
> the world—No European museum, castle . . . can match the
> scholarship and treasures that have gone into Winterthur. . . .
>
> I went to see him in Boca Grande, Florida—armed with about
> 40 books and articles—all bookmarked in the parts I was inter-
> ested in—where I thought there were things we could still trace
> before they disappeared forever to the past—and return to the
> White House.
>
> He was charming—all he wanted to know was if I was truly se-
> rious about the project—When he saw I was and that I would
> work with him night and day until we accomplished something
> we could be proud of—he accepted the chairmanship immedi-
> ately—and all the energy that he had used to form Winterthur—
> he then used to get this started and has worked with me on it
> constantly ever since.[25]

One month after the inauguration, the new first lady announced
the appointment of the Committee of the Fine Arts Commission for
the White House, chaired by du Pont, with the expressed purpose of
locating "authentic furniture of the date of the building of the White

House (1802) and the raising of funds to purchase this furniture as gifts to the White House. It is planned to place this authentic early American and other period pieces in the White House where they will remain permanently. No furniture will be put into the White House until it has been photographed, authenticated and picked by the Committee and then approved by the Fine Arts Commission." The press release quoted the commission's chairman, David Finley, as being "especially gratified that Mrs. Kennedy has seen fit to give leadership to this project."[26]

The new Fine Arts Committee for the White House (as it came to be called) had a membership, widely reported in the press, that consisted of a Who's Who list of seven women and five men with extensive curatorial and/or collecting experience. In addition to du Pont, the committee included Charles Adams (descendant of the Adams presidents), Mrs. C. Douglas Dillon (wife of JFK's Secretary of the Treasury and collector of eighteenth-century furniture and art), Mrs. Charles W. Engelhard (member of the International Council of the Museum of Modern Art in New York), David Finley (former director of the National Gallery of Art and chair of the Fine Arts Commission), Mrs. Albert Lasker (trustee of the Museum of Modern Art and collector of French art), John Loeb (benefactor of the Metropolitan Museum and collector of French Impressionist paintings), Mrs. Paul Mellon (daughter-in-law of the National Art Gallery's founder), Mrs. Henry Parish II (interior decorator), John Walker (director of the National Gallery of Art), Mrs. George Warren (former trustee of the Museum of Modern Art and benefactor of colonial America preservation efforts), and Mrs. Charles Wrightsman (member of the Metropolitan Opera Board and collector of eighteenth-century French paintings and furniture).[27]

Although several members of the Fine Arts Committee had formal museum experience, most of those chosen to serve were valued for what today would be called "development" potential — that is, their own sources of wealth and associations with other monied elites. This element of the project dovetailed perfectly with Jacqueline Kennedy's New York, Newport, Paris, Palm Beach, and Georgetown connections. In the winter of 1961 the White House circulated a list of antique furniture among Palm Beach society, suggesting opportunities for underwriting the acquisitions.

Mrs. Kennedy also used her personal charm to solicit donations. A prominent New York physician told *Newsweek* that the first lady "talked to me for hours [at the White House], showing me how sad and forlorn various rooms looked. She never once asked me to do anything about it, but when I left I found myself promising her a mirror for which I had turned down a $20,000 offer. I went home and told my wife I was even considering throwing in George Washington's field bed—one designed by Thomas Jefferson and absolutely priceless!"[28]

Jackie had to use her diplomatic skills to soothe Adlai Stevenson's feelings over the acquisition of a settee and chairs associated with Abraham Lincoln. Stevenson, the former governor of Illinois and the United States' ambassador to the United Nations in the Kennedy administration, seemed a logical choice to approach regarding purchasing furniture once acquired by another celebrated inhabitant of the Prairie State. Mary Lasker of the White House Fine Arts Committee did just that, and Stevenson responded with a check for $450, the purchase price of the Lincoln items. Lasker had not coordinated the deal with Mrs. Kennedy, however, who had already arranged for another donor to buy the settee and chairs for placement in the White House's Lincoln Bedroom. Stevenson was yet another older man Jacqueline Kennedy had charmed over the years. Their correspondence was filled with mutual admiration and often signed "affectionately" or "with love." In an era before sexual harassment had entered the legal lexicon, Jackie and Adlai, a divorced ladies' man, seemed to enjoy a quaintly flirtatious relationship. He was thirty years her senior, so the coquetry appeared utterly innocent. "I am heartbroken to be writing you this—because you were so fantastic to respond so quickly and generously to Mary Lasker's plea—and because it would have been so fitting to have you give the Lincoln settee and chairs—" the first lady wrote to Ambassador Stevenson. "I got someone to give them—probably the very day Mary wrote to you—as I was so scared we would lose them. I really jumped the gun on myself. So I sadly return your check with my deepest thanks." Jackie offered hope that Adlai could still participate in decorating the Lincoln Bedroom: "Something else will turn up [to purchase] and I will ask you the very first one if you would like to give it— Think of the meaning it will have and how proud Illinois will be—"

Mrs. Kennedy displays a silver pitcher presented to the White House,
December 1961. (Photo by Abbie Rowe, White House. JFK Library, Boston)

She closed her handwritten note with an act of contrition. "Please forgive my predatory instincts for the White House—I did think of asking you but then decided I didn't dare—as it would be an imposition—I hope Lincoln will forgive me—and that you will too—Always affectionately, Jackie." Stevenson harbored no hard feelings about the snafu. Shortly thereafter, he visited President and Mrs. Kennedy on Cape Cod and wrote in a subsequent thank-you note to Jackie, "You and the President have a genius for making people feel relaxed and at home, and I wish I had more opportunity to practice such arts on you here in New York."[29]

In a memo to the first lady, Nicholas Katzenbach, assistant attorney general in the Department of Justice's Office of Legal Counsel, spelled out the legal status and ramifications of the Fine Arts Committee. He cautioned that, because the committee was a private entity, under law, it could not accept property or donations on behalf of the government. Katzenbach outlined the legal channels through which the committee could work.[30]

Yet even donations that passed legal muster might run afoul of public ethics. Maxine Cheshire, a society-page journalist for the *Washington Post*, had once been a police reporter, and she relished investigative stories. In addition, she was an antiques collector who had a number of contacts in the business. A page-one article she wrote for the *Post* in May 1961 derailed a $500,000 furniture gift from Fine Arts Committee member Jayne Wrightsman and her oilman husband Charles. Cheshire had heard that President Kennedy was "worried [about the Wrightsmans' furniture gift] because he was afraid it would be viewed as an attempt by the oil lobby to buy influence in the White House." After Cheshire's story appeared, "the Wrightsmans were asked by [Jack] Kennedy to abandon the idea."[31]

Bolstering the professional and scholarly facet of the restoration project was yet another panel, this one also chaired by du Pont and named the Fine Arts Advisory Committee, consisting of sixteen museum curators or directors and two scholars. The latter, Julian Boyd, editor of the Jefferson Papers at Princeton University, and Lyman Butterfield, editor of the Adams Papers at the Massachusetts Historical Society, immediately set to work on a short memo, "The White House as a Symbol," which outlined "a statement of philosophy" to "underlie the work" of the three committees/commission charged with restoring and redecorating the White House. Circulated to the panels' members, with a cover memo by du Pont on May 3, 1961, the Boyd/Butterfield white paper on the White House succinctly captured the nuances of the building's functional and symbolic roles. "It would . . . be highly inadvisable, even if it were possible, to fix on a single style of decoration and furnishings for a building that ought to reflect the whole history of the Presidency. . . . [T]o furnish the White House uniformly in the eighteenth-century style current when it was built would give a static even monotonous air to a house whose history is by no means finished. . . . [I]t will therefore be necessary to be eclectic." While conceding that "it would seem proper to favor early periods and American furnishings," Boyd and Butterfield asserted that "it would be a mistake to exclude *all* representation of the latter nineteenth and early twentieth centuries. . . . Perhaps the line could be drawn at 1910 or 1920. . . . We assume that in the end the choices will be made by the mistress of the White House in consultation with the advisers she has enlisted."[32]

And choose she did, but not always as eclectically as Boyd and Butterfield advised. The committees themselves were not particularly diverse, reflecting a bias in their membership toward early American decorative arts or eighteenth- and nineteenth-century French style. Ultimately, three advisors came to the fore in guiding Mrs. Kennedy's decisions: Sister Parish, Henry du Pont, and Stéphane Boudin. Having worked with her before coming to the White House, Mrs. Kennedy felt comfortable with Parish, but her classic country, chintz-laden interiors were simply not suited to the stately public rooms of the White House. Consequently, her work was primarily confined to the second-floor hallways and family quarters, including the Yellow Oval Room (used as a semiformal drawing room by the Kennedys), although she initially decorated the Oval Office too. Du Pont, as Jackie herself described him so enthusiastically, was *the* expert on American decorative arts (specializing in objects from 1640 to 1860), so she could not easily ignore him. Yet not surprisingly, in light of her Eurocentric, and particularly her French, travels and education, her tastes were more Continental. Jayne Wrightsman, Jackie's friend who had introduced her to du Pont, also arranged a connection to Boudin, president of the Paris-based decorating firm of Maison/Jansen. Decorator for the Duke and Duchess of Windsor and stately homes throughout England, he more precisely represented Mrs. Kennedy's evolving tastes than Parish or du Pont. She naturally gravitated toward his European designs. Supervising this trio of decorators sorely tested her management talents, charm, diplomacy, determination, and knowledge. The first lady had to guide the restoration process through the shoals of contrary tastes, monumental egos, and political pitfalls—including the occasional public relations glitches, as when a donated "antique" desk turned out to be a fake, or when the White House accepted a gift of restored wallpaper from the National Society of Interior Designers, which had paid $12,500 for it, only to learn that its seller had purchased it for $50. Boudin's French pedigree posed a potential political headache for the White House, which was "reluctant to advertise the fact that a foreigner [was] taking such a large part in renovating a U.S. shrine. . . . 'That's Mr. Boudin, but we *never* introduce him,' the White House curator told a VIP she was escorting through the mansion."[33]

The first lady used flattery to placate the octogenarian du Pont, who was often at odds with Boudin. Writing to du Pont in September 1963 from Hammersmith Farm, where she was still recovering from the death of her infant son six weeks earlier, she composed a cheery letter of gratitude in her own hand. She shared with him her detailed opinions on where a certain antique wallpaper should go—*not* on the ground floor of the White House where "it would be smudged and scraped in eight months—and that paper which survived a century—would be ruined forever." Perhaps Blair House should be its new home, she concluded, seeming to decide, while seeking his advice, or at least appearing to do so. She also declared that visiting foreign dignitaries should "go to Winterthur first, not Williamsburg!" Finally, she expressed her appreciation that he, a Republican, had given so generously of his talents to her, a Democrat. She then slipped into her trademark submissive role, so effective with members of the opposite sex: "I am rather confused about political parties right now—having been brought up in one and married into another. All I care about is my husband—whom [*sic*] I think can save the world—but everyone should think that about their husband."[34]

Ironically, by the time Jackie penned this missive, Boudin had won the contest for her allegiance. A box score of decorator "wins" would show the Frenchman clearly in the lead by November 1963. Of the three "colored" state chambers on the first floor, Boudin's designs had triumphed in the Red and Blue Rooms, as well as the East Room and the Oval Office (which he had redecorated in a post-Parish design and completed during JFK's fateful trip to Texas), and even the first lady's bedroom, which Boudin had begun to transform. Du Pont's vision was partially victorious in the Green Room, where he planned the acquisition of furniture and its upholstery and placement. Still, Boudin designed the chamber's wall and window treatments, based on one of his favorite paradigms, Leeds Castle in England. The State Dining Room's final rendition was a draw between du Pont and Boudin. The ground floor chambers were split between the influence of du Pont (the Diplomatic Reception Room and the Library) and Boudin (the Vermeil Room and the China Room). Parish ran a distant third, with her Oval Office and some family quarters designs disappearing by late 1963. Her Yellow Oval Room was a more lasting success.

If the well-received results of Boudin's influence over the redecoration project illustrate both Mrs. Kennedy's good taste and adept managerial skills, her favoritism toward the Frenchman also helped her to achieve another of her goals: creating a showplace for the presidency. In 1980 the former first lady remarked that "[t]he Blue Room was Boudin's masterpiece. [It] is a formal reception room, and so you have to have a sense of state, ceremony, arrival, and grandeur.... [He] gave it that, and he did it all so simply." Seale describes Boudin's designs as "not unlike stage scenery, meant to serve ceremony and to inspire those who experienced the rooms with the flavor of the American past. He [Boudin] brought to the state rooms the French taste for pageantry." Just as her husband's New Frontier political metaphor was meant to adapt the best of the American past to contemporary challenges,[35] the Kennedy White House redecoration wove historical images into fresh and creative interpretations.

Jacqueline Kennedy was clearly aware of the potential strength of this symbolism on the world political stage. In her September 1963 note to du Pont, she wrote that she was embarrassed by Blair House, with its "peeling walls wire coat hangers, stuffed furniture and a ghastly television set." She worried about what visiting chiefs of state thought of the "President's Guest House." "I cringe to imagine—All during their visits here, we are telling them that they should choose to go with us and not the Russians—They have probably just slept in gilded beds and eaten off Ivan the Terrible gold plates in the Kremlin—So it is important how you first affect them when they reach this country."[36]

Aside from entertaining visiting foreign dignitaries, Mrs. Kennedy succeeded in disseminating the refurbished White House image to the general public through a host of channels. The one that she thought most important was the establishment of the White House Historical Association (WHHA) "because it will last forever—to oversee the guidebook [another of her enterprises] and other publications about the White House." The idea originated with Nash Castro, in 1961 an assistant superintendent of the National Capital Parks and liaison between the Park Service and the White House. He suggested the founding of a nonprofit corporation to be called the White House Historical Association, which would oversee publications about the Executive Mansion. Mrs. Kennedy approved the general concept but suggested that Nash confer with legal counsel, Clark Clifford, about the idea. Having researched the status of the White House vis-à-vis the Park Service, Clifford determined that the relationship should be clarified by law.[37]

As special assistant to JFK, and a favorite professional confidante of the first lady, Arthur Schlesinger Jr. (whose office was in the East Wing) kept track of legislative details for Jackie. After meeting with Mrs. Kennedy at the White House, New Mexico Senator Clinton Anderson, chair of the Senate Interior and Insular Affairs Committee, introduced a bill in August 1961 to establish the Executive Mansion as a national monument under the auspices of the National Park System. President Kennedy did not want to reside in a national monument, however, so the bill's language was amended to confirm the name of the president's official residence as the "White House," to be administered by the National Park System. The legislation, which also declared that "primary attention shall be given to the preservation and interpretation of the museum character of the principal corridor on the ground floor and the principal public rooms on the first floor of the White House," embodied the heart of Mrs. Kennedy's project for preserving the White House and its interiors.[38]

In addition, the act protected the "furniture, fixtures, and decorative objects of the White House [either currently in its possession or acquired in the future]" by labeling them as "inalienable and the property of the White House" when the president declared them "to be of historic or artistic interest." Such items were to be preserved by the Smithsonian when not in use by the White House. Mrs. Kennedy particularly lauded the act's "arranging that the Smithsonian would be in a way the watchdog—or at least keep the furniture no longer needed in the White House—so that nothing—no matter of how little value—would ever be sold or thrown away [as previous administrations had done]. . . . This was one of the most important things I think—as it ensures historical preservation."[39]

Granting the White House museum status, under the National Park System's administration, rendered any donations to the mansion tax deductible. *Newsweek* wrote that the first lady had attracted "the interest of those citizens most prone to make tax-deductible gifts." Yet some charitable contributions to Mrs. Kennedy's cause raised ethical concerns. Jules Stein, chairman of the board of the Music Corporation of America, and his wife offered to furnish the long gallery on the White House's second floor. Their donation was worth approximately $100,000. When the Kennedy Justice Department issued an antitrust complaint against the MCA, however, Stein deferred the offer to avoid embarrassing the White House.[40]

Now that the White House's status was legally defined, Castro prepared a letter from the National Park Service to Mrs. Kennedy outlining the plan to create the White House Historical Association. She approved, and Castro accepted the responsibility of supervising creation of the association's charter and bylaws. On November 3, 1961, the WHHA was chartered. Among the founding members of its board of directors, approved by the first lady, were John Walker, director of the National Gallery of Art, David Finley, former director of that institution and chairman of the Fine Arts Commission (both members of the new Fine Arts Committee for the White House), Clark Clifford, and Melville Grosvenor, president and editor of the National Geographic Society. The media release from the first lady's Assistant Social Secretary for the Press Pam Turnure led with the announcement that the WHHA would "undertake to enhance visitor understanding, appreciation, and enjoyment of the Executive Mansion." Slightly exaggerating Jackie's role in the concept's genesis, the statement continued, "The idea for such an association stemmed from Mrs. Kennedy, who is anxious that the White House and its history should be better understood by the hundreds of thousands of visitors who come to see it each year."[41]

The WHHA's first agenda item was production of a White House guidebook. Mrs. Kennedy had originally considered having postcards or brochures printed of the mansion's restored state rooms and art objects to be sold to tourists visiting the presidential home. She also conceived the idea of using proceeds from these sales to purchase furniture and artwork for the White House. The concept evolved into producing a booklet, "for there had been no *official* guidebook before." Castro later conferred "ultimate credit for the guidebook [on] Mrs. Kennedy, because from the very beginning she gave the project her full support and constant encouragement." She was proud of the fact that, as she stated, "I worked hard on [the guidebook]—went over every detail of the text—chose the pictures—worked on the layouts—wrote some of the captions."[42]

The National Geographic Society offered to assist the WHHA in producing the book and underwriting, as a public service, editorial and photographic costs. Society employees prepared a mock-up of the publication, and White House Curator Lorraine Pearce drafted the text. In early 1962 they met with Mrs. Kennedy, along with Castro and J. B. West, chief White House usher. Castro later remembered, "We met for more than two hours. No one could have been more interested than the First Lady. Mrs. Kennedy studied every page of the [mock-up] with great care and thoroughness, making many suggestions, bringing to bear her own professional background in journalism. She performed a vital role in establishing the now well-known 'look' of the White House guidebook."[43]

For help with the publication, Mrs. Kennedy again prevailed upon Arthur Schlesinger, apologizing "to impose on you—but you are the only person who can do it—and the only one who is always kind enough to help me with whatever project I need help with." The book venture was moving far too slowly for the impatient first lady, who told Schlesinger:

> We have to get this finished *soon* so it can be printed by this spring and we can make some money—it is where all our funds will come from—more hemming and hawing has gone on for a year with everyone thinking someone else was doing it. At last Lorraine Pearce has written the text. The National Geographic is printing it—their text was so corny it was impossible (please don't tell anyone that)—all about little Caroline and orchid corsages—[44]

Lorraine will give you her text—with illustrations—I would be so grateful if you could polish it up a bit—with some stirring phrases. You don't have to do any research as all facts will be correct—but I so badly want it to be something we can be proud of— that scholars will want instead of students—so any additions, deletions and beautiful words—. . . you can add—I would be so grateful for. As it can't wait till I get back from India for me to see—I will tell Lorraine that your word is the final law—and they can rush it off to the press. (I have OK'd Lorraine's version.)[45]

Just before departing for India, the first lady wielded her red editor's pencil once more, this time on Pearce's draft of the guidebook's introduction. Mrs. Kennedy added a note about the new law designating the Smithsonian "the watchdog" over White House furnishings so that they would not disappear. She then chastised Pearce for making the introduction "too long" and not ghost-writing it for the first lady: "[T]his must not sound as if it's written by you." In yet another memo to Schlesinger, Jackie termed the Pearce iteration "ghastly—uncoordinated and conceited." In numerical order the first lady spelled out her ideas for the introduction, which she wanted to be no more than one page long, but she assumed a deferential tone with Schlesinger ("any ideas you have will be considered better than mine"):

1. This is 1st guidebook at W.H. It was made to give the millions of people who come here—something to take away—so the things they had seen would not just be a blur in their minds—but they could go home and look up history behind it. It is especially done for children—(though not written down to them) in hopes it will stimulate their interest in U.S. hist[ory].
2. What W.H. means . . . in your language and thoughts.
3. Something about effort to bring back historical things— without making one sound conceited—a quote you might use from T.R.'s message to Congress [about the White House; Mrs. Kennedy even provided a citation for Schlesinger] . . . OK any quote you know from any President which says about W.H. what I am trying to say!
Marvelous closing sentence worthy of Euripides.[46]

Schlesinger prepared an introduction that followed most of the first lady's directives, but ultimately, she approved the following foreword, typed on White House stationery over her signature, for the guidebook's first page. It reflects her breezy style in contrast to Schlesinger's more erudite tone:

> This guidebook is for all the people who visit the White House each year.
>
> It was planned—at first—for the children. It seemed such a shame that they should have nothing to take away with them, to help sort out the impressions received on an often crowded visit. It was hoped that they would go over the book at home and read more about the Presidents who interested them most. Its purpose was to stimulate their sense of history and their pride in their country.
>
> But as research went on and so many little-known facts were gleaned from forgotten papers, it was decided to make it a book that could be of profit to adults and scholars also.
>
> On the theory that it never hurts a child to read something that may be above his head, and that books written down for children often do not awaken a dormant curiosity, this guidebook took its present form.
>
> I hope our young visitors will vindicate this theory, find pleasure in the book, and know that they were its inspiration.
>
> To their elders, may it remind you that First Families loved this house—and that each and every one left something of themselves behind in it—as you do now by the effort you have made to come here.[47]

In 1963 Mrs. Kennedy described the rationale for producing the guidebook: "Besides the obvious reason of having an authoritative book on the White House—and something that the children especially could take home with them—I knew it would eventually be a source of revenue—so that we would not have to beg and borrow for every item desired—so many things we wanted slipped away because we could not produce the money at the time."[48]

Her proposal to sell the book in the White House, however, was nearly as controversial as her plan to restore the mansion had been initially. For security reasons the Secret Service and White House police opposed the idea, arguing that a moving crowd is easier to control than one that is at a standstill, stopping to purchase souvenirs. Both security forces warned that the number of visitors touring the White House would have to be reduced in order to accommodate the new bottleneck, in direct conflict with President Kennedy's desire to increase the number of tourists allowed on tours. Major Ralph Stover of the White House Police noted that members of Congress, in charge of procuring White House passes for their constituents, would surely complain if the numbers were reduced. A member of JFK's staff, John McNally Jr., summarized these concerns for the president and added that the press, public, and foreign dignitaries might be offended by such a commercial enterprise operating in the "President's House." In 1963 Mrs. Kennedy recalled her reaction to these opponents: "Again I had a score of protests from many people a long time in government that it would be a sacrilege to sell anything in the White House—to let money change hands there—I knew how much I had always wanted a guide—so I was stubborn and said just let me try it for a little while—if there are protests—we will sell it in the bookstores or somewhere else. I did this over rather violent objections and it was a success from the first day."[49]

The White House: An Historic Guide debuted on June 28, 1962, with a small West Wing ceremony. National Geographic Society President Melville Grosvenor and JFK both praised the first lady for her efforts in bringing the project to fruition. Press reports of the ceremony noted that "the book takes readers not only through the handsomely refurbished State Rooms, including the dining room where the tables are set for a state dinner, but upstairs to the President's Dining Room, the Lincoln, the Rose Guest Room, in which visiting queens have slept, the Empire Guest Room, and the historic Treaty Room reopened only yesterday after undergoing restoration." At the Treaty Room's unveiling Vice President Lyndon Johnson remarked that Mrs. Kennedy had "electrified America" with her restoration of the White House. The first lady's labors were indeed garnering positive headlines for her and the projects she supervised.[50]

Presented in the glossy, colorful style of the National Geographic Society, the guidebook's slick photos were accompanied by a lively, yet informative, text, which gave the reader an overview of the White

House's architectural, decorative, and presidential history—all packed into 132 pages. Selling for $1.00, as of July 4, 1962, the book's first printing of 250,000 copies was depleted within three months. (Advance orders had numbered 10,000.) After only eighteen months on the market, the book generated nearly $59,000 for the Fine Arts Committee for the White House.[51]

At first the White House Historical Association sold the book in the East Wing's ground floor entrance, used by visitors starting their tour of the mansion. Then a member of the president's staff suggested that sales might go even higher if tourists could purchase the souvenir as they exited the White House. Immediately, the first lady drafted a detailed memo to J. B. West, describing just what type of table, and its covering ("red felt same color as ground floor screen"), should be used to display and sell the books in the first floor's north entrance hall. "[B]ut let us start at once with any table available until you get the right one (Use old kneehole desk that was in 2nd floor hall under Eisenhower to start with . . .) as every penny is needed—do let me know as soon as you start this & how much we sell."[52]

Sales were destined to rise with the increase in tourists visiting the White House. During the last year of the Eisenhower administration in 1960, fewer than one million people toured the Executive Mansion. In 1961 the number rose by several hundred thousand; the total figure in 1963 approached two million. Two more printings of Mrs. Kennedy's edition of the guidebook were necessary to keep pace with demand.[53] By 2001 the book, updated in its twenty-first edition, maintaining its initial format, and selling for $6.00, had sold millions of copies through the White House Historical Association.

While Mrs. Kennedy worked on the White House guidebook, she decided that the WHHA should also produce a similar book on the presidents. After reviewing a National Geographic mock-up of the presidential volume, she again cajoled Arthur Schlesinger into helping, only this time she requested that he draft the entire text. "Could you write the biog[raphical] sketch of each President and decide which things in their terms should be highlighted—I send you a booklet of Mt. Vernon. One thing I like in it which would be nice if you could use it the quotation at the bottom of every other page—there could be one from each President and not the obvious ones—but significant ones that you will know and readers will discover with joy—"[54]

In a subsequent letter to Schlesinger, the first lady outlined in detail the entire format of the presidential book from cover to cover, explaining, "What I want it to be is a brief booklet where someone like me can get a vague but interesting idea of each President (for instance I haven't a clue what party Pierce or Buchanan were of or what they did—except fail)[.] It must be short enough so people will read it all—in other words [a biography] all on one page. . . . So many people and children are lazy—if they can learn something in a glance at a page—they will do it—rather than thumb through a history book—" Mrs. Kennedy instructed Schlesinger to compose "[l]ively even controversial biog[graphical] sketch[es]—(not just born, married, made Monroe Doctrine, died)—with some description of their character—Say two black and white inserts of significant happenings on their term." The first lady even included small sketches of a sample layout for the entries. As a bantering aside, which often marked her correspondence with Schlesinger, she concluded, "Dear Arthur if you can do all this I will carve your name on the Blue Room mantelpiece. Its [*sic*] your penance for not coming to India when we were there[.] Affec[tionately] Jackie." The former Harvard professor and noted historian always responded with the utmost professionalism, but he sometimes signed his business letters, "Much love, Arthur Schlesinger, Jr.," revealing a reciprocal affection for the first lady.[55]

The WHHA continues to publish *The Presidents of the United States of America*, the 2001 edition written by Frank Freidel and Hugh Sidey, with a similar format to that suggested forty years previously by Mrs. Kennedy. In addition to it and the guidebook, the association also offers a companion book, *First Ladies of the United States of America*, by Margaret Brown Klapthor and Allida Black. Sales of these booklets, as well as recent WHHA-sponsored coffee-table publications, totaled eight million by 2001. The association also publishes the journal *White House History*. Like U.S. Supreme Court and U.S. Capitol historical societies, the WHHA distributes videos and other educational materials around the country, sponsors lectures, exhibits, and other outreach programs, and commissions Christmas ornaments, sculptures, paintings, and jewelry based on historical themes and emblems. As of 2001 the White House Historical Association had generated "more than $18 million [for] preserving the White House, acquiring and conserving its furnishings, and educating the public about this national treasure."[56] Jacqueline Kennedy's mission has undoubtedly been accomplished and exceeded.

In her 1963 litany of how she was achieving her goals, the first lady included two more elements: the establishment of the Paintings Committee and the funding of a White House curator and registrar. She praised the chairman of the Paintings Committee James Fosburgh: "He has accomplished the most extraordinary things and is as tireless as Mr. du Pont . . . [in acquiring] all the pictures and engravings (some of them extremely rare) . . . in just two years." By September 1963 *Time* reported that "more than 150 works of art, or the funds to buy them, ha[d] been donated."[57]

In a meeting between the first lady and Henry du Pont, at his Florida residence on March 6, 1961, they considered the necessity of creating a permanent curator position for the White House to supervise the mansion's furnishings, art, and decorations. Without a curator or registrar, Chief Usher West had to keep track of such items, in addition to his many other administrative duties. With her initial inclination toward American decorative arts, Mrs. Kennedy expressed her preference for a Winterthur graduate, and du Pont obliged, recommending his protégée, Lorraine Waxman Pearce. Coincidentally, Pearce had studied the French influence on American decorative arts, so she seemed a perfect match for the first lady. The news release announcing Pearce's appointment as curator for the White House delineated her job description: "Mrs. Pearce will study and register all items of interest presently in the White House, as well as any new acquisitions. As soon as possible, she will compile a catalogue of these items which will be available to the public. She will also work in conjunction with the Fine Arts Committee for the White House of which Mrs. Kennedy is honorary chairman." The new Curator's Office also included a secretary to the Fine Arts Committee and, eventually, a registrar, William Elder, to catalog the White House collection. In August 1963 Elder advised Mrs. Kennedy that all items acquired for the White House during the Kennedy administration had been recorded, along with 50 percent of the objects in the mansion before 1961.[58]

At only twenty-six-years of age, Pearce possessed the necessary energy, along with the knowledge, to meet the first lady's demands as she progressed with the refurbishing and acquisitions projects. Pearce also presented the restoration venture to the outside world, via articles in professional journals and lecture/slide presentations, containing nearly a hundred photographs of redecorated White House rooms and items acquired/donated through the Fine Arts and Painting Committees' efforts. She even offered to present the slide show to President Kennedy to keep him updated on his wife's project. The curator sent the president her lecture script with a cover memo: "I thought this would give you some view of the changes that have been made and the historical principles that are guiding our choice." Despite Pearce's effusive praise of the first lady in her public presentations, the curator began to violate Mrs. Kennedy's #1 rule for subordinates: Keep a low profile. Moreover, Pearce was caught between the diverging decorating philosophies of her mentor, du Pont, and the first lady, as Jackie moved into the Boudin orbit. Mrs. Kennedy suggested that Pearce be eased out of the curator's position by focusing full-time on writing the White House guidebook's text. A frustrated Pearce was happy to comply. Even then, as noted above, Mrs. Kennedy still found reason to complain about Pearce's failure to subordinate her voice in the book's introduction. Nonetheless, the August 1962 press release announcing Pearce's resignation "for personal reasons" graciously praised her "knowledge, time and enthusiasm" contributed "in the early difficult days of establishing the restoration program, and . . . the scholarship which she devoted to the writing of the White House Guidebook. . . . Mrs. Kennedy further stated that she was delighted that she could continue to call on Mrs. Pearce in an advisory capacity, but as a mother, herself, she could well understand Mrs. Pearce's wish to be able to have more time for her young son." William Elder received a promotion to curator, where he served until the fall of 1963. In 1964 a presidential Executive Order established a permanent office of the White House curator, and the position survives to this day as a crucial element of the White House's museum status.[59]

Mrs. Kennedy's concerns with Pearce's public presentations are illustrative of the first lady's larger considerations over how to introduce her work to the public and the press. She had several very practical reasons for wanting to maintain control over how her White House restoration story was told: (1) avoiding criticism from those who had initially been opposed to her project; (2) preventing inflation of prices for items desired by the White House Fine Arts and Paintings Committees; and (3) diverting Congress's attention from refurbishing costs and purchase of European products. She was only too happy to announce, via press releases from the office of the assistant social secretary for the press, the completion of each refurbished room and acquisition of donated treasures—but on her own terms. When Pierre Salinger, JFK's press secretary, allowed *Washington Post* reporter Maxine Cheshire to visit the government storage area at Fort Washington, Mrs. Kennedy phoned him from Hyannis Port to express her displeasure. Lorraine Pearce followed with a memo to Salinger "to express Mrs. Kennedy's wish that no articles or photographs concerning the refurnishing project of The White House be authorized by our office without Mrs. Kennedy's approval." Salinger testily responded to Pearce that he had already heard from Mrs. Kennedy on this matter, he had only granted Cheshire's request after clearing it through the first lady's Social Office, and he had determined that a federal government storage facility filled with public property could not be considered off-limits to the press. "For six months this office has scrupulously cooperated with Mrs. Kennedy in not divulging any details of her work at the White House in the furnishing lines unless directed to do so by Mrs. Kennedy," Salinger concluded.[60]

The printed press disseminated stories of Mrs. Kennedy's White House restoration successes and occasional missteps (like the "antique" desk fraud and overpriced wallpaper scandals noted above). The *Washington Post* reported the administrative details of establishing the Fine Arts Committee and the White House Historical Association, as well as the publication of the guidebook, the hiring and subsequent resignation of Curator Lorraine Pearce, and the periodic acquisition of antiques and paintings. The *Post*'s daily "For and About Women" section carried florid descriptions of the three "colored" salons on the mansion's first floor as they were reopened to the public. Women's section reporter Marie Smith gushed over the new Red Room's walls "covered in American Empire Red silk—a shade currently called magenta—with a gold scroll border" and "handsome silk draperies that hang on gold rings from a gold rail." Smith remarked on the pedigrees of two sofas in the room, one that had belonged to Nellie Custis and another to Dolley Madison. The first acquisition of the Paintings Committee, a work entitled *Cannonading on the Potomac* by A. Wordsworth Thompson, was displayed on the wall above the Madison sofa. Mrs. Kennedy even loaned some antiques from her own collection, including a pair of obelisks that she placed on the mantle. While not citing dollar figures, Smith noted that the White House staff confirmed that the refurbished Red Room was "the most expensively furnished."[61]

Smith also authored the *Post*'s report on the Blue and Green Rooms' unveilings. The darker stains on the wooden floors were among the most striking changes, she announced. While the Blue Room had been returned to the Empire style of the Monroe era, its Boudin-inspired cream-colored walls were Madisonian in origin. The first lady sidestepped another potential controversy over the Blue Room's neutral wall covering. During a series of investigative reports by Cheshire in late summer 1962 that criticized some of the restoration efforts, both President and Mrs. Kennedy urged Press Secretary Pierre Salinger to emphasize to the media that "the Blue Room will always remain the Blue Room."[62]

A white-tie dinner party for members of the legislative and judicial branches, hosted by the Kennedys, was the gala occasion for reopening the Blue and Green Rooms and the subject of another *Post* article, adjacent to the Smith piece. Speaker of the House of Representatives John McCormack warmly toasted the first lady in his tribute "to womanhood in general and Mrs. Kennedy in particular," proclaiming that she "has done more for the White House than any other First Lady before her." As White House Curator Betty Monkman reported in 2001, "So strong was the perception of [Mrs. Kennedy's restoration] project that many Americans believe that White House interiors have not changed since 1963."[63]

Surely the media—from newspapers to glossy magazines to news periodicals to television—helped to establish that impression. The *Saturday Evening Post, Life,* and *Look* ran glitzy features on the first lady's White House restoration. According to *Look,* which included beautiful colored photographs of remodeled White House rooms in its January 1962 feature, "Mrs. Kennedy and her talented aides have deftly combined history with taste to bring to 1600 Pennsylvania Avenue a new sense of warmth, elegance and beauty." Of the seventeen articles on Jacqueline Kennedy published during her first ladyship by *Time* magazine, five highlighted her White House refurbishing enterprise, always in laudatory fashion. The most acclamatory piece ran in September 1963: "What was neglected [by previous presidents] was the ideal: the White House as a monument, as a symbol of the nation's continuity under all administrations. That no longer is true. First Lady Jacqueline Kennedy conceived an ideal of what the White House ought to be and translated her vision into reality. She has redecorated the public rooms in authentic period styles and arranged in them a treasure of newly acquired paintings and sculptures by U.S. artists. She has made the White House a repository of history preserved in art."[64]

Newsweek, which reported more critically on the first lady's project, praised her "efficiency and professionalism that even her husband might envy." The magazine noted that "the White House has resisted all attempts by the press to compile facts and figures that would give a clear picture of how much the program has cost, who pays the bills, and how the money is spent." Yet it concluded that, "[b]y educating the public through print and television, by involving Congress and a nationwide string of historians and art patrons," Mrs. Kennedy "hopes to set up a system of checks and balances so powerful that no one ever again will be able to let the White House become a frumpish, second-rate building."[65]

The most lasting imprint of Mrs. Kennedy's work resulted from her February 14, 1962, broadcast (on all three television networks at that time) of *A Tour of the White House with Mrs. John F. Kennedy.* To polite questions posed by veteran CBS correspondent Charles Collingwood, the first lady expounded on every detail as the tour moved from the state rooms on the ground and first floors to the historic chambers upstairs. Nothing was too esoteric for Mrs. Kennedy's presentation or memory; she recalled, without cue cards, minutiae about presidential preferences and stories of her restoration adventures. In the Lincoln Bedroom, Collingwood inquired about "detective work" that had resulted in discoveries of notable furnishings. The first lady's delight is evident even in the printed transcript of her response: "Yes, these two chairs are an example of that. We found one at Fort Washington, which is the storehouse; so battered, all the stuffing coming out. But we just thought it looked of the Lincoln period so we dragged it home. And we found from an engraving that it was. And then out of the blue a Mrs. Millard Black of Arlington sent us its exact pair. And then a Mrs. Burton Cohen from New Jersey sent us some Victorian green and yellow Morris velvet and it was just enough to cover the two chairs. So here they are, Lincoln's chairs."[66]

In the final scene of the hour-long documentary, President Kennedy made a cameo appearance in which he praised his wife's efforts, encouraged visitors to come see the results of her White House project, and slipped in some subtle Cold War rhetoric about the United States' longevity. "When we were founded, there was a king in France, a czar in Russia, an emperor in Peking. Today all that's been wiped away—and yet this country continues. It makes us feel that we will continue in the future. . . . Anything which dramatizes the great story of the United States—as I think the White House does—is worthy of the closest attention and respect by the Americans who live here and who are part of our citizenry. That's why I am glad Jackie is making the effort she is making. I know other First Ladies have done it; and I know that those who come after us will continue to try to make this the center of a sense of American historical life."[67]

An estimated three out of four Americans viewed the program, and the United States Information Service then released it for televised showings and public screenings in 106 countries, including six behind the Iron Curtain. By today's standards Mrs. Kennedy's performance appears stilted, her whispery voice a distraction, but she was an unqualified hit with viewers forty years ago. She received 10,000 fan letters, including one from future first lady Barbara Bush. One little boy wrote, on tablet paper that he decorated with his rendition of the White House and presidential helicopters, "Dear Mrs. Kennedy, I enjoyed your program. It was exciting." Then he added with childlike frankness, "My dad was going to watch Maverick [a popular TV Western at the time]." *Time* magazine effused, "With a tiny microphone and transmitter hidden under her blouse, Jackie commented on everything from the curator's basement headquarters to the Lincoln Bedroom upstairs. So skilled was her performance that only one retake was ordered—and that simply because one of the television cameras had gone out of whack." In describing the feelings of the documentary's crew, Collingwood captured the essence of television's new frontier: "Everyone from the lowliest porter to the director felt they had been involved in one of the landmarks of this infant [TV] business."[68]

Indeed they had been. In 1952, when President Harry Truman had guided Walter Cronkite around the refurbished White House in its first televised tour, less than 20 percent of American households had television sets. When Mrs. Kennedy made her broadcast presentation, nearly 90 percent had them.[69] The event was emblematic of the era and the first lady's indelible mark on it. Her youthful, knowledgeable, and elegant style reinforced that of her husband. She embodied the very image that she sought to project for the White House: a place of excellence, perfection, historicism, beauty, and radiance. The telegenic first lady beamed these symbols into American living rooms and throughout the free and communist worlds. She had woven the Kennedy mystique and aura into the fabric of one of the nation's most potent political icons.

Eight presidents and their wives have lived in the White House since the Kennedy years. They have continued the historical precedent of redecorating the mansion's public and private spaces to counter wear and tear and meet their professional and personal needs. Pat Nixon expanded the Executive Mansion's furniture and fine arts collection. She also opened the White House grounds to the public for special spring and fall tours ofthe gardens. Rosalynn Carter established the White House Endowment Fund, a nonprofit organization to raise private money for restoration projects. Barbara Bush and Hillary Clinton helped the fund to meet and exceed its original endowment goal of $25 million.[70] Forty years after Jacqueline Kennedy moved out of the White House, her legacy to the president's home remains intact. Most of the public interiors have been remodeled numerous times, but the Red Room, her favorite state chamber, displays the same furniture and decorative arts she chose for it. In addition, the Clintons returned her elegant swag pattern for the Blue Room wall treatments. The foundation she created for supporting the White House's history and image, the Historical Association, continues to thrive. Its revised versions of her White House publications have provided millions of dollars for continuing her policy of collecting only the "best" furniture and art for display in the president's home. The curator's office, which she established, is a crucial element in preserving the Executive Mansion and its possessions. Mrs. Kennedy's goal of creating a sophisticated stage, rooted in history, for the modern presidency constitutes the most enduring contribution of her brief tenure as first lady.

CHAPTER 5

PROMOTING THE ARTS AND CULTURE

Mona Lisa, Mona Lisa, men have named you.
You're so like the lady with the mystic smile.
Is it only 'cause you're lonely, they have blamed you,
for that Mona Lisa strangeness in your style?
Do you smile to tempt a lover, Mona Lisa?
Or is this your way to hide a broken heart?
Many dreams have been brought to your doorstep.
They just lie there and they die there.
Are you warm? Are you real, Mona Lisa?
Or just a cold and lonely, lovely work of art?
—Jay Livingston, "Mona Lisa"

The 1950s ballad "Mona Lisa," crooned by Nat King Cole, could have served as the theme for a highlight of the Kennedy administration's courting of the art world. The lyrics capture the popular magic of da Vinci's masterpiece; and the mysterious object of the balladeer's affections might well have been Jacqueline Kennedy, with her enigmatic smile, flirtatious demeanor, and iconic status. The link between the first lady and the portrait, Mona Lisa, was sealed in 1963 when she facilitated a trip to the United States for the Louvre's most famous painting.

The genesis of the idea to bring *La Gioconda*, the portrait's formal title (based on the family name of its Florentine subject), to

Washington's National Gallery lay with *Washington Post* White House reporter Edward Folliard. As early as the 1930s, when the gallery was merely a proposal in the mind of its patron, Paul Mellon, Folliard dreamed of attracting the world's greatest masterpieces to it. He considered the Mona Lisa the ultimate artistic accomplishment, and he began to lobby the French for a loan of the portrait as early as 1950. The catalyst for Folliard's eventual success was First Lady Jacqueline Kennedy. Her triumphant state visit to Paris with her husband in 1961 included cordial meetings with French Minister of State for Cultural Affairs André Malraux. They developed a mutual admiration during their conversations and trips to Parisian art museums, particularly the Jeu de Paume's Impressionist exhibits. Jackie was especially touched by Malraux's hospitality in light of the fact that he was mourning the recent loss of his two sons in a fatal automobile accident.[1]

The next year Mrs. Kennedy invited Malraux and his wife to the United States and staged a gala state dinner for them. The first lady sparkled in a light pink strapless silk gown and an antique diamond sunburst pin in her hair. Photos show her standing close to Malraux and smiling during their tête-à-tête, her left shoulder nearly tucked under the Frenchman's right arm. "I think Jackie had a crush [on Malraux], and vice versa, at least in an intellectual sense," Tish Baldrige remembers. By mail, the first lady received some criticism of her revealing evening attire, but she told Baldrige to respond by saying that future gowns would be cut even lower! Ignoring her boss's pique, the social secretary instructed the correspondence staff to answer critiques more diplomatically: "Mrs. Kennedy was interested to hear your opinion, and she has asked me to send you very best wishes." The White House assembled an American cultural pantheon among the 168 guests at the Malraux dinner, which included authors Saul Bellow, Robert Penn Warren, and Thornton Wilder, poets Robert Lowell and Archibald MacLeish, painters Andrew Wyeth and Mark Rothko, playwrights Arthur Miller and Tennessee Williams, movie director Elia Kazan, composer/conductor Leonard Bernstein, actresses Julie Harris and Geraldine Page, and choreographers Agnes de Mille and George Balanchine.[2]

Page wrote a gushing thank-you note to her hostess: "Dear First Lady, I hope you are First Lady for the next three hundred years at

least! . . . All the life-renewing myths are brought to mind by the stirring and awakening and coming to life all over the country and all
around the world that is taking place because *you two are where you
are.* You remind us all who we can be and the reestablishing of values is bringing us all to life again." Violinist Isaac Stern performed at
the Malraux dinner. He had previously written to Mrs. Kennedy, "It
would be difficult to tell you how refreshing, how heartening it is to
find such serious attention and respect for the arts in the White
House. To many of us it is one of the most exciting developments on
the present American cultural scene."[3]

At a luncheon for the French culture minister and the press, Folliard queried Malraux, "Wouldn't it be a wonderful thing if the
Mona Lisa could be shown in the National Gallery?" The Frenchman agreed, adding, "France feels that these masterpieces belong to
mankind. She [France] has no copyright on them." Folliard credited
Mrs. Kennedy with seconding his idea during her visit with Malraux
to the National Gallery of Art. In December 1962, when the French
government approved the unprecedented display of their national
masterpiece in Washington, D.C., and New York City, through a
loan of the painting directly to President Kennedy, JFK replied,
"Mrs. Kennedy and I particularly want to thank President de Gaulle
for his generous gesture in making possible this historic loan, and
Mr. Andre Malraux, the distinguished French Minister of Cultural
Affairs, for his good offices in the matter."[4]

Opening the Mona Lisa's four-week exhibit at the National Gallery of Art, on January 8, 1963, President Kennedy eloquently summarized its symbolism for the world of art, culture, and international politics. Before an excited throng of 1,500 American and
French invitees, JFK observed,

[W]e in the United States are grateful for this loan from the leading artistic power in the world, France. . . . [G]rateful as we are
for this painting, we will continue to press ahead with the effort
to develop an independent artistic force and power of our
own. . . . Our two nations have fought on the same side in four
wars during a span of the last 185 years. Each has been delivered
from the foreign rule of another by the other's friendship and
courage. Our two revolutions helped define the meaning of de-

Unveiling of the Mona Lisa at Washington's National Gallery of Art,
with French Minister of Culture André Malraux, to Mrs. Kennedy's right,
January 1963. (Photo by Robert Knudsen, White House. JFK Library, Boston)

mocracy and freedom which are so much contested in the world
today. Today, here in this Gallery, in front of this great painting,
we are renewing our commitment to those ideals which have
proved such a strong link through so many hazards. . . . We are
here tonight . . . to pay homage to this great creation of the civilization which we share, the beliefs which we protect, and the aspirations toward which we together strive.[5]

The first lady left the public pronouncements to her husband,
but she attracted the spotlight in her strapless pink silk chiffon
gown, patterned with porcelain beads and rhinestones. *Life* magazine exclaimed, "It was a long awaited reunion [between Mrs. Kennedy and the Mona Lisa], and both ladies were at their glowing

best." Postcards, featuring the famous da Vinci portrait, appeared with the caption, "Mona Lisa, We salute the first lady of the land, Mrs. John F. Kennedy, for bringing to America the first lady of the world." Ultimately, more than 600,000 visitors to the National Gallery viewed the painting; another million would see it at the Metropolitan Museum of Art in New York. Combining the epitome of the Renaissance with pioneering space-age technology, the portrait appeared on the first live television broadcast from the United States to Europe, via the Relay satellite.[6]

The Kennedys' outreach to "creative Americans in the arts, sciences, and the humanities" had begun when the Inaugural Committee launched a project to issue invitations from President-elect and Mrs. Kennedy to 168 distinguished artists, scientists, and intellectuals. Fifty-eight of the invitees attended the inauguration, despite the snowy weather that made travel difficult. Author John Steinbeck "expressed the general spirit of the group when he said he was so astonished and thrilled to have been invited that he was quite willing to mush to every event." Many of the laureates "revealed delight that President and Mrs. Kennedy were moved to consider them the equals of the politicians." Poet Robert Frost composed a verse for the event, which began,

> Summoning artists to participate
> In the august occasions of the state
> Seems something artists ought to celebrate.

It concluded,

> A golden age of poetry and power
> Of which this noonday's the beginning hour.

On the inaugural stand, Frost struggled in vain against the winter sun's bright glare to read his composition; he finally recited from memory his poem "The Gift Outright." The elderly poet, bundled against the cold, as the young new president and his wife looked on, would become another of the indelible images of the Kennedy inauguration. Years later, in a book of her mother's favorite poetry, Caroline Kennedy wrote, "Throughout her life, my mother took great pride in the role of poetry and the arts in my father's administration. She celebrated American arts and artists in the White House, believing, as my father did, that America's artistic achievements were equal to her political and military power, and that American civilization had come of age."[7]

Recognition of what the Kennedy Inaugural Committee labeled the "Eminent Group" continued until the end of the administration. In addition to fêting them at the Malraux dinner, the White House had celebrated Nobel Prize winners of the Western Hemisphere in April 1962. August Heckscher, President Kennedy's special consultant on the arts, suggested that Mrs. Kennedy host a dinner at the Executive Mansion in the spring of 1963 for winners of the major awards in literature and allied fields. Tish Baldrige later notified Heckscher's office that the first lady had decided not to hold the literary prize dinner because it was "too controversial and complicated" to determine which winners should be included in the event. Arthur Schlesinger had advised the first lady, "On the social/cultural front, I agree that it is hard to envisage another big cultural dinner which did not draw on much the same people as the Malraux dinner last year." Nevertheless, the Kennedys designed a special medallion for the Presidential Medal of Freedom. Established by President Truman in 1945 to honor civilians for their service during World War II, the award was reinstated by President Kennedy. It was presented to thirty-one honorees in the arts, sciences, humanities, and public service on Mrs. Kennedy's last day in the White House, December 6, 1963. Recipients from the arts and humanities included singer Marian Anderson, cellist Pablo Casals, architect Ludwig Mies Van Der Rohe, pianist Rudolf Serkin, essayist E. B. White, author Thornton Wilder, writer Edmund Wilson, and painter Andrew Wyeth. The former first lady watched the ceremony, dressed in widow's black and screened from the guests in the State Dining Room. Her assassinated husband received the award posthumously; his brother, Bobby, accepted on the late president's behalf.[8]

By the time Jacqueline Kennedy left the White House, she had shaped a legacy in the arts and humanities that included promoting the performing arts through White House–sponsored entertainment and the fund drive for the National Cultural Center, focusing on the fine arts through her Paintings Committee, bolstering historic preservation in her White House restoration and Lafayette

Square projects, and emphasizing the American literary tradition by revitalizing the Executive Mansion's library.

President Kennedy summarized one aspect of his wife's efforts: "Her emphasis upon culture at White House functions is an expression of her feeling that the White House ought to be the center of excellence." She took her cue from choreographer George Balanchine of the New York City ballet, who encouraged the new first lady "to distinguish between material things and things of the spirit— art, beauty." Because Washington, D.C., offered no national performing arts venue, the Kennedy White House literally provided a stage for musicians, singers, dancers, and actors. The National Park Service constructed for the East Room a portable platform that stood nearly a foot and a half off the floor, with a backdrop of panels, all swathed in rich red velvet.[9]

The American presidency has had a long and illustrious association with music through the personal tastes of its incumbents and their public preferences in entertainment. Starting with George Washington, numerous chief executives have found amusement, joy, comfort, and solace in playing instruments, dancing, and listening to a variety of musical forms. By no means was the Kennedy White House the first to present musical entertainment. During his term in the early 1840s, President John Tyler began the tradition of inviting performing artists to entertain at the Executive Mansion. Abraham Lincoln adored classical opera, which proved a much-needed distraction for him during the Civil War. He was also the first president to invite an opera singer to perform at the White House. In the postbellum era President Rutherford Hayes and his wife instituted the musicale, "a short concert with social overtones that was popular in Europe at the time." Grover Cleveland loved operettas, especially those by Gilbert and Sullivan, and requested selections from their *Mikado* for the U.S. Marine Band to play at his White House wedding reception in 1886. Theodore Roosevelt's administration, an activist presidency in so many realms, was no exception in supporting the performing arts. In 1903 Steinway donated a concert grand piano to the president for use in East Room entertainment, and the piano company organized most of the White House's concerts in the first half of the twentieth century. In the first Roosevelt administration alone, the president and first lady hosted celebrated pianists Paderewski, Busoni, Hofmann, and Rachmaninoff. Yet T.R. and Edith were just as delighted by Scott Joplin's ragtime tunes, played by the Marine Band, as they were by classical sonatas presented by young Spanish cellist Pablo Casals. The Roosevelts also had elegant programs printed for their White House concerts. Calvin Coolidge and Herbert Hoover continued the practice of inviting virtuosos to the president's home, and First Lady Lou Henry Hoover inaugurated the custom of presenting guest artists to perform for visiting heads of state. The Franklin Roosevelts' twelve-year tenure in the White House occasioned the opportunity to mount more than three hundred concerts, despite economic and wartime crises. Not surprisingly, given the diversity of the New Deal coalition, FDR and Eleanor hosted an eclectic array of black, American Indian, women, and folk music performers, in addition to mainstream classical programs. Harry Truman, an avid amateur pianist, adored classical music and embraced every opportunity to display his musical talents, including when the Kennedys threw a state dinner in his honor. Highbrow observers, including Arthur Schlesinger Jr., criticized the Eisenhowers' allegedly pedestrian preferences for military bands, swing music, and Broadway productions, but Ike and Mamie also presented a White House concert by renowned pianist Artur Rubinstein. In truth, Jack Kennedy's taste in music was less than sophisticated. He even had to arrange a signal from Tish Baldrige to alert him when to applaud at symphony concerts. He was tempted to clap after movements ended—a violation of audience protocol.[10]

For each of their sixteen state dinners, the Kennedys offered musical or theatrical entertainment. They began more traditionally with a military tattoo for their first evening in honor of a visiting head of state, the president of Tunisia, in May 1961. At the incomparable Mount Vernon soirée for the president of Pakistan in the summer of 1961, the Kennedys featured a concert by the National Symphony Orchestra, which presented Mozart and Debussy, as well as Gershwin's "American in Paris." The *Washington Post* published a front-page report on the evening's festivities. Staff reporters Marie Smith and Maxine Cheshire who usually wrote on the first lady for the *Post*'s women's section, reported that, from start to finish, the state event at Mount Vernon "was a flawless spectacle Hollywood

couldn't surpass. . . . After the dinner, the National Symphony Orchestra assembled for an outdoor concert that could be heard far
out over the countryside in the balmy night breezes."[11]

That fall the president and first lady hosted two state dinners, one
for the president of Peru, at which Metropolitan Opera stars Jerome
Hines and Roberta Peters sang, and another for Sudan's president,
capped by the American Shakespeare Festival's presentation of
scenes and excerpts from the Bard's plays. The debut of the East
Room's new stage captivated *Washington Post* reporters: "For President and Mrs. Kennedy's 100 guests, their first glimpse of the trans-
formed White House ballroom last night was a moment almost as
dramatic as the Shakespearean scenes about to unfold there in
honor of Sudan's President Aboud. . . . The President and First Lady,
who share a passionate absorption with the written and spoken
word, had set a scene for their English-speaking guest of honor,
which they intend to repeat often in the future on this same collap-
sible stage."[12] A proud member of the audience was Mrs. Kennedy's
Shakespeare professor from Vassar.

In November 1961 pianist Eugene List, who had played for Harry
Truman, Winston Churchill, and Joseph Stalin at the 1945 Potsdam
Conference, provided after-dinner entertainment at the state event
celebrating Truman's return to the White House. List performed the
former president's favorite Chopin and Mozart compositions and
then turned the Steinway over to a delighted Truman.[13]

The 1961 state social season climaxed with a return engagement
by eighty-five-year-old cellist Pablo Casals, more than a half century
after his first White House concert for Theodore Roosevelt, at the
dinner for Puerto Rico's governor. Casals, who made his home in
Puerto Rico after the Spanish Civil War, ended his self-imposed ban
on performing in the United States. He had established the mora-
torium when the United States recognized the fascist regime of
Francisco Franco in the cellist's native Spain. Ignoring the uncom-
fortable fact that the United States continued to support right-wing
regimes as counterpoints to Marxist movements throughout the
Cold War, President Kennedy used the occasion to extol the
evening's cultural and political symbolism. "Music and the arts are
an integral part of a free society," remarked the president, "and the
artist must be a free man." A music critic summed up the concert by

"one of the immortals of the art," and its political implications: "The sounds that were heard last night, as well as the meaning bound up in the entire evening, will be with us for a long time."[14]

Early in 1962 the White House presented the American debut of Grace Bumbry, a twenty-four-year-old black mezzo-soprano from Saint Louis, who had already earned acclaim in Europe and who would subsequently star at the Met. She sang a variety of operatic and classical pieces after a dinner in honor of the U.S. vice president, speaker of the House of Representatives, and chief justice. In light of the growing struggle over civil rights, her minority racial status infused the performance with political symbolism. Two months later the Kennedys welcomed the shah and empress of Iran to a state dinner, followed by excerpts from Jerome Robbins' American contemporary dance company, Ballets: USA.

Less than three weeks later the White House honored the Western Hemisphere's forty-nine living Nobel Prize winners at a gala dinner, after which actor Fredric March read excerpts from the works of deceased American Nobel laureates, including Ernest Hemingway, who had only recently committed suicide. His widow listened to March's presentation as a member of the illustrious audience. (Years later she donated Hemingway's papers to the Kennedy Library.) In his toast to the prizewinners, JFK joked that a Canadian journalist had labeled the event "the President's Easter egghead roll on the lawn of the White House." But the chief executive emphasized the more serious purpose that he and Mrs. Kennedy had in saluting United States achievement in science, literature, and world peace: "I think the pursuit of knowledge, the pursuit of peace, are very basic pressures in this life of ours, and this dinner is an attempt to recognize those great efforts, to encourage young Americans and young people in this Hemisphere to develop the same drive and deep desire for knowledge and peace."[15]

The Malraux dinner followed the Nobel evening a mere eleven days later, prompting the president to quip, "This is becoming a sort of eating place for artists. But they never ask us out." An interval of only eleven more days passed before the next state dinner, this one for the Ivory Coast's president. The Kennedys invited the American Ballet Theatre to stage Aaron Copland's *Billy the Kid.* To accommodate the native language of the African guests, the White House printed complete programs of this quintessentially American ballet in French. President and Mrs. Kennedy presented the African head of state with a stereo and a record collection of American music, including the Copland ballet. That fall the Kennedys planned to host the grand duchess of Luxembourg at a state dinner, with internationally known American pianist Byron Janis to present a special program. The Cuban missile crisis postponed the event.[16]

Not until March 1963 did President and Mrs. Kennedy hold another state dinner for a foreign leader, this time the king of Morocco. The New York City Center Light Opera Company performed scenes from the musical *Brigadoon*. The production required symphonic accompaniment, but the East Room could not accommodate even a small orchestra, along with the stage and dancers. So Tish Baldrige arranged to have the score piped in via a tape recorder. The president worried about a machine malfunction, but Baldrige assured him that she had the military's Signal Corps prepare a backup. She had not anticipated a blown fuse in the middle of the performance, however. The music stopped and the East Room was plunged into darkness. Consummate troupers, the dancers froze in their positions, where they remained until the lights and music returned. An embarrassed JFK turned to the king of Morocco and said, "Of course, you see, Your Highness, that's all part of our ballet." The perplexed guest apparently accepted his host's explanation, but President Kennedy instructed Baldrige afterward, "Don't let that happen again. We don't like sitting in the dark in the middle of entertainment. At least have an accordionist there or somebody to entertain when all the lights go out and all the music stops."[17]

A month later the White House held the rescheduled dinner for Luxembourg's grand duchess and offered a different entertainment segment from the one originally planned. British stage and screen star Basil Rathbone, accompanied by singers and musicians, presented a program of Elizabethan poetry and music. Caroline Kennedy has described the production as "one of my mother's favorite White House events. . . . She worked hard on every detail of the evening, choosing the music to be played on Elizabethan instruments and overruling the Library of Congress and other Shakespearean scholars to make sure that her favorite poems were included in the program. 'I have loaded it with love sonnets,' she wrote in a triumphant memo discussing the pros and cons of various passages."[18]

Mrs. Kennedy's last public event before the anticipated birth of her baby in late summer 1963 was a June state dinner for the president of India. The Opera Society of Washington presented act 1's finale from Mozart's opera, *The Magic Flute*. To an Opera Society trustee Jackie remarked, "Tish [Baldrige] tells me this is going to be the most beautiful thing we've staged yet in the White House." The press praised Baldrige "for her last night in a role that has never before been filled so imaginatively and creatively." In her subsequent memoir the former social secretary asserted that Mrs. Kennedy "began to resent press clips that mentioned my influence on the entertaining after dinner."[19]

The first lady thought that her baby's birth would preclude her attendance at a September state dinner for the king and queen of Afghanistan, but she suggested to her new social secretary, Nancy Tuckerman, that Washington's late summer weather would allow "outside entertainment. Perfect for [the king] would be the exact same tattoo on the lawn we had for [the president] of Tunisia—all the military bands, bagpipes, etc." The last state dinner held in the Kennedy White House, for Ethiopia's emperor in October 1963, featured two original works by the Robert Joffrey Ballet. Mrs. Kennedy, vacationing abroad after the death of her infant son, did not attend.[20]

Jackie Kennedy also targeted youthful performers and audiences. Labeled "Mrs. Kennedy's Concerts for Children by Children," they were inaugurated with an August 22, 1961, concert on the White House lawn, given by the Transylvania Orchestra, a youth ensemble from Brevard, North Carolina. Despite her official sponsorship of the performance, the first lady did not attend. She was spending a six-week vacation at the Kennedy summer home in Hyannis Port. Her husband was careful to emphasize his substitution for her in welcoming remarks to the musicians and their audience of handicapped children from Washington, D.C. The training of young American musicians "all across the United States . . . is a great national cultural asset," the president observed, "and therefore it is a great source of satisfaction to me, representing as I do today my wife, to welcome all of you here today at the White House."[21]

The second of Mrs. Kennedy's youth programs consisted of a performance by the young Metropolitan Opera Guild singers of *Cosi Fan Tutte* in the White House's East Room. They presented the opera for children of foreign ambassadors posted to Washington's embassies. After the performance, one of the singers, arrayed in an elaborate turban decorated with ostrich feathers, stood too close to a candle-lit wall sconce, which ignited his headpiece. A vigilant Secret Service agent extinguished the flames before any injuries occurred, and the president's laughter at the mishap relieved the tension among the children, who joined in with giggles.[22]

In the spring of 1962 the White House hosted Mrs. Kennedy's third youth program featuring the Greater Boston Youth Symphony and the Breckinridge Boys Choir. That summer the National High School Symphony Orchestra from the famed National Music Camp at Interlochen, Michigan, performed for the fourth of the first lady's youth concerts. The fifth program, in the fall of 1962, presented the Paul Winter Sextet, a jazz ensemble of young American musicians, and Korean pianist Tong Il Han, who performed a classical program. He and the jazz band played in the East Room for the children of Washington's foreign ambassadors, as well as the offspring of Cabinet and State Department officials. The sixth in Mrs. Kennedy's series was held in the spring of 1963. The first lady attended the concert presented by Kentucky's Youth Symphony Orchestra and the Berea College Country Dancers.

During her three years in the White House, Jackie Kennedy sponsored two additional arts series. She served as the honorary chair for "evenings with artists," presented by the president's Cabinet in the State Department Auditorium. Cabinet members, Mrs. Kennedy, and her staff suggested performers for the program. In 1961–62 presenters included Robert Frost, Carl Sandburg, Marian Anderson, and Thornton Wilder. In 1963 the series attracted noted artists from other countries: Britain's Royal Shakespeare Company, Spain's guitarist Andres Segovia, Chile's pianist Claudio Arrau, and the Soviet Union's violinist David Oistrakh.

Yet another performance for which Mrs. Kennedy served as patron was a filmed presentation of excerpts from "The Festival of Performing Arts." Rather than present a live performance, this program took advantage of previously televised concerts and dramatic productions, underwritten by Standard Oil, which were preserved on tape and projected on a giant screen at the 6,000-seat Watergate outdoor band shell, located along the Potomac at the foot of the Lincoln Memorial. Primarily for students in the Washington area, the program on June 17, 1963, included Yehudi Menuhin, Paul Scofield, and

Pablo Casals, who performed a portion of the program he had presented at the White House in 1961.

A more personal mode of supporting arts and culture during her husband's administration was Mrs. Kennedy's attendance at live performances and exhibits in the nation's capital and beyond. During her tenure as first lady, she appeared at eighteen such programs (not counting those cultural events she attended abroad). In addition to her role in presenting the Mona Lisa, she previewed paintings at Washington's Corcoran Gallery, attended the opening of the Schlumberger exhibit at New York's Wildenstein Gallery, opened the show Tutankhamun's Treasures at the National Gallery of Art, inaugurated a show of Latin American paintings at the Pan American Union, toured the National Gallery with André Malraux, and attended the opening of the Meyers' exhibit there. For the performing arts she attended the Washington Opera with West German Chancellor Konrad Adenauer, spent an evening at the Washington Ballet and attended their reception, opened the National Symphony Orchestra's 1961 season, attended "An Evening with Oscar Wilde" at the Library of Congress (which must have been a treat, given her selection of the Irish playwright as one of the three artists she wished she had known for her application essay in *Vogue*'s 1951 Prix de Paris competition), went to theatrical performances of *Joan of Arc* and *Irma La Douce,* attended the opening of Lincoln Center's Philharmonic Hall in New York, took Caroline to the Washington School of Ballet to see a rehearsal of the Bolshoi Ballet and attended its opening-night performance, greeted the Bolshoi's dancers at the White House and gave them a tour of the mansion, went to a performance by the American Ballet Theatre, and attended the opening night of Irving Berlin's musical, *Mr. President.* Her attentiveness to the 120 members of the Bolshoi Ballet, who appeared in Washington and visited the White House a scant month after the Cuban missile crisis, was a remarkable cultural exchange. Producer Sol Hurak concluded after the troupe's tour of the White House and aperitifs in the State Dining Room with the first lady, "[T]hey will bring back to Moscow a marvelous message of good will." It must have brought special pleasure to Mrs. Kennedy, who had written about Russian ballet impresario, Serge Diaghileff, in her 1951 *Vogue* essay, that he "dealt not with the interaction of the senses but with the interaction of the arts, an interaction of the cultures of East and West."[23]

Jacqueline Kennedy's most tangible and enduring contribution to the performing arts was the role she played in the establishment of a national cultural center. Though less hands-on than her work in the White House restoration project, the lending of her name and stature to the enterprise was crucial in resuscitating a stagnant initiative left over from the Eisenhower era. Even indirectly, her emphasis on artistic presentations at the White House (complete with the new portable stage), and her attendance at performances in Washington, underscored the point that the nation's capital had no grand theater, no large concert hall, no magnificent opera house, in stark contrast to capital cities around the world. In 1958 Congress had passed legislation, which Senator John F. Kennedy supported and President Dwight Eisenhower signed, establishing the National Cultural Center as a bureau of the Smithsonian Institution, to be directed by a Board of Trustees. The Board's mission, as delineated by Congress, was to present classical and contemporary music, opera, drama, dance, and poetry from the United States and other countries; arrange lectures and other programs; develop series for children, youth, and the elderly in arts designed specifically for their participation, education, and recreation; and provide facilities for other civic activities. Congress granted the site for the center, ten acres in the District, just north of the Theodore Roosevelt Bridge, along the Potomac River. Washington builders argued—presciently, it turned out—that planned expressways and highway interchanges would eventually isolate the setting. The local construction industry urged Congress to build the center in downtown Washington in order to spur development in the decaying central city. Despite such opposition, Congress refused to shift the site.[24]

Controversy also ensued over the building's design and cost. In 1962 the Center's Board of Trustees asked architect Edward Durell Stone to combine his three proposed halls (a 1,200-seat theater; 2,750-seat symphony hall; and 2,500-seat house for opera, ballet, and musical theater) under one roof, instead of placing them in separate edifices. The new plan slashed the $75-million proposal by more than half. Nevertheless, the building itself was an "unfunded mandate," for the national legislature dictated that construction funds should be raised by the voluntary contributions of the

American people.[25] That effort had made little progress by the time the Kennedy administration came to power. A presidency devoted to artistic and cultural promotion provided a fortuitous boost for the fund-raising process.

In a bipartisan effort, President Kennedy appointed his wife and former first lady Mamie Eisenhower honorary cochairs of the Cultural Center's Board of Trustees. Mrs. Kennedy's first public event for the cause was a tea she hosted at the White House on June 22, 1962, for Mrs. Eisenhower and other supporters, including the first lady's mother, Janet Auchincloss, the chair of the new Greater Washington Committee for the National Cultural Center. The Auchincloss Committee was charged with the daunting responsibility of raising $7.5 million, one-quarter of the Center's total cost. Late that summer in Newport Mrs. Kennedy unveiled architect Stone's scale model of the white marble building. Before an audience of 300 community fund-raising chairs from thirty-five states, the first lady spoke in the ballroom of The Elms, a Newport mansion designed as a French chateau, which had just opened its rooms and artwork to the public. "It is no secret that Washington needs this Cultural Center," the first lady began. "Washington has more visitors than any other city in the land. I hope that seeing this model will do for all of you what it has done for me. I hope that the people of the country seeing this model—and it will tour the U.S.—will think it worth their effort to contribute to the building of the center." Actor/comedian Danny Kaye joined her in promoting the center, telling the audience that President and Mrs. Kennedy "have made poets, actors, writers, and musicians feel ten feet tall. They have made actors feel as important as architects and artists and agricultural workers." Six weeks later, in the midst of the Cuban missile crisis, the first lady kept the only appointment on her public calendar not canceled by the international emergency. She met with NBC's Sander Vanocur for a television interview on the Cultural Center.[26]

In November 1962 the White House held a reception for the President's Business Committee, a group led by the director of Trans World Airlines, to seek contributions for the Center from American industry and commerce. Their goal was $6 million, one-fifth of the total to be raised. The meeting was followed by an even more important event for the cause on November 29, 1962. That night the Washington National Guard Armory ("a site which of itself dramatize[d] the need for the Cultural Center") was the main venue for a $100-per-plate dinner and an "American Pageant of the Arts" to kick off the $30 million campaign. Broadcast via closed-circuit television to eight other sites in Washington, as well as to local fund-raising committees across the country, the occasion featured host Leonard Bernstein and an eclectic cast of performers—Frederic March, Jason Robards, Bradford Dillman (reprising their Broadway roles in a scene from *Long Day's Journey into Night*), Hal Holbrook (presenting a portion of his one-man show on Mark Twain), Harry Belafonte, Marian Anderson, Pablo Casals, Van Cliburn, Colleen Dewhurst, Robert Frost, Benny Goodman, Gene Kelly, Danny Kaye, and the National Symphony Orchestra.[27]

In his remarks to the on-site and television audiences President Kennedy began with his usual bow to good humor. "I want to assure the officials of my administration tonight that this demonstration of support for the arts is modest and painless compared to what has been required of past governments and administrations." He wryly observed that France's Louis XVI, to encourage the arts, "donned brilliant tights and played in a drama called *Furious Roland*," for which "he drafted the highest offices of his administration," who "all clad in brilliant tights themselves." JFK continued, "This was suggested tonight but for some reason or other the [dinner] committee turned it down!"[28]

The president then returned to the serious purpose for the evening's festivities—the promotion of art as a source of "national greatness and national achievement. . . . If we can make our country one of the great schools of civilization, then on that achievement will surely rest our claim to the ultimate gratitude of the mankind. . . . Moreover, as a great democratic society, we have a special responsibility to the arts, for art is the great democrat calling forth creative genius from every sector of society, disregarding race or religion or wealth or color. . . . What freedom alone can bring is the liberation of the human mind and spirit which finds its greatest flowering in the free society."[29] Once more, the president tied support of artistic merit to the Cold War struggle between the free world and closed societies.

True to form, the first lady kept her public presentation to a bare minimum. Following her husband's introduction, she commented, "Tonight seems to be at long last the beginning of what for so long has really been just a hope or a dream. I know there still is an enormous amount of work to be done before Mr. Stone's beautiful building rises beside the Potomac, but I hope that by this spring ground will be broken and they will start to build a wall of the Center, for that will be a reward to all who have worked so hard for tonight, and it will be an encouragement to all of us who must keep on working until the Center truly exists." With that, she introduced Mrs. Eisenhower, with the encomium, "no one cares more about [the Center's] completion than she does." Ike and Mamie appeared via television hookup from their home in Augusta, Georgia. The successful event raised a million dollars.[30]

In addition to the president's Business Committee and local community structures, the fund-raising also encompassed a "seat endowment campaign," in which individuals and organizations could sponsor a permanent seat in one of the Center's three performance halls. A tax-deductible $1,000 donation entitled the donor to recognition as a "founder" of the Center, to be acknowledged by a bronze plaque affixed to the back of the seat. RCA Victor recorded music from the four U.S. military bands and offered the records for public sale, with all profits going to the Center. In March 1963 the Ford Foundation awarded a matching grant of $5 million, payable when the Center reached the halfway point toward its funding goal. And the government of Italy donated marble to be used in the building's construction. By mid-1963 the fund-raising effort had achieved one third of the total funds required, but Congress's five-year deadline for meeting the goal, set in the original 1958 legislation, had to be extended to 1966.[31]

Mrs. Kennedy discovered a unique way to combine two of her interests, painting and promoting the Center, into one fund-raising effort. In September 1963 the White House announced that the first lady had painted a pair of Christmas scenes that Hallmark would produce as holiday cards and contribute the net proceeds to the Cultural Center. She initialed the watercolors, entitled "The Journey of the Magi" and "Glad Tidings," to be used for the cards' designs. Mrs. Kennedy also agreed to donate her fees for *McCall's* December publication of the paintings.[32]

Jackie's delegation of the Washington fund-raising committee's leadership to her mother was typical of the first lady's approach to these types of more time-consuming responsibilities. Except for the minutiae of her White House restoration project, along with her detailed planning of White House state functions and her official trips abroad, she simply did not want to overextend herself with what she viewed as intrusive administrative duties or excessive public appearances. Only three weeks after she became first lady, Mrs. Kennedy received a letter from Congressman Carroll Kearns (R.-Pa.) asking her to become the honorary chair of a proposed National Committee for the Arts. Kearns tried every form of flattery, so characteristic of congressional puffery, to persuade the first lady. He referred to her husband as "my good friend, Jack, with whom I served for six years on the House Education and Labor Committee." Then he heaped praise on the first lady: "There is great cause for rejoicing . . . that you are so deeply interested in the arts." "Mrs. Kennedy," the congressman implored, "if you were willing to serve as honorary chairman of this highly important National Committee, I am most confident that it could be organized quickly and become firmly established, and the cultural, civic and political leaders of the fifty States (including the Governors) would consider it an honor and privilege to serve with you. . . . I am sure your illustrious husband would approve your support of this worthy objective." Kearns's Capitol Hill office then issued a press release announcing his invitation to Mrs. Kennedy, including the full text of his letter to her.[33]

In turn, the first lady responded with the kind of politely supportive, yet noncommittal, message that politicians and their staffs have perfected. "Thank you for your letter . . . with its most stimulating contents," Mrs. Kennedy began, probably using wording suggested by Tish Baldrige. "Both the President and I were interested in your exposition of the past and present status of Executive participation in cultural affairs. We are in complete agreement with you that 'the unfinished cultural business' is most important. I would like to study your letter in relation to current projects. I will be in touch with you at a future date on the whole subject. Again, thank you for bringing this matter to our attention."[34] It is unclear if the first lady was ever subsequently in touch with Kearns about his effort to establish a National Committee for the Arts; the Committee failed to materialize under the Kennedy administration.

Nevertheless, President Kennedy created an executive branch structure for the support of art and culture. He named the president's first special consultant on the arts—albeit as a temporary and part-time position. August Heckscher, the Yale- and Harvard-trained director of the Twentieth Century Fund, was highly competent and productive in the role. He diplomatically expressed some frustration, however, when, eight months after taking the position (which initially was only supposed to last six months), he wrote to Mrs. Kennedy: "In my work here I have felt it a lack not knowing your own views on some of the matters in the cultural field with which I am dealing. Could I come by for a talk with you? I am in Washington usually two days a week."[35]

Heckscher managed to schedule a meeting with the first lady approximately six weeks later. His assistant, Barbara Donald, prepared talking points for him that went to the heart of the positive public reaction to the Kennedys' support for artists and the potentially crucial role that the first lady could play in expanding that patronage. Donald wrote to Heckscher:

> I suppose your talk would focus on Mrs. Kennedy's role as First Lady in relation to the arts; the importance as a *political* and *cultural* fact of the tremendous public response and delight which has been engendered by the various expressions of interest and recognition of artists and the arts manifested by the President and Mrs. Kennedy personally beginning with the Inauguration ceremonies. Cannot overestimate the terrific boost to morale, to rising expectations, and the general ferment of excitement and hope for new era of cultural activity on the part of the general public and the professional arts world (letters re Mrs. Kennedy's telecast on Cultural Center [in October 1962] are examples of public response). Danger is that through inadvertence and pressure of other duties this enthusiasm, interest and momentum may be dampened or disappointed.[36]

Donald's memo observed that, presently, "*the only tangible ways of showing continuing* [Kennedy] Administration interest" were through White House entertainment and the Cabinet Artist Series. Therefore, Heckscher suggested that the first lady support the arts additionally through a policy of "White House Recognition," described as performances (presumably at the White House); invitations to individuals for dinner or luncheon; receptions for small groups of leaders in artistic organizations; special dinners or receptions for groups of prize winners; attendance at performances around Washington; messages and honorary sponsorship; and entertainment of foreign visitors and/or performances of foreign groups. The talking points anticipated Mrs. Kennedy's response to the suggestions that she do more for the arts. Wrote Donald: "[We] fully recognize problem of engaging in these different types of recognition on any broad scale on top of multitude of other social, political and personal commitments. In view of importance, however, perhaps some program or policies can be worked out which would minimize burden."[37]

According to Donald, the first lady liked the idea of holding a White House dinner for literary prize winners. (Six weeks later she begged off the project.) "Mrs. Kennedy also expressed her willingness to receive the ANTA [American National Theatre and Academy] convention on March 11 [1963]," wrote Donald. (Just before the convention the *Washington Post* reported that the first lady would probably *not* greet the ANTA members; Tish Baldrige would perform the duty.) Donald also noted that Mrs. Kennedy had said in her meeting with Heckscher that "she welcomed suggestions as to appropriate White House entertainments and affirmed her willingness to help in any she could by attending performances, receiving individuals, etc." (Though the White House would not officially announce her condition until April 1963, the first lady was in the first trimester of pregnancy early in 1963, which limited her official duties—only a few months after Heckscher had urged to do more.)[38]

Heckscher later remembered, "Mrs. Kennedy was awfully nice to me. She said, 'Mr. Heckscher, I will do anything for the arts you want.' (She said it, but it didn't work out that way, and wisely perhaps.) She added characteristically, 'Except read [legislative] bills.' I told Mrs. Kennedy, 'Don't worry about the bills. . . . ' Then she did go on . . . 'But, of course, I can't be away too much from the children, and I can't be present at too many cultural events.' Then with sort of a smile, she said, 'After all, I'm *not* Mrs. Roosevelt.' I couldn't help but laugh at that."[39]

It was clear from her June 1962 note to Bill Walton that Jackie Kennedy was simply not going to assume any more official duties than she wished to, merely to fulfill others' expectations of her or her office. As Baldrige wrote to Heckscher about the many requests they received to invite Mrs. Kennedy to appear at artistic events, "We are bombarded every week by requests of this nature—every piano prize, art exhibit, charity concert, from Alaska to British Guinea. So we have to be tough and 'Neigh' [*sic*] all of them. Sorry!" Mrs. Kennedy's personal role in promotion of the arts, described above, offers an accurate picture of her activism, which was less than Heckscher, Baldrige, and many artists hoped for, but more than her subsequent critics sometimes acknowledge. She could always point to her maternal obligations, and the president validated that reason for the constraints on her time. "If Jackie were older," he told a reporter in 1962, "and our children older, she would have more time for public things. But she is concentrating on trying to live as normally as possible in abnormal circumstances, for the sake of our children." Reflecting a traditional view of the female role, he observed, "And by carrying out her primary responsibility to support her husband and care for her children well, she is doing her real job as a woman."[40]

President Kennedy met with Heckscher several times and accepted a comprehensive report from him on "the arts and national government," which the special consultant on the arts submitted with his resignation from the temporary position. JFK followed Heckscher's recommendation to create a President's Advisory Council on the Arts and permanently establish the special consultant's job as a full-time position. On June 12, 1963, via executive order, the president founded the Arts Council, consisting of Cabinet members and other government officials, as well as members of the private sector, to encourage development of the arts and cultural life.[41]

Later that summer the press reported that Richard Goodwin, then head of the Peace Corps' international secretariat, might become JFK's new special consultant on the arts. The *New York Times* commented on the president's concern over the link between cultural accomplishments and the competition for the allegiance of the developing world, especially in Latin America. Reported the *Times*, "It has been a recurring criticism that Washington has abysmally underestimated the importance that Latin Americans attach to cultural expressions as a key to better international understanding. Actually, while the Soviet Union is staging a major cultural drive to impress Latin America with its ballet groups, symphony orchestras and concert artists, Congress and the State Department have curbed funds for this type of activity." The press announced Goodwin's new assignment on November 22, 1963. That day's tragic events in Dallas, however, aborted his service as President Kennedy's arts consultant.[42]

Not long after Jacqueline Kennedy arrived at the White House as first lady, she discovered that the National Gallery of Art had in its board room eight Cézanne paintings, bequeathed to the White House by Charles Loeser. Harry Truman had rejected them for display in the Executive Mansion because "they weren't American." Former National Gallery Director Carter Brown recalled in 1994 that, as a new first lady, Mrs. Kennedy visited the Gallery, and "she went like hunting dogs to the best [of the Cézannes]." She chose four of the eight paintings to be exhibited at the White House, with the balance on loan to the National Gallery. When the Kennedys entertained the president of Tunisia in May 1961, they proudly showed their guests two of the Cézannes, which had been hung in the Green Room. The first lady commented that she hoped the Loeser bequest would "serve as an example to other collectors so that one day this much-loved house will be as great a repository of historical and beautiful objects as any other official residence in the world."[43]

Thus Mrs. Kennedy's primary focus in the fine arts was the attraction of museum-quality paintings, drawings, and sculptures to the Executive Mansion. She took a dual approach to her goal. As first lady she could request art objects from museums around the nation. Perry Rathbone, director of Boston's Museum of Fine Arts in the early 1960s, described Mrs. Kennedy as "the Nation's No. 1 art lover" after she asked to borrow eleven paintings and watercolors from his museum. Rathbone labeled her taste in American art "discriminating"; she chose some pieces for their historical subjects (a portrait of Daniel Webster), others for the fame of their artists (Winslow Homer), and some for their contemporary themes (paintings by Edward Hopper).[44] She also borrowed paintings, especially by American artist Maurice Pendergast, from the private collection of Duncan Phillips in Washington.

The first lady's second approach to art collection was to encourage donations, initially through her Fine Arts Committee and its Advisory Committee. On the job only three months, Mrs. Kennedy accepted the Committee's first major artistic acquisition for the White House on May 2, 1961. It was a signed pencil and sepia allegorical drawing of Benjamin Franklin by French master Jean Honoré Fragonard. Appraised at $30,000, the drawing was a gift of Georges Wildenstein, an art historian and dealer. The first lady placed it in the Blue Room. That summer the White House Fine Arts Advisory Committee announced its first windfall of antiques and art, including paintings, watercolors, engravings, and sculptures. Some were loans; others were gifts to the White House.[45]

In September 1961 Mrs. Kennedy wrote to James Whitney Fosburgh, a New York artist, lecturer on art, and staff member of the Frick Collection, to ask him to chair the new Special Committee for White House Paintings, an adjunct of the Fine Arts Committee. In her handwritten letter she cited "the crying need for some good American pictures [in the White House]" as there was "really nothing but late nineteenth century Presidents in black. . . . It is my greatest hope to acquire permanently for the White House all the finest from this country's past. I think it should have pictures by Stuart, Trumbull, Peale, Hicks, Audubon, Sargent, Whistler, Homer Eakins, Currier & Ives (bedrooms), Mary Cassatt, Remington—and so many others that I am sure you will be able to think of—All the most important periods should be represented—except the really modern ones—as it is a period house—or will be—but we can think of some solution to that." Within two months the White House announced the formation of the Paintings Committee, with Fosburgh chairing a group of art historians and collectors whose mission was to expand the White House's collection. Members included Mrs. Joseph Alsop, Mrs. J. Cheever Cowdin, Lawrence Fleischman, Mrs. Walter Halle, Stanley Marcus, Mrs. William S. Paley, Vincent Price, Joseph Pulitzer Jr., Nathaniel Saltonstall, and Mrs. Suzette Morton Zurcher.[46]

The first lady and the Paintings Committee developed criteria for acquiring artwork. Paintings and sculptures were, with few exceptions, to be American, that is, *by* a U.S. artist and *of* a U.S. subject. Ideally, the subject was to have some relationship to the White House or the federal government. Work by living artists was excluded from the collection. The Committee's first acquisition, announced in January 1962, was A. Wordsworth Thompson's Civil

War battlescape, *Cannonading on the Potomac,* which was displayed in the first restored White House chamber, the Red Room. By February 1962 Mrs. Kennedy and Mr. Fosburgh announced donations, purchases, or loans of eighteen additional paintings. Trumpeted the first lady's press secretary, "The paintings have been given by nonpartisans from all parts of the country—a fact of which Mrs. Kennedy and the [Paintings] Committee are very proud. It is their hope that these generous gifts will be added to by others so that in time a collection may be assembled for posterity that will be worthy of the dignity of the Presidential Mansion."[47]

Throughout the second and third years of the Kennedy administration, gifts and acquisitions of oil paintings, watercolors, and drawings arrived at the White House. Among the most historically significant were the life portraits of Thomas Jefferson by Rembrandt Peale, James Monroe by Samuel F. B. Morse, and Andrew Jackson by John Wesley Jarvis. Until then, the White House's only portraits from life of the first six presidents had been those of George Washington. Mrs. Kennedy proudly hung the new acquisitions of the presidential portraits in the redecorated Blue Room to complete a set of the first seven presidents. She hoped to acquire life portraits of John Adams, James Madison, and John Quincy Adams to replace the paintings of them executed after their deaths. The first lady also gratefully accepted five oil paintings of American Indians. The subjects of the 1821 portraits, members of Great Plains tribes, were depicted by artist Charles Bird King as they appeared at a special council at the White House, convened by President Monroe. Actor Vincent Price, an art connoisseur and member of the Paintings Committee, had discovered the Indian portraits' availability and alerted the White House. Sears Roebuck underwrote their purchase and, in a populist twist, donated them on behalf of its employees. The paintings became focal points of the White House's restored library. Another special donation to the White House, accepted by Mrs. Kennedy, was an original portrait of Benjamin Franklin. Publisher Walter Annenberg donated the painting, valued at over $250,000, after the first lady told him that he and Franklin were both "great Philadephia citizens." She hung the portrait over the refurbished Green Room's mantel. By September 1963 *Time* reported that "more than 150 works of art, or the funds to buy them," had been donated to Mrs. Kennedy's committees. "The paintings already acquired constitute a priceless national heritage," the magazine concluded.[48]

Another element of the White House restoration that elevated the mansion's cultural tone was the decorative and bibliographic refurbishment of the library. When the Kennedys arrived in the White House, the ground-floor library looked like a gentlemen's club, with its dark, knotty-pine paneling and drab wingback chairs. The American Institute of Interior Designers offered to redecorate the room, and White House Fine Arts Committee Chairman Henry du Pont recommended that the paneling be painted a pale yellow and highlighted in ivory and antique gold. The new wall treatment then accommodated early nineteenth-century furniture to complete the look. Highlights among the acquisitions were a suite of caned-seated furniture, rendered by master craftsman Duncan Phyfe, and an early nineteenth-century mahogany library table, with a green tooled leather top. Random-width hardwood floors replaced the Truman-era tile, and an Aubusson rug of rust, blue, green, and yellow completed the floor treatment. Gold-on-ivory medallion-patterned curtains added to the library's new elegant ambiance. A donated watercolor, *The Signing of the Declaration of Independence,* by a French artist, graced the space above the mantel.[49]

In presenting the redecorated room to the public in June 1962, Mrs. Kennedy announced that the library would "acquire the books most essential to an understanding of our National experience." She did not see the collection as static, however, commenting that "all libraries must grow and so must this one if it is truly to reflect our national experience." Before 1930 the White House did not have a "home library," as Herbert Hoover and his family discovered when they took possession in 1929. Attempting to remedy this deficiency, the American Booksellers Association made an initial gift of 500 books to the White House in 1930 and supplemented the collection with 200 new titles every four years. The donated books were meant to portray a "model home library . . . representative of the best books published in the United States."[50]

In the summer of 1961 Julian Boyd, editor of the Jefferson Papers at Princeton, and Lyman Butterfield, editor of the Adams Papers at the Massachusetts Historical Society, both members of the White

House Fine Arts Advisory Committee, strongly urged Henry du Pont "that particular attention be given to the selection of the books for [the White House library]." Boyd, writing to Mrs. Kennedy several months later, asserted, "It seems to me that this library could do for learning what your excellent efforts have already done for the decorative arts." By the end of 1961 the first lady had authorized Boyd and Butterfield to establish a committee of librarians and history scholars to select the books for the White House library. Mrs. Kennedy once again called on her reliable friend and consultant in all things academic, Arthur Schlesinger Jr., special assistant to the president, "to handle this whole problem of the library for me."51

The ad hoc Library Committee, chaired by Yale University Librarian James Babb, labored and agonized for over a year to compile a list of titles for the White House. The Library of Congress prepared the first selection of books, which Boyd, Butterfield, and Schlesinger reviewed. They then compiled a revised preliminary list and submitted it to at least twenty-five prominent historians for their responses and suggestions. Schlesinger distributed the list with a cover letter that began, "As you know, Mrs. Kennedy is deeply interested in realizing the full potentialities of the White House as an expression of American culture and the American experience. Her redecoration program has included the library on the ground floor; and it is her hope that this library may contain the books which will best represent the history and culture of the United States." Babb and his colleagues at Yale then reviewed the historians' contributions to the endeavor.52

Schlesinger attempted to keep Mrs. Kennedy apprised of the process. She left the substantive decisions on which books to include to the scholars, but she joined in the discussion on the procedural and aesthetic aspects of the library. She had the White House press release for the library's opening sent to Boyd, Butterfield, and Babb "so they will all know . . . where I stand on the library—I don't want a lot of priceless books we have to lock up. It's the content and a decent—preferably old binding I care about—not the rarity of the edition—though a couple of these would be OK."53

As 1963 dawned, the first lady confided to Schlesinger, "I am ashamed to say I really don't know what is happening on our Library Committee except that absolutely no progress is being made. . . . Do you think you could give me a brief memo, in Telegram-ese, telling me these things: (a) Who is on the Committee—(b) Have we accomplished anything—and, as we only have room for 2,500 books, what exactly should be done?" Mrs. Kennedy offered to write to Babb or speak to him in person, so "I can get this thing moving. . . . It is so silly to form a Committee and, then, have zero happen." Schlesinger assured her, "Do not despair about the Library." He reported that the basic list of books was complete and was being put in proper bibliographic format, an acquisitions committee had been named, and a bookplate was being considered.[54]

The discussions among the Library Committee dragged in to 1963, however, and Babb contacted Mrs. Kennedy directly in April to ascertain her views on the library's mission. Should it be an exhibition of "great American books" in their original editions or a "fine, but small, reference library for the President, his family, and the official White House staff"? Babb asked the first lady. She responded at length with one of her rambling handwritten missives:

> We have had so little contact—that there has been a lot of confusion on the library—This is what I think it should be—. . . I NEVER thought or would let it be a reference library for W.H. staff—It could never be big enough—all the books would have to have those awful numbers on the back and no one would ever return them! They have the Library of Congress and they would never use this library anyway. I think it should be . . . a library of significant American (mainly dealing with government, I suppose—as do we have enough room for novels?—) & writings that have influenced American thinking—Locke etc.—all books by Presidents—Grant's memoirs etc.
>
> I wanted old books in their bindings whenever possible . . . I don't think it necessary to search for rare rare first editions—They cost even more than furniture—& it was a back breaking job & we are still in debt—to get the furniture we have gotten. . . . If we go in for rare editions, we will have to put up grilles which I HATE—it gives a prison look—& never raise the money & I would love to get it done next year—
>
> I think the list of the books in the library will be most impressive to people & we should make that public—so do send me a

memo on what books we should have and how you plan to go
about it—The only money I have for you is the $5,000 or was it
$2,500 from Doubleday—The rest will have to be raised or do-
nated—so I hope you can persuade people—or form a committee to—as I have hit rock bottom & touched every possible donor
I can think of.

I am so anxious to have this well under way by fall—so do let's
start—I wasn't mad about the book plate. I agree with you [that]
it shouldn't be fancy—but it should say The White House—&
not W.H. Hist. Assoc.—

I would like to design it myself which I will have plenty of time
to do this summer—& once I get something decent I'll send it to
you for suggestions or approval—. . . .

Don't worry—The thought of the W.H. staff using it for reference fills me with . . . horror . . . so that will never [underlined
three times] happen![55]

As always, Schlesinger wrote a carefully crafted letter to Jackie, as-
similating her thoughts and Babb's, while seemingly smoothing
over any concerns she had expressed about the nature of the library.
Finally, on August 15, 1963, the Library Committee released its list of
1,780 books, comprising thirty-two categories. The *New York Times*
printed each title, its author, publisher, and publication year. Acquisitions were well underway by the fall of 1963. President Kennedy's
death produced contradictory outcomes for the project. At first, the
White House curator's office received numerous books and mone-
tary donations in JFK's memory for the library. Mrs. Kennedy's departure from the White House, however, created a perception that
the project, which she had directed, might be truncated. In February
1964 President Johnson announced that he and Lady Bird intended
to complete the planned library. In fact, he added a dozen University
of Texas Press publications to the collection. Arthur Schlesinger,
who had resigned from his White House post, wrote to James Babb
that he thought LBJ definitely wanted the library to continue, but
Schlesinger added, "I do hope we can avoid twelve volumes covering the social, economic and natural history of Texas!"[56]

Throughout Jacqueline Kennedy's three years in the White
House, she turned to William Walton, a longtime friend of the first

couple, for consultation on numerous aspects of the arts. A former reporter, Walton was a self-taught painter who produced modern abstract art in his Georgetown home studio. At President Kennedy's request he had joined the 1960 campaign to help in the Wisconsin and West Virginia primaries, and serve as manager of the JFK organization in New York. He first met Jacqueline Bouvier during her stint as the inquiring photographer for the *Times-Herald.* "She had the same intense interest in books and art and the same curiosity about ideas she has now [in the White House]. She also had that fey, elfin quality that is part of her charm," Walton recalled in an early 1960s interview. Mrs. Kennedy clearly enjoyed her breezy, bantering friendship with the divorced Walton, pouring out her thoughts to him in lengthy late-night notes.[57]

The first lady encouraged Walton to become chair of the Fine Arts Commission. Established by Congress in 1910, the FAC's mission was to advise the federal and District of Columbia governments on the aesthetics of the nation's capital, particularly its architecture. Without veto or enforcement power, the commission had to rely on its powers of persuasion. Mrs. Kennedy reported to Walton that she and the president "adore[d]" David Finley, who had been chair of the commission when they came to the White House. "I want [Finley] to know how grateful we are for all his help & backing of my little projects & have a touching farewell in the Rose Garden (if he wouldn't mind)." Jackie thought Walton would be the perfect replacement for Finley if he retired. She also wanted a woman on the commission, which

is . . . going to be involved with all the things we care about—when Jack is gone—so he won't be able to help you—& lovely buildings will be torn down—& cheesy skyscrapers go up—Perhaps saving old buildings & having the new one be right isn't the most important thing in the world—if you are waiting for the bomb—but I think we are always going to be waiting for the bomb & it won't ever come & so to save the old—& to make the new beautiful is terribly important—. . . You mustn't ever be stopped from painting—or your whole disorganized life—or you will be miserable—But you are needed for the clinches and you know it—. . . I remember reading last y[ea]r that of 133 buildings the FAC opposed tearing

down, 131 went down—That is a tragic record—& the real estate
operators are your enemy—. . . It is a wonderful thing to find you
can have the best of both worlds—I got that by forethought—. . . If
I can do it Billy so can you! . . . I just realized I have written a 12 page
letter! Don't ever do that
   XO Jackie[58]

In the summer of 1963 President Kennedy had the opportunity to
name five members of the Fine Arts Commission, and Walton was
among them, along with another Kennedy friend, architect John
Carl Warnecke of San Francisco. Mrs. Kennedy's desire to see a
woman appointed to the FAC was also fulfilled. After Finley's term
expired, the seven-person commission voted Walton chair. The first
lady's wish had come true. Apparently one of Walton's first concerns
were the guard houses surrounding the White House—"charming
little details," Jackie called his initial project. In a series of notes and
letters to Walton, Mrs. Kennedy spelled out her ideas for the sentry
boxes; she wanted to make sure that they did not look like "out-
houses," "Army camouflage buildings," or "telephone booths."[59]
   The first lady and Walton were associated with a more significant and enduring project: the preservation of Lafayette Square.
Part of the original President's Park, an 82-acre preserve delineated
by George Washington when the capital city was surveyed in 1792,
the parcel had a colorful history. Located just north of the White
House, the land, before 1824, had been at various times an apple or-
chard, racecourse, construction site (for tradesmen working on the
Executive Mansion), neglected eyesore, city market, town common,
and militia parade ground. Charles Bulfinch, the Capitol's architect,
oversaw landscaping of the six-acre tract starting in 1818. By the time
it was completed in 1824, the square had been named in honor of the
French general, Lafayette, and subsequently acquired the name Lafayette Park. Bounded initially by wooden fences and then iron en-
closures, the park reflected landscape architectural trends of several
eras. By the antebellum period, fashionable Washington homes surrounded the square, which took on an even grander ambiance with
the erection of the monumental equestrian statue of Andrew Jackson in the 1850s. When the White House grounds closed to unofficial visitors during the Grant administration, as a response to the

Architect John Carle Warnecke discusses his plan for preserving
Lafayette Square with Mrs. Kennedy, September 1962.
(Photo by Robert Knudsen, White House. JFK Library, Boston)

first lady's concerns for her children's privacy, Lafayette Park became a surrogate for civic space close to the Executive Mansion.
Between 1891 and 1910 each of the park's four corners received a
statue representing a quartet of foreign-born heroes of the American Revolution, signifying "a new international view of America's
place in the world and of Washington as capital." The square began
to reflect the neoclassical touches of Europe's great public land-
scapes. In the 1930s the National Park Service, which had managed
the square since the turn of the century, simplified the park's landscaping and maintained its formal look with manicured grass
between the walkways.[60]

The federal government's twentieth-century proliferation ultimately necessitated additional office space in Washington. During

the Eisenhower administration, architects began to design plans for razing the buildings (regardless of vintage) surrounding Lafayette Park and erecting in their place modern low- and high-rise office blocks. In his first month as president, JFK summoned Walton to the Oval Office and asked him to examine the problem. Later they studied the square's buildings from the second floor of the White House and during a drive around the park's perimeter. Yet they could not solve the conundrum of how to preserve the nineteenth-century edifices while creating space for new government office buildings. The president discussed the predicament with his wife, "whose interest in the problem," Walton remembered, "was . . . very deep and very intuitive." Walton admitted, though, that he and JFK "gave up and thought that the destruction of the few remaining houses on Lafayette Square was inevitable. We had reckoned without Jacqueline Kennedy. 'The wreckers haven't started yet,' she said, 'and until they do, it can be saved.' She stood in the middle of the Lafayette Park with David Finley . . . and outlined to him her views. He was in complete agreement with her. Still we didn't have any solution on paper."[61]

Yet before destructive action could be taken, Mrs. Kennedy, at David Finley's suggestion, wrote to Administrator of the General Services Administration Bernard Boutin, an old friend of the first lady. To him she pleaded her case for saving the historic and picturesque square across from the White House. In her March 6, 1962, missive, dispatched just before her trip to South Asia, she included a letter from her ally, Finley, as well as design alternatives for the new buildings. Stressing that she and the president had a keen "interest in history and preservation," the first lady asserted, "it really matters a great deal to the president and myself that this [the Lafayette Square project] be done well; we have received so much mail on the subject."[62]

Mrs. Kennedy took the unusual step of publicly acknowledging that her husband had erred in letting the plans go forward. She reportedly received his permission to reveal the mistake. As she informed Boutin, "Unfortunately, last summer the president okayed some plans for buildings; he was in a hurry, he doesn't have time to bother himself with details like this, he trusted the advice of a friend . . . and I really don't think it was the right advice. With all he has to do, at least I can spare him some minor problems like this. So, I turn to you for help." Jackie critiqued the proposed "hideous white modern court building" that would dominate Madison Place along the eastern edge of the park," and she called the planned edifice for Jackson Place on the park's west side an "unsuitable, violently modern building." She emphasized that any new structures should be "more in keeping with the 19th century" styles of existing facades that faced the park. The first lady included a supplication for preserving the Old Court of Claims at the corner of 17th Street and Pennsylvania Avenue. Once the Corcoran Gallery of Art, which had moved one block south on 17th Street, the building traced its origins to ancestors of David Finley's wife. Mrs. Kennedy admitted to Boutin that the court building "might look like a Victorian horror, but it is really quite lovely and a precious example of architecture which is fast disappearing. I so strongly feel that the White House should give the example in preserving our nation's past. Now we think of saving old buildings like Mount Vernon and tear down everything in the 19th century—but in the next hundred years, the 19th century will be of great interest and there will be none of it left, just plain glass skyscrapers."[63]

Mrs. Kennedy then exercised the written version of her feminine flattery in telling Boutin that "Bobby [Kennedy] says you are the most wonderful head of GSA there ever was or ever will be. I am sure this is true, and I cannot tell you how much I am counting on you . . . before you know it, everything is ripped down and horrible things put up in their place. I simply panic at the thought of this and decided to make a last-ditch appeal."[64]

While the first lady was in India and Pakistan, the president renewed an acquaintance with West Coast architect John Carl Warnecke, who happened to be in Washington. JFK asked him to explore the Lafayette Square matter. When Mrs. Kennedy returned from abroad, she penned a letter to Finley, expressing her gratitude that he had suggested she contact Boutin. She praised the GSA's director: "I just think you should know how extraordinary this man [Boutin] is—. . . out of the morass of conflicting opinions—so many cooks in the broth—all things that upset you and me—all the long delays and despair that our hope for Lafayette Square would ever be realized—and we would just have to give up and let it turn into a modern square—he has brought order and in two weeks will have definite plans for your approval." Boutin later recalled that "the President and Mrs. Kennedy deserve[d] full credit" for turning Lafayette Square into "a showplace for all Americans!" The first lady was so involved in the planning process that when Boutin would bring his voluminous plans for the square to the White House, "we'd spread them on the floor and would go on hands and knees from one plan to another looking at them with Mrs. Kennedy."[65]

The first lady revealed to Finley her view of political potency: "I so admire people who can use power efficiently and wisely—and cut through red tape—and I just wanted you to know what a godsend this man is—in case there are other preservation problems you may have that I don't know about—this is the man to solve them." Jackie instructed Finley, "Hold your breath—because this is what is going to happen—all our wildest dreams come true. I dictated him [Boutin] a long letter the afternoon of our trip around Lafayette Square—"[66]

She outlined plans for the square, using multiple exclamation points and asterisks to emphasize her approval and enthusiasm:

1) The new court building will be 19th century in feeling. . . .

2) *The Dolley Madison and Tayloe houses will be saved!!!

3) The Court of Claims will be saved—It will be I think turned into a Museum of Modern Art which people are trying to get started here and which I said I would sponsor—as I think it is wrong to identify oneself solely with art of the past—and never encourage what is happening now. So it will be used as it used to be [when it was the Corcoran Art Gallery].

4) The whole Decatur House side facades will be saved except for the two tall modern buildings [constructed in the 1920s]!!!*** Some will be used as extension of guest facilities at Blair House—the rest offices—So Theodore Roosevelt's old house—and place where National Gallery was born will be preserved—This is what delights me the most—Everyone wants to raze things and build efficient new buildings—Bernard Boutin is a preservationist and also he says it will be cheaper! Who else would ever have said that! None of those naughty show-off architects! The gaps that are left will be filled with some 19th century D.C. houses that he

will have moved there. So if you know any special ones you want saved—tell him.

5) On 17th Street a big building will go up to provide space for Bureau of the Budget or whoever it is who wants all this space—

He has found a brilliant architect to help him whom [*sic*] I imagine will work with the ones already signed up under previous administrations—or rather tell them what to do. It is time someone acted with authority—before they happily destroyed the most historical part of Washington—and at last we found him—

I was so excited when I heard this I just had to tell you—[67]

Five months later Warnecke and his San Francisco firm had already completed a preliminary model of the Lafayette Square project to show Mrs. Kennedy. Her press secretary reported that the first lady was "very enthusiastic and extremely interested in the blending of old and new buildings." By placing the proposed mid-rise federal office building and federal courts edifice *behind* the facades of the nineteenth-century buildings, Warnecke had solved the riddle of blending the historic with the modern. President Kennedy called the plan a model for urban renewal and redevelopment projects throughout the land, commenting, "I believe that the importance of Lafayette Square lies in the fact that we were not willing to destroy our cultural and historic heritage but that we were willing to find means of preserving it while still meeting the requirements of growth in government."[68]

By constructing the new buildings out of brick (a little-used medium in modern architecture), instead of stone or glass, the project's proposed budget actually was $9 million less than the amount appropriated by Congress. Warnecke recommended to President Kennedy that the difference could be applied to the rehabilitation and rebuilding of the historic structures surrounding the park. In 1963 Jackie, her friend Bunny Mellon, and architect Harold Adams walked through Lafayette Park and suggested that the color of brick used in constructing the new buildings should match that used in the square's paths—another step in unifying the park and its modern edifices. The National Park Service asked Warnecke's firm to revitalize the park's landscape, which was showing the wear and tear of crowds who flocked to the site. Bunny and Paul Mellon eventually provided funding, through one of their philanthropic foundations, to redo the park's landscape and plantings. They were completed in the spring of 1970.[69]

JFK died before work began on Lafayette Square, but Warnecke maintained contact with President Johnson, updating him on the plan's status just two months after the assassination. In the spring of 1965 Warnecke's firm reported that construction on both the office building and court edifice was progressing. Both were completed by 1968. Then demolition of the twentieth-century buildings began, followed by preservation of the historic structures. The new court building was not an immediate critical success, however. Warnecke recalls over a quarter century later that in 1967 *Newsweek* labeled it a "noble failure." Whatever one's view of the new buildings' architecture, they accomplished President and Mrs. Kennedy's goal of serving function without destroying the historic form surrounding them. Jacqueline Kennedy would be especially pleased by one historian's observation of Lafayette Square's role at the turn of the twenty-first century: "It is of the White House, being a feature of the President's Park, but even more, it is adjunct to the White House, rather an open anteroom, in which one enjoys a strong sense of place and history."[70]

Mrs. Kennedy also ensured that land on the other side of the White House, the South Lawn, was revitalized. In one of her many detailed memos to Chief Usher J. B. West, she delineated the problems and possible solutions:

> The White House Lawns are a disgrace. I am sure you are working on them—but something truly drastic must be done by Fall—
>   1. It is a sea of brown as one looks across the South Lawn.
>   2. Clover, weeds, and crab grass are mixed in.
>   3. On the hillsides there is a completely different type of stringy, long green grass.—It is driving the President crazy—and I agree with him. In Glen Ora where we have one man who cuts the lawn every two weeks, it looks like green velvet—and this place does not look as well as cowfields in Virginia.
>   Months ago the complaint of crab grass came up—the lawns are worse than ever—and patches of soggy, dying, expensive turf are not solving the question. This summer please solve this.

1. Probably the lawns need to be reseeded—the proper seed must be found. Surely some expert in the Agriculture Department—Park Service can provide advice—

2. A method to water the lawn must be found—and not by having miles of snakelike green hose everywhere—with sprays shooting up so no one can walk near them—also it is ugly and undignified for the President's house.

3. Is sinking water spouts too expensive? It is done in Palm Beach but I don't know if that is practical this far north—

If helicopters leave a mark perhaps a piece of canvas could be laid to protect the grass.

I have never bothered much about lawns—but every place I have lived—with a part time gardener—the lawn has been beautiful—so surely with twelve gardeners that is possible at the White House—

By the East Wing—the hill and gardens are truly atrocious—we are on our way to restoring the White House now—so please make a major effort this summer on the lawns—

AND—the big problem is the LAWNS—[I] am sure you will solve it—

Thanks, JBK[71]

Horticulture experts examined the pitiful turf and determined that all of the topsoil (to the depth of one foot) must be dug up, sterilized, replaced, and reseeded. Bunny Mellon, a talented gardener, took on the project of redesigning the East Garden, after completing the new Rose Garden for President Kennedy outside the West Wing. She drew plans for a whimsical space with seasonal flowers, topiaries, low hedges, a pergola, wicker chaises, Victorian benches from the Benjamin Harrison and Lincoln administrations, and a croquet lawn. Jackie responded enthusiastically to Mellon's designs: "I have complete confidence in your East Garden. All I would do is to look at your plans and just agree with them, so go ahead—you have so much sense of which is fitting for the White House—dignified but not elaborate with scriggly [*sic*] French beds everywhere—so I know what you will do there will be divine." The enchanting garden, completed during the Johnson presidency, was appropriately named for Mrs. Kennedy. Tourists visiting the Executive Mansion, and heads of state greeted on its South Lawn, beheld a fitting setting for the leader of the free world. Jacqueline Kennedy's vision for restoring the White House and the spaces surrounding it revitalized historical presidential images for a new age.

The first lady's struggle to preserve and revive the areas around the Executive Mansion foreshadowed her successor's commitment to "the whole field of conservation and beautification," as Lady Bird Johnson described her top policy priority. She expanded Jackie's vision to include all of Washington, D.C., which Lady Bird was determined to transform into "'a garden city' whose floral displays and plantings would make a handsome model for America." Eventually, Mrs. Johnson literally took her contributions to a Great Society on the road, guiding highway beautification legislation through Congress by force of her sharp political acumen and her delightful Southern charm.[72] Americans can thank Lady Bird Johnson for the dearth of billboards and profusion of wildflowers along the nation's byways—and Jackie Kennedy's efforts that laid the groundwork.

CHAPTER 6

KEEPING
THE FLAME

In the winter of 1963 the Kennedys were overjoyed to learn that they would welcome a new member to the first family in early September. For the first time since President Grover Cleveland was in office, an incumbent first lady was expecting a baby. Once again Jackie feared the prospect of a troubled pregnancy, and she reduced her spring schedule. Even so, after the announcement of her upcoming "blessed event," she appeared at a state dinner for the grand duchess of Luxembourg in a pale mauve Cassini sleeveless gown. Its skirt, gathered at the waist in a soft ruffle and bow, concealed her five-month pregnancy, and she looked anything but matronly. Her final public event before her due date was a state dinner for the president of India on June 3.[1]

The occasion was Tish Baldrige's last in her capacity as chief of staff and social secretary to Mrs. Kennedy. Baldrige had considered leaving the White House in late 1961. She was exhausted after planning and executing the first lady's European trip that summer, and Mrs. Kennedy complained about the work load that Baldrige sent to her, even though it was "only a fifth of the decisions to be made." Baldrige expressed her discontent directly to the president, and he persuaded her to stay, arguing: "I need you . . . in the East Wing, in that very spot. I want Jackie to feel protected and not persecuted by the demands of her job. I want you to keep doing the terrific things you do. Just lighten up on the workload, and it'll make things easier on both of you. She [Jackie] gets pressured very easily. Come to me when there are problems. You don't have to suffer in silence. But don't leave now." Yet Baldrige continued to have a different vision for the first lady's role. The dynamic social secretary "wanted [Mrs. Kennedy] to do more, knowing that her power to help her husband and the country was unlimited. She had a real opportunity to change history in her interpretation of her role in the White House. She flashed angry eyes at [Baldrige] once and said, 'Not everyone has your energy, you know. I certainly don't. I don't want to do all those things. Keep it away!'" Jackie recalled in a 1962 letter to her friend, Bill Walton, "I was tired—and I wanted to see my children— so I just told Tish—who nearly died from the shock—that I would NEVER go out—lunches, teas, degrees, speeches, etc. For two months there was a flap—Now it is a precedent established—If you can just diabolically figure out a way where you get the right person as your assistant—. . . Look how Pam [Turnure, the first lady's press assistant] helps me—because she answers every question exactly as I would—I know she will do it correctly—so we don't even communicate for weeks on end—. . . Mummy and Tish prefer frenzy—but that is all they have to fill their lives—"[2]

After nearly three years of "frenzy," Baldrige decided it was time to leave the White House, and she took a position at the Kennedy family's Merchandise Mart in Chicago. The first lady hired her prep-school roommate, Nancy Tuckerman, to serve not as chief of staff, but as White House social secretary. Chief Usher J. B. West, while giving Baldrige credit for her "inner sense of what would catch the public's eye, and . . . how to use entertaining to build an image for the First Lady," believed that Mrs. Kennedy's routine and demeanor were more placid under the Tuckerman regime. The new social secretary simply did not prod the first lady to accept unwanted responsibilities. In fact, Jackie instructed Tuckerman, "Don't bring any questions to me because Mr. West knows what can or can't be accomplished." The relationship was so felicitous that Tuckerman stayed on as Mrs. Kennedy's personal assistant until the former first lady's death more than thirty years later.[3]

Just after Baldrige's departure, Jackie retired to Hyannis Port, where she and the president had rented a home on Squaw Island, near the Kennedy compound. In between his political forays at home (to Texas, Colorado, California, and Hawaii) and state trips abroad (to Germany, Ireland, England, and Italy), and his work in Washington, the president visited his family on weekends. Before leaving for her summer on Cape Cod, the first lady drafted a typically detailed memo to West about how to decorate a nursery for the new baby. She requested that a small room used by Caroline and John for their meals be converted to a baby's bedroom, complete with the family's crib, white curtains, and a white "shaggy inexpensive" rug, "which we can throw in [the] washing machine." She teased West at the end of the memo: "Next y[ea]r I won't do one single thing & recuperate for 6 months—and you will have that to look forward to—Thank you—JBK." Once she arrived at the beach, she set to work on her gift to JFK for their tenth wedding anniversary, to be celebrated on September 12, 1963. With West's help she prepared three scrapbooks, entitled, "The White House—Before and After," "The President's Park," and "The Making of a Garden." She personally selected all of the photographs to document JFK's nearly three years as president.[4]

The first lady did not remove herself completely from official duties. In June and July she wrote a series of memos from the Cape to her new social secretary on the state dinner to be held for the king and queen of Afghanistan on September 5. Because her baby was due that month, Jackie knew she could not attend. That fact did not stop her from planning every conceivable component of the event, from entertainment by military bands, to weather contingencies, to types of dining tables, to suggestions for decorative trees. When Nancy Tuckerman responded with a description of arrangements she had made with the chief usher, Mrs. Kennedy wrote at the end of the memo, "Fine. Sounds marvelous. JBK."[5]

On the morning of August 7 Mrs. Kennedy suddenly experienced labor pains, and her obstetrician ordered her to Otis Air Force Base on the Cape, where a special hospital unit had been prepared in case of such an emergency. Alerted in Washington, the president flew to his wife's side immediately, but he arrived after the cesarean birth. The baby boy, baptized Patrick Bouvier Kennedy, was five weeks premature and weighed less than five pounds. Like his brother, John Jr., he developed neonatal breathing problems. They were more severe, however, and the doctors suggested that Patrick be flown to Boston for specialized care. His condition, diagnosed as hyaline membrane disease, was once a common affliction of premature infants. Its primary symptom was a coating of the lungs' air sacs with thick fluid, which limited oxygen transfer to the bloodstream. The condition, now preventable through medication, was then particularly perilous to premature babies, whose lungs are typically underdeveloped. As a last resort, physicians placed Patrick in a high-pressure chamber to force air into his lungs. President Kennedy divided his time between keeping vigil over his ill son and comforting his wife. He told his mother-in-law, Janet Auchincloss, "Oh, nothing must happen to Patrick because I just can't bear to think of the effect it might have on Jackie."[6]

In the early hours of August 9, doctors summoned JFK to Patrick's side as the infant's heart failed and his brief life came to an end. Jack Kennedy, not known for emotional displays, sobbed over his son's death. The president flew back to the Cape to inform his wife of the sad news. Too weak to leave the base hospital, Jackie missed the child's private funeral, held in Cardinal Richard Cushing's Boston residence. President Kennedy clung to the small casket before it was interred at the Kennedy family plot in Brookline. When Jackie left the hospital several days later, looking pale but composed, the president uncharacteristically held her hand and then steadied her as she disembarked from the helicopter at Hyannis Port. There they consoled themselves, as well as Caroline and John Jr., who had so eagerly anticipated a new brother or sister.[7]

As news of the Kennedy tragedy spread, condolences poured in from the around the world. A London paper starkly headlined, "Jackie's Baby Dies." The first lady continued to recuperate at the Cape and then traveled to Hammersmith Farm to celebrate her wedding anniversary on September 12. She gave the president the White House scrapbooks that she had meticulously composed, as well as a St. Christopher medal to replace the one she had given him for a wedding present, and which he had placed in Patrick's coffin. Jack presented her with a gold ring containing emerald chips that symbolized the lost baby. The president also offered her a list of antiquities from a New York dealer and told her to choose one. JFK, always concerned about his wife's extravagant spending habits, jokingly

The first family at Hyannis Port one week after the death of infant Patrick,
August 1963. (Photo by Cecil Stoughton, White House, JFK Library, Boston)

steered her away from the most expensive objets d'art. She selected a
simple coiled serpent bracelet.[8]

Kennedy friends, Ben Bradlee and his wife, attended the anniversary dinner, and they observed, "This was the first time we had seen
Jackie since the death of little Patrick, and she greeted JFK [upon his
arrival at Hammersmith] with by far the most affectionate embrace
we had ever seen them give each other. They are not normally de-
monstrative people, period." Jackie's mother also thought that the
first couple

> were closer [on their tenth anniversary]. They'd certainly been
> through as much as people can go through together in ten years:
> tragedy and joy and their children's births and deaths and then
> Jack's illnesses and Jackie's cesarean operations, and then the
> campaigning and occupying the highest office in the world. I
> can't think of two people who had packed more into ten years of
> marriage than they had. And I felt that their strains and stresses,

which any sensitive people have in a marriage, had eased to a
point where they were terribly close to each other. I almost can't
think of any married couple I've ever known that had greater
understanding of each other, in spite of Jackie's introver[sion],
stiffness—I mean that it's difficult for her to show her feelings. I
think one felt in those rare moments when one could be alone
with them on a quiet evening when there weren't a million pressures pending—that they were very, very, very close to each other
and understood each other wonderfully. He appreciated her gifts
and she worshiped him and appreciated his humor and his kindness, and they really had fun together.

White House correspondent Robert Pierpoint, who thought Jacqueline Kennedy was a "strange" and moody woman and who knew
of her husband's womanizing (although, like the rest of the mainstream press, he did not report it), concluded that "for some time
[prior to Patrick's death] they were estranged really. But then, after
the baby died, the rest of the summer they seemed closer together." If
indeed they were experiencing a newfound closeness, it apparently
did not curtail Jack's womanizing. Marion Fahnstock revealed in
2003 that she "was involved in a sexual relationship with President
Kennedy" from June 1962 until November 1963. JFK also reportedly
resumed his affair with Ben Bradlee's sister and engaged in dalliances
while traveling in Florida just before his fatal trip to Dallas.[9]

After three months away from the White House, the first lady finally returned on September 23 and greeted Ethiopian Emperor
Haile Selassie when he arrived at Washington's Union Station the
next day. She excused herself, however, from the state dinner in his
honor, telling him at a private tea, "*Je suis comblée*" (I am overcome)—so *comblée*, apparently, that she left immediately for a
sixteen-day vacation abroad. *Time* magazine reported that the first
lady was literally overcome on her transatlantic flight and was administered oxygen. Her sister Lee Radziwill had arranged invitations
for herself and Jackie to sail on board Greek shipping tycoon Aristotle Onassis's yacht, described in the press as a "325-foot pleasure
palace." Before setting sail on October 4, Mrs. Kennedy recovered
from her jet lag for several days at a Greek villa near Athens, where
she had stayed during her 1961 trip. She paused from her respite to

have tea with Greece's King Paul and Queen Frederika. JFK, hoping that the holiday would restore his wife's physical and mental health, sent Undersecretary of Commerce Franklin D. Roosevelt Jr. and his wife along on the journey to add an air of legitimacy. *Time* bought the ruse, reporting that FDR Jr. "was in Greece to discuss trade matters with local officials." President Kennedy's aides cautioned him that the first lady's socializing with Onassis, an infamous womanizer and outlaw businessman, could have political repercussions, but JFK maintained his hope that the trip would distract Jackie's morbid thoughts about her deceased baby.[10]

The first lady certainly had plenty to take her mind off her sadness. The *Washington Post*, noting the color and styles of Jackie's bathing suits, reported that she and her sister swam and motorboated before boarding Onassis's yacht for a cruise through the Aegean Sea to Istanbul, Turkey. Jackie also hosted a shipboard dinner party and dance. The *Post* benignly characterized the trip as a "two-week vacation rest after the death of her infant son recently." Stressing the link between the first lady and the president, the paper concluded, "Informed sources said Mrs. Kennedy had spoken with her husband twice by telephone since her arrival. But Athens circles were discounting rumors of a brief flying visit by President Kennedy as only 'wishful thinking.'"[11]

Despite the troubled history of her marriage, Jackie wrote tender, soulful letters to JFK during the Aegean cruise. "I think that I am lucky to miss you—I know I always exaggerate—but I pity everybody else who is married. . . . I have never realized the enormous stress you are under—but there I can't help you, therefore I shall give you the only thing I can give you: I think of you. . . . I'll show you how much I love you when I get back. I hope you are not making a speech in Arkansas."[12]

The first lady had one more stop on her holiday's itinerary before returning home. As *Time* described it, "In the black, silver-sequined tent of a Moroccan chieftain sat a dark-haired beauty. . . . She might have been a desert princess—but she was not. She was the First Lady of the U.S. . . . A guest of King Hassan II on the last leg of her 16-day vacation, Jackie apparently could have taken home most of Morocco just for the asking. At Hassan's invitation, she visited the King's cloistered wife Lalla Latifa, 19—the only foreigner ever to do so. . . . Home was an apartment in Hassan's Bahia Palace, furnished in white leather and looking out over vast palm groves toward the Atlas Mountains. There a French hair stylist called frequently, [and] did Jackie's hair in a fetching 'Parisian nymph' style."[13]

The first lady returned to Washington via Paris. President Charles de Gaulle was on a state visit to Iran, but he arranged to have a bouquet of roses and orchids presented to Mrs. Kennedy as she changed planes. She also purchased a dozen neckties for her husband from a Christian Dior collection that was brought to the airport for her shopping convenience. When the first lady's plane touched down at Washington's National Airport, on October 17, the president, Caroline, and John Jr. were waiting for her, and the children excitedly raced up the steps to greet their mother. The little boy scrambled to the plane on all fours. The *Washington Post* reported the details of the first lady's travel outfit, as well as the clothing worn by her children for their mother's homecoming.[14]

The press took advantage of these rare public sightings of Caroline and John to relate their appearance, behavior, and antics. On November 13, when Jackie attended her first official event since Patrick's death, the *Washington Post*'s women's section published four photographs, along with its narrative. The first family sat closely together on the Truman Balcony to observe the Black Watch, the storied Scottish Highland Regiment, perform for 1,700 underprivileged Washington children on the South Lawn of the White House. John Jr. snuggled on his mother's lap; Caroline balanced on the arm of her father's chair and curled her arm around his neck. At their parents' urging, each child shook hands with a member of the Regiment posted on the balcony. Jackie had taught Caroline to curtsey and John to bow from the waist when meeting official visitors, and the children's impeccable manners were on display. At the performance's conclusion the first family walked down the steps to mingle with some of the visiting children. The president had told them earlier that, when he was their age, the "green and misty country" of Scotland had enthralled him. He shook hands with several of the bolder children who pushed toward him while he clutched young John in his other arm. Caroline and her mother strolled along hand in hand.[15]

After so much time apart over the previous several months, and such sadness over Patrick's death, the family seemed to be enjoying their togetherness. They had spent the previous weekend at their new home, Wexford, in the Virginia countryside. Pictures and videos, captured by White House photographer Cecil Stoughton, display vignettes of the first lady gracefully hurtling over fences on horseback, Caroline and John playing with their dad on the new terrace, Jackie teaching her son how to salute, and the president sitting on the grass and playfully fighting off Caroline's pony as it nuzzled his neck.[16]

Mrs. Kennedy was gradually returning to the official social scene after her long hiatus from Washington. On November 20 she and the president hosted a buffet reception for members of the U.S. Supreme Court, lower-court judges, and their spouses. Five days later a state dinner for Ludwig Erhard, the new chancellor of West Germany, was planned for the White House. Before it, the Kennedys were to make a three-day trip to Texas, where the president hoped to raise money and mend political fences between squabbling factions of the Democratic party in the Lone Star State—a key component of his electoral strategy for the 1964 presidential contest. The first lady, who had eschewed domestic political trips with her husband throughout his presidency, surprisingly agreed to accompany him for whirlwind stops in San Antonio, Houston, Fort Worth, Dallas, and Austin, and at Vice President Lyndon Johnson's ranch. Ben Bradlee recalled that after Jackie's return from her October cruise, she and the president had commented at a private dinner party about some of the unflattering press reports of the hijinks aboard Onassis's yacht. According to Bradlee, Jackie "seem[ed] a little remorseful about all the publicity." She remarked that her husband was being "really nice and understanding" about it. Nevertheless, President Kennedy, attuned to potential political fallout from his wife's associations with Onassis, declared that the Greek tycoon should not travel to the United States until after the 1964 presidential election. JFK impishly noted that "Jackie's guilt feelings" might reap rewards for him. Smiling at his wife, Jack reportedly teased, "Maybe now you'll come with us to Texas next month." "Sure I will, Jack," the first lady is said to have replied. She even called Tish Baldrige, now at her new job in Chicago, to exclaim, "You won't believe it, but I'm going campaigning to Texas with Jack next week, and I'm doing it because I want to. I'm even glad I'm going! I know this is hard to believe, but believe it. I'm anxious to hit the campaign trail again. Did you ever expect to hear me say that, Tish?" Baldrige, "de-lighted to hear the note of genuine happiness in [Jackie's] voice," re-sponded that it certainly was amazing, "knowing how much she hated political campaigns and this was the start of a new one and she was thrilled to be going on it!"[17]

Robert Pierpoint was "very, very struck by how suddenly she [Mrs. Kennedy] had decided to become the good political wife and decided to do the right thing and was trying very hard and even managing to make it appear that she was enjoying this political jaunt [in Texas]. . . . I thought she felt awkward and ill-at-ease [at previous political events]."[18]

Expecting cool autumn weather in the week before Thanksgiv-ing, the first lady had chosen a primarily neutral or dark color pal-ette for her Texas wardrobe: a cream coat, a white dress, a black suit. Her hair was nearly shoulder-length now and more naturally styled, without the bouffant she had made famous. The Texas winds were blustery, though, and her new hairdo was less resilient than her shorter, sprayed version. Consequently, she looked more tousled for the outdoor events on this trip. She worried about the several motorcades in open cars with her husband, where her hair would be subject to the elements. The president had told her to look particularly stylish in Dallas to impress "the rich Republican women at that lunch," where he was to speak on Friday afternoon, November 22. They would be "wearing mink coats and diamond bracelets," but, JFK instructed his wife, "be simple—show these Texans what good taste really is." The first couple decided that a mainstay from Mrs. Kennedy's wardrobe would be perfect—a pink Chanel suit, trimmed in navy, and topped with a matching pillbox hat. The first lady had been photographed wearing it numerous times: in London on the way home from her 1962 trip to South Asia, inspecting the architectural plans for preserving Lafayette Park, holding John Jr. on the South Lawn during a welcoming ceremony, and posing with the maharajah and maharani of Jaipur after the Cuban missile crisis postponed the planned White House dinner dance in their honor.[19]

The Texas weather was warmer than first predicted, as were the crowds. Despite a few negative placards, Jackie and the president beamed at the enthusiastic welcome they received in San Antonio and Houston on their first day of the trip. They both appeared in good spirits. At their stop in Houston, the Kennedys made a brief visit at the meeting of the League of United Latin American Citizens (LULAC). The president proudly introduced his wife to say a few words in Spanish. "Looking radiant in a black velvet suit [with] not a hair out of place," according to the *Washington Post,* Jackie spoke slowly, "I am very happy to be in the great state of Texas, and I am especially pleased to be with you who are part of the noble Spanish tradition which has contributed so much to Texas. You are working for Texas and the United States. Thank you and viva to Las LU-LACs!" The ecstatic audience gave her a standing ovation.[20]

The next morning in Fort Worth, the president appeared before a crowd of union workers outside his hotel. They shouted a greeting he was now long used to: "Where's Jackie?" He sheepishly pointed toward her room and replied, "Mrs. Kennedy is organizing herself. It takes her a little longer, but, of course, she looks better than we do when she does it!" In fact, it took her so long that she was twenty minutes late to the Chamber of Commerce breakfast, but no one would have known it from her husband's reaction as she made her way to the dais. He smiled warmly and applauded with the crowd as she came toward him in the pink outfit they had selected for the day's events. She took her seat and widened her eyes in amazement at the tumultuous applause. Correspondent Pierpoint observed that Mrs. Kennedy "really looked and acted like one who was very much in love with her husband and even in love with the fact that he's a politician, and she wants to be a good politician's wife. [S]uddenly she had gotten into it." The president's trademark wit was in top form. When cheers for the first lady's entrance at the Fort Worth breakfast died down, he began, "Two years ago I introduced myself in Paris by saying that I was the man who had accompanied Mrs. Kennedy to Paris. I am getting somewhat the same sensation as I travel around Texas." Comedic pause. "Nobody wonders what Lyndon and I wear!" The self-deprecation and gentle joshing over his wife's fashion were irresistible to the attendees. When the master of ceremonies presented the hat-phobic president with a white Stetson, JFK deflected cries of "put it on!" "I'll put it on in the White House on Monday. If you'll come up, you'll have a chance to see it then!" His gracious grin mellowed the hosts' ten-gallon Texas egos.

Earlier he had quipped, "I know now why everyone in Ft. Worth is so thin, having gotten up and down about nine times. This is what you do every morning!" The breakfast crowd broke into peals of laughter at his informal banter.[21]

The next stop was Dallas, the most worrisome destination on the president's itinerary for its right-wing and sometimes violent propensities. JFK described it as "nut country" to his wife. A damper on the otherwise sunny start to the visit in "Big D" was a nasty ad, bordered by funereal black, in the *Dallas Morning News,* accusing him of a litany of leftist sins, as perceived by the ultraconservative "American Fact-Finding Committee." So the Kennedys were pleasantly surprised and relieved at another warm Texas welcome, this time at Dallas's Love Field. Flashing their dazzling smiles, they moved along the fence, shaking hands with spectators. The bright sun highlighted the president's suntan and the raspberry tones of the first lady's suit and hat. They seemed to be "shimmering," in the words William Styron had used to describe the couple's appearance on the night of the White House dinner for Nobel Prize winners.[22]

The motorcade route to the Dallas Trade Mart, where JFK would deliver his luncheon speech, was seven miles long. Crowds were sparse along the sections between the airport and downtown. Once the cavalcade reached the city center, however, the number of spectators swelled and their greetings were friendly and boisterous. The Kennedys smiled and waved from each side of their open Lincoln Continental. Texas Governor John Connally and his wife, Nellie, were riding in the same car, ahead of the first couple in the limousine's jump seats. Mrs. Connally was elated over the outpouring of affection for the Kennedys. Years later she remembered, "I wanted Texas to love them and . . . I wanted the Kennedys to respond like they knew they were being loved." As they approached the last block of the parade route, Mrs. Connally thought she would sum up the visit thus far: "Mr. President, you certainly can't say that Dallas doesn't love you." Just then Mrs. Kennedy heard a sound that she presumed was a police motorcycle backfiring. She turned toward her husband, who had raised his hands reflexively to his throat, his elbows outstretched to either side. As he began to slump forward, the first lady grabbed his left arm. At that moment the right side of his skull shattered, and the

President and Mrs. Kennedy arrive in Dallas, November 22, 1963.
(Photo by Cecil Stoughton, White House. JFK Library, Boston)

president's limp body pitched toward his wife. Showered in blood and brain tissue, she screamed, "Oh, no, no, no! Oh, my God, they have shot my husband!" Pivoting toward the back of the limousine, she raised herself up on her elbow and began crawling across the broad trunk deck of the Lincoln. The driver, now recognizing that they were under fire, mashed the accelerator to the floor. Clint Hill, a Secret Service agent positioned behind the president's vehicle, raced toward the rear bumper, planted his foot, and grabbed the handhold. Despite the car's rapid acceleration, he managed to lock hands with Mrs. Kennedy and push her back into her seat, where he sheltered her and the president.[23]

Jackie cradled her husband in her lap on the horrific six-minute ride to Parkland Memorial Hospital. "Jack. Jack. Jack, can you hear me? I love you, Jack," she repeated, but she knew he was dead. The first lady, who had tried so hard to protect her family's privacy, now attempted to shelter the president's gruesome head wound. Only when Agent Hill wrapped his suit coat around President Kennedy's head did Mrs. Kennedy release her grip. Mrs. Connally, whose husband had also been wounded in the ambush but would survive, and Jackie sat in the hall outside the trauma rooms where their spouses lay. As medical personnel performed futile life-saving efforts on her husband, the first lady looked utterly devastated, but she did not cry. Two local Catholic priests, one of whom had cheered the motorcade as it passed his parish, were summoned to administer the last rites of the Church. Jackie joined them and held her deceased husband's hand during the brief administration of the sacrament. "Thank you for taking care of the president. Please pray for him," she said softly to the clerics.[24]

The head physician who had attended her husband tried to spare the new widow the arrival of the casket that would bear her husband back to Washington. Quite logically, she countered, "Do you think seeing the coffin can upset me, Doctor? I've seen my husband die, shot in my arms. His blood, his brains are all over me. How can I see anything worse than I've seen?" She then decided that she wanted to leave something of herself with her spouse's body, so she slipped off her wedding band and placed it on his finger. Despite pleas that she should return to the airport immediately, she insisted on remaining with her husband. Finally, the casket was loaded into a hearse, and she accompanied it to Love Field.[25]

Back on Air Force One, several members of her entourage suggested that Mrs. Kennedy change from her bloodstained suit. She refused to do so, telling Lady Bird Johnson, "I want them to see what they have done to Jack." In the plane's main cabin, she stood, dazed but stoic, next to Lyndon Johnson as he was sworn in as thirty-sixth president of the United States. The White House photographer captured the scene, which flashed around the world via the Associated Press. Lyndon Johnson's longtime friend, Jack Valenti, an eyewitness to the historic scene, remembers: "[Mrs. Kennedy's] pink blouse was splattered with blood and white flecks of her husband's brain. She stood beside the new president, eyes opaque, cast downward, her hands clasped in front of her, her whole figure a resolve cast in grace and dignity." Then she returned to the rear compartment to keep vigil over her husband's coffin.[26]

When Air Force One landed at Andrews Air Force Base outside Washington, television viewers and spectators waiting on the tarmac were stunned to see Mrs. Kennedy emerge into the spotlights still wearing the suit and hosiery streaked with blood. Even on black-and-white TVs, the spectacle was shocking. As Lady Bird Johnson, the new first lady, remembered, "Somehow that was one of the most poignant sights—that immaculate woman exquisitely dressed and caked in blood." She could have returned directly to the White House, but she insisted on accompanying her husband's remains to Bethesda Naval Hospital, where she wanted the autopsy to be performed because of his service in the Navy.[27]

With family members and close friends gathered to comfort her at the hospital, she finally broke down and sobbed. As Ben Bradlee saw the terrible scene, "There was this totally doomed child, with that God-awful skirt, not saying anything, looking burned alive." When her brother-in-law, Attorney General Robert Kennedy, reported that Lee Harvey Oswald, an avowed communist, had been arrested in Dallas for the murder of her husband, she remarked disgustedly, "[Jack] didn't even have the satisfaction of being killed for civil rights. It had to be some silly little Communist."[28]

The former first lady took it upon herself to infuse her husband's death with meaning and establish the symbols of his postpresidency. In doing so, Jacqueline Kennedy's own image of glamour, youth, sophistication, and elegance would become inextricably bound with the emblems of courage and dignity. Her shock induced scramble to the trunk deck of the limousine below the sniper's nest was her last unthinking act on November 22, 1963, and the days of mourning that followed. Summoning the strength to stand with the new president for his oath-taking, and choosing to wear her bloodstained suit for the return to Washington, seared her portrait in the public mind. Although she was surrounded by a legion of loyal helpmates, led by her brothers-in-law, Bobby Kennedy and Sargent Shriver, she made several of the most important decisions about how the nation and the world would grieve her husband and view her last official acts.

Although she was vague about the details, Jackie referred to the funeral arrangements made for another assassinated president, Abraham Lincoln, which were partially depicted in her White House

*Two hours after witnessing her husband's assassination in a
Dallas motorcade, Mrs. Kennedy watches as Lyndon Johnson takes the
presidential oath of office aboard Air Force One, November 22, 1963.
(Photo by Cecil Stoughton, White House. JFK Library, Boston)*

guidebook. Historian and presidential aide Arthur Schlesinger Jr.
called the head of the Library of Congress, who formed a team of librarians to research the Lincoln rites. The Kennedy planning group
then adapted them to the ceremonies for JFK. An early decision by
Mrs. Kennedy, to have her husband lie in state with the coffin closed
(a departure from the Lincoln funeral), assured that his living image
would supersede the undertaker's efforts. She told Secretary of Defense Robert McNamara, another crucial actor in the funeral planning, "[T]hey have to remember Jack alive." Her appearance on the
White House's North Portico with her children on Sunday, November 24, after a private day of grieving that Saturday, created an un-
forgettable portrait, wired around the planet by UPI. Ahead of her, a
military honor guard carried the flag-enshrouded casket from the
Executive Mansion, where it had lain in the East Room, and placed
it on a horse-drawn caisson for a procession to the Capitol. Mrs.
Kennedy's face, framed in a black lace mantilla, was a study in fa-
tigue and desolation. She remained composed, however, grasping

the hands of Caroline and John Jr. The children wore the same matching powder-blue coats in which they had been photographed observing the Black Watch performance with their parents on the South Portico just eleven days before.[29]

Mrs. Kennedy's resolve broke only once before the cameras on Sunday. Waiting at the foot of the Capitol steps for her husband's casket to be borne to the Rotunda, she bowed her head and wept softly as the military band struck up "Hail to the Chief." Yet during the ceremony inside the Capitol, she maintained her composure, even when Senate Majority Leader Mike Mansfield took as the theme of his eulogy the placement of her wedding band on her husband's finger at Parkland Hospital. (In fact, Jackie had second thoughts about relinquishing the symbol of her union with JFK, and she asked that the wedding band be returned to her at Bethesda Naval Hospital. With Bobby Kennedy by her side in the White House East Room, she had placed inside the casket the president's favorite pair of gold cufflinks, which she had given to him early in their courtship, and letters from herself and the children. Bobby added his PT-109 tie clip and a silver rosary his wife had presented to him at their wedding. Jackie then took a lock of her husband's hair, and the coffin was closed for the last time.) Before leaving the Rotunda ceremony, Mrs. Kennedy walked with Caroline to the casket, where they knelt and kissed the American flag covering it. The *Washington Post* wrote, "Jacqueline Kennedy led a grieving people to the bier of her slain husband with matchless courage. . . . Her silent strength was matched by her tender solicitude for her children. . . . She bore the 90-minute ordeal of the procession to the Capitol, the ceremonies and return to the White House with an unspoken sadness and bravery that brought tears to the eyes of spectators and television viewers."[30]

Jackie was adamant that her husband's funeral mass should occur at St. Matthew's Cathedral in Washington. It was only half as large as the cavernous National Shrine of the Immaculate Conception on the campus of Catholic University in the northeast section of the nation's capital, but St. Matthew's was just six blocks from the White House. Its close proximity was determinative. Mrs. Kennedy had decided that she would walk behind her husband's caisson from the White House to his funeral. Her family and friends attempted to

Mrs. Kennedy, her children, and Attorney General Robert F. Kennedy
leave the Capitol, where President Kennedy lay in state, November 24, 1963.
(Photo by Abbie Rowe, White House. JFK Library, Boston)

dissuade her, citing the security risks, not only for herself, but the heads of state who would feel obliged to process with the widow. She prevailed. On that sunny, crisp day, November 25, shrouded in a flowing sheer black veil, Jacqueline Kennedy marched at the head of the procession with her husband's surviving brothers, Robert and Edward, to St. Matthew's. Following were the new president and first lady, Lyndon and Lady Bird Johnson, and every attending head of state who was mobile. The most recognized among the foreign dignitaries were Charles De Gaulle, Haile Selassie, and Prince Philip, each bedecked in full military regalia. West German Chancellor Ludwig Erhard, who was to have dined with President Kennedy that very night, was instead marching to his funeral. The mournful tones of the Black Watch, another poignant touch requested by Mrs. Kennedy, piped the cortege up Connecticut Avenue.[31]

The widow of the first Roman Catholic president of the United States asked that Kennedy family prelate, Cardinal Cushing, celebrate a low mass, rather than the more elaborate and solemn high service. Conducted in Latin, a pre–Vatican II relic, the televised requiem mass lasted but an hour and included a reading of JFK's inaugural address by Auxiliary Bishop of Washington Philip Hannan. Cushing departed from prescribed liturgy with an English paraphrase of the Catholic blessing for the deceased and an added tribute to his friend, "May the angels, dear Jack, lead you into Paradise. May the martyrs receive you at your coming. May the spirit of God embrace you, and mayest thou, with all those who made the supreme sacrifice of dying for others, receive eternal rest and peace. Amen."[32]

At that tender and graceful prayer for her husband, the former first lady dissolved into tears, but she recovered for the recessional from the cathedral. She and her children stood hand in hand at the bottom of the stairs while the casket was again placed on the caisson for its final journey to interment. She then prompted the most shattering and lasting image of the ordeal. Leaning over John Jr., she whispered, "You can salute Daddy now and say good-bye to him." The little boy, who turned three that day, took a step from his mother, came to attention, and raised his right hand in a perfect military salute.[33]

Jacqueline Kennedy was not responsible for the initial inspiration to bury President Kennedy at Arlington National Cemetery. Robert Kennedy and his sisters, along with Kennedy's "Irish mafia," wanted JFK's remains returned to his native Massachusetts. Defense Secretary McNamara disagreed and reconnoitered Arlington for an appropriate setting. He found it in the sloping lawn below the Custis-Lee Mansion, overlooking the Potomac River and the monuments of Washington. After viewing his find, Jackie, Bobby, and the Kennedy sisters agreed that it was the perfect final resting place for the slain president.[34]

Mrs. Kennedy's deft touch in the creation of funereal iconography was ultimately evident in the closing and lasting tribute to her husband at the graveside service. After the prayers, the "missing man" formation of the flyover, the twenty-one-gun salute, the playing of taps, the folding and presentment of the flag, she departed from standard religious and military ritual to light an "eternal flame" over her husband's grave. Reminiscent of the fire that burns at the Tomb of the Unknown Soldier under Paris's Arc de Triomphe, the one at JFK's burial site recalls the metaphorical torch, passed to a new generation, that he hailed in his inaugural address. After lighting the flame, Jackie, looking utterly stricken behind her veil, turned and walked from the grave, clutching the folded American flag. The president's brother, Bobby, equally devastated, clasped her free hand and guided her passage from the site. Returning to the White House, they greeted foreign dignitaries, held an Irish wake, and celebrated little John's birthday as best they could. Then the heartbroken pair paid a sorrowful midnight visit to the new grave.[35]

Mrs. Kennedy's contributions to her husband's legend, all captured on television and then embellished by media stories that she alone had planned every detail of the funeral with the efficiency of a CEO, enhanced her own public standing. She added one more lasting imprint on the Kennedy narrative. Summoning Theodore H. White, author of *The Making of the President 1960,* to Hyannis Port, where the widow was spending Thanksgiving one week after the assassination, she begged him to write her version of the Kennedy epilogue. She compared her husband's 1,000-day administration to the "one brief shining moment that was known as Camelot," quoting from the popular Broadway musical about the legendary King Arthur. Whether JFK in fact liked the lyric, as his distraught widow asserted, is immaterial. For *Life m*agazine, White eloquently and movingly penned the Kennedy administration's epitaph as its first lady wished. Camelot—the evocative label for the Kennedy era—resonated with a grieving public and endured, despite subsequent revelations about JFK's philandering and the inevitable iconoclasm that followed.[36]

In mid-1962 Jackie had written her friend, Bill Walton, who years later described the feelings expressed in the letter as "the real [Jackie]." Pouring out her thoughts in a late-night note, the first lady had told Walton, "I have learned one thing—and now my life here [in the White House] which I dreaded—and which at first overwhelmed me—is now all under control and the happiest time I have known—not for the position—but for the closeness of one's family—the last thing I expected to find in the W. House. And do you know what did it—once I pulled myself together? Organisation [*sic*]—I like to live in a disorganised [*sic*]—or free way . . . —and I still do—But I spent about 1 week organising [*sic*] things as well as Field Marshal Rommel ever did—And now my life is the way I want it—though deadly little details always do crop up—but not enough to spoil the atmosphere I want for Jack & me & our children—" As of November 22, 1963, the life that she had constructed, the "happiest" she had known, was gone. As one writer put it, "In an instant of pure and almost unimaginable carnage, Jackie Kennedy lost her husband, her job, and her house."[37] Nine days after the assassination, Jackie wrote to Nellie Connally about their shared experience: "We loved [our husbands] every way that a woman can love a man, haven't we, and so fortunate to have them in our arms at that terrible time."[38]

President and Mrs. Johnson were exceptionally patient with the traumatized first lady. She met with the new president in the Oval Office and asked if he would rename Cape Canaveral, Florida, site of NASA's space launches, Cape Kennedy. Jackie remembered the "first speech Jack made in Texas . . . that there would be a rocket one day that would go to the moon. I kept thinking, 'That's going to be forgotten, and his dreams are going to be forgotten.' I had this terrible fear then that he'd be forgotten, and I thought, 'Well, maybe they'll remember some day that this man did dream that.'" The Johnsons told Mrs. Kennedy to take the time she needed to find a new home for her children and Caroline's White House school. In turn, she expressed her appreciation to them. She wrote to LBJ, thanking him for "walking . . . behind Jack" in the funeral procession, despite the security risk. When she moved from the White House on December 6, she took time to write a welcome note to Lady Bird. Before the inauguration, the Kennedys had sold their Georgetown home, so Jackie, Caroline, and John had no place of their own to settle in Washington. But the former first lady told Ted White, "I'm going to live in the places I lived with Jack. In Georgetown, and with the Kennedys at Cape Cod." She gratefully accepted Undersecretary of State Averell Harriman's offer of his Georgetown home, just three blocks from her previous N Street address, as a temporary solution. A few months later she purchased, redecorated, and moved into a house across the street. Congress voted unanimously to pay for President Kennedy's funeral expenses, temporary office space for the former first lady, her personal staff and Secret Service protection, $10,000 annually for her widow's pension, and a lifetime franking privilege. Her annual income from a Kennedy trust fund was approximately $150,000, and Bobby provided another $50,000.[39]

The former first lady could not escape the horrid memories of November 22. She received nearly 800,000 condolence letters and appeared on national television to thank all those who had written. Her eyes brimming, she mourned her husband and "all his light gone from this world." She personally penned responses to many of the sympathy notes from people she knew. To Richard Nixon she wrote: "We never value life enough when we have it—and I would not have had Jack live his life any other way—though I know his death could have been prevented, and I will never cease to torture myself with that—" A friend, actress Kitty Carlisle Hart, remembered that Jackie repeatedly replayed the assassination in her mind and wondered whether she could have saved her husband by reacting more quickly to the first rifle shot. She wrote to the Bradlees, "I consider my life is over and I will spend the rest of it waiting for it really to be over."[40]

The former first lady even contemplated suicide, according to a Catholic priest she consulted in the spring of 1964. "Do you think God would separate me from my husband if I killed myself?" Jackie asked the Rev. Richard T. McSorley, a theology professor at Georgetown University, who met with her at Bobby Kennedy's urging. "I feel as though I am going out of my mind at times. Wouldn't God understand that I just want to be with him [JFK]?" she queried the priest. McSorley reminded the widow of her maternal obligations and of Catholic teaching that the faithful will be resurrected after death and reunited with loved ones. Several weeks later Jackie told him, "I know I'll never do it. I know it's wrong. It's just a way out." Yet she was filled with sadness that she had not been able to tell her husband goodbye and guilt that she had not made his life happier while he was alive. She confided in Fr. McSorley: "I was melancholy after the death of our baby [Patrick] and I stayed away [on her holiday with Aristotle Onassis] . . . longer than I needed to. I could have made his life so much happier, especially for the last few weeks. I could have tried harder to get over my melancholy."[41]

Jackie's old friend, Adlai Stevenson, sent her loving and comforting notes to assuage her grief. "There is radiance and glory in the darkness, could we but see. And you *can see*," he consoled her. Less than two weeks after the assassination, she responded with a personal note in her own hand. "I do thank you for your letter," she began. "I was going through Jack's things—he had so little that was of any value—I had wanted to give people something to remember him by—but there was so little. In the studbox I gave him—which was always in his top drawer, the box he kept the few nice things he had in—I found this silver shoe. It must be from your campaign. I would like you to have it back—How much has happened since those days. With my love, Jackie." (The shoe became a symbol of Stevenson's presidential campaigns in the 1950s when a photographer captured him with his feet propped up and a hole in the bottom of his sole.)

In Hyannis Port with Caroline and John the summer after JFK's death, Jackie composed a wistful lament for her husband, later published in a *Look* memorial issue about him:

> It is nearly a year since he has been gone.
>
> On so many days—his birthday, an anniversary, watching his children running to the sea—I have thought, "But this day last year was his last to see that." He was so full of love and life on all those days. He seems so vulnerable now, when you think that each one was his last time. . . .
>
> Now I think that I should have known he was magic all along. I did know it—but I should have guessed that it could not last.
>
> So now he is a legend when he would have preferred to be a man.[42]

Stevenson invited his grief-stricken friend to come to Pennsylvania with him in May 1964 to see the unveiling of a bronze statue of JFK. Jackie sent regrets to Adlai: "I do not feel I can see it at this particular time. It still pains me so much—whenever I see portraits or busts of the President." Haunted by memories of her slain spouse, hounded by packs of tourists and photographers (even on her doorstep), treated as the nation's widow-in-chief, in 1964 she escaped to New York City and the familiar territory of her childhood. She purchased a sprawling Fifth Avenue apartment and focused on raising her children. Her goal was to have them remember their father fondly and be proud of his accomplishments, but not be defined by his death. She had so wanted them to have a normal life, even in the White House, but after President Kennedy's passing, she worried, "The world is pouring terrible adoration at the feet of my children and I fear for them, for this awful exposure. How can I bring them up normally? We would never even have named John for his father had we known." For herself, she resolved to observe an official year of mourning, wearing black, writing on black-bordered stationery, and remaining in the United States. Bobby Kennedy, who resigned as attorney general and successfully ran for the U.S. Senate from New York in 1964, was a reliable source of support and stability for Jackie and her children. Gossip linked her romantically to her brother-in-law, but the historical record contains no such evidence. When she began to travel abroad again, she did so frequently. She seemed restless, and the press (especially tabloids) linked her to several suitors, including Lord Harlech (David Ormsby-Gore, former British ambassador to the United States), Roswell Gilpatrick (deputy secretary of defense), and John Carl Warnecke (architect on the Lafayette Square project and the Kennedy gravesite).[43]

Upon her move to New York City, Adlai Stevenson wrote, "Jackie dear—Welcome to New York! I hope you can find some peace here. I haven't! And I will give you none—until you set aside an evening for me—alone, small group, medium, large—whatever and whoever you wish. Love always, Adlai." French newspapers photographed the couple together, noting Jackie's hand clasping Adlai's arm, and speculated on whether they might marry. Stevenson sent the clipping to Jackie, and she returned it, "for your scrapbook," along with a playful note. It was her last missive to him.[44] Shortly thereafter, Stevenson collapsed and died of a heart attack on a London sidewalk, in the company of another of his many female admirers.

In addition to raising her children successfully, memorializing her husband was Mrs. Kennedy's other primary raison d'être after his death. Amidst coverage of his funeral in the *Washington Post* on November 26, 1963, was a brief announcement that "a bipartisan move [in Congress] is under way to have the National Cultural Center named the John Fitzgerald Kennedy Memorial Center for the Performing Arts." Congress did so, and President Lyndon Johnson signed the legislation in 1964, designating the center the sole official memorial to JFK in the nation's capital and authorizing federal matching funds for construction. On December 2, 1964, LBJ broke ground on the site of the officially named John F. Kennedy Center for the Performing Arts, along the banks of the Potomac River, just north of the

Theodore Roosevelt Bridge. Mrs. Kennedy, as well as first lady Lady
Bird Johnson and former first lady Mamie Eisenhower, became "honorary chairmen" of the Center's Board of Trustees. Jackie was also an
active member of the Program Committee of the Kennedy Center,
which held its first meeting in January 1965 to establish the center's
mission and agenda. Architect Edward Durrell Stone designed the
center's simple classical form, rendered in Italian marble. The center's
opening night, September 8, 1971, was marked by the premier of Leonard Bernstein's "Mass," composed for the occasion. The JFK Center's
performance spaces include a concert hall and opera house, each seating over 2,000, and the Eisenhower Theater, which comprises 1,100
seats for theater, opera, and dance productions.[45]

The Kennedy Library was the first memorial to her husband that
Mrs. Kennedy promoted publically. In her television address to the
American people on January 14, 1964, thanking them for their condolences, she noted, "Your letters will be placed with his papers in
the library to be erected in his memory. I hope that in years to come,
many of you and your children will be able to visit the Kennedy Library. It will be, we hope, not only a memorial to President Kennedy
but a living center of study of the times in which he lived and a center for young people and for scholars from all over the world."[46]

At a preliminary meeting of the Committee on Arts and Architecture for the Kennedy Library in early 1964, the former first lady
revealed her determination to define JFK's martyrdom. She told the
committee that the library "must express the beliefs that Jack gave
his life for. [W]e want people to enter the memorial part [of the li-
brary], and see what Jack *was*."[47]

The library project was plagued by obstacles, including problems
finding a site for the structure. President Kennedy had wanted the library affiliated with his alma mater, Harvard, and he preferred a lo-
cale for it near the university's campus. After JFK's death Robert
Kennedy led the John F. Kennedy Library Corporation, whose mission was to raise funds for the project, determine the site, and select
an architect. Kennedy friend and architect, Jack Warnecke, hoped to
receive the commission. He had traveled with President Kennedy to
Boston in May 1963 to look for potential library locations. But in late
1964 the Kennedy family, after consultation with a number of architects, chose I. M. Pei to design the building. By 1970 acquisition of a

site near the famous Harvard Yard seemed assured, and plans were made to begin constructing the JFK Library. Cambridge residents, already stymied by traffic gridlock around the Harvard campus, however, protested the additional congestion sure to result from the tourist site.[48]

On the tenth anniversary of JFK's assassination, ground had yet to be broken on the library. Jackie took the opportunity to publish an article in the November 1973 issue of *McCall's* magazine, advocating the completion of her late husband's memorial and archives. Entitled "The Bright Light of His Days," the short tribute declared, "For those of us who shared his days it is too painful to look back. But for the young it can be helpful. That is why I care about his Library. It can't replace him, but it can help people who believe ''tis not too late to seek a newer world.' God grant us always young people who feel that way. That is my prayer. If they care, then in his Library they can find ways of solving problems through government."[49] After five years of wrangling with Cambridge residents, the Library Corporation abandoned the Harvard site in 1975 and accepted an invitation to build the memorial to President Kennedy on twelve acres of land adjacent to the University of Massachusetts's Boston campus. The $12 million John F. Kennedy Library and Museum ultimately opened on October 20, 1979, at Columbia Point on Dorchester Bay. Pei's modern ten-story building, consisting of white poured concrete and glass, rises dramatically at the water's edge and overlooks the Boston skyline.

Although Mrs. Kennedy's initial preference for building the library at her husband's beloved Harvard did not materialize, the university became the home of the John F. Kennedy School of Government (previously the Graduate School of Public Administration). Dedicated in October 1978, it houses the Institute of Politics. The latter, founded in 1966 as a living memorial to JFK, supports Mrs. Kennedy's wish to inspire and train students interested in public service. The Institute's mission is to link scholars and practitioners of government, who can encourage students to think creatively about politics and public policy. Professor Richard Neustadt, a Kennedy advisor, whose book *Presidential Power* was considered a must-read in the administration, served as the Institute's founding director. He worked closely with Mrs. Kennedy, who took an active role in setting criteria for a diverse student body and participating in seminars on current political issues. Neustadt remembered that Jackie hoped to duplicate at the Kennedy School and Institute the kinds of stimulating dialogues she had loved during her college year in Paris. In 1985 Mrs. Onassis attended a ground-breaking ceremony for a five-acre public park, dedicated to President Kennedy and adjacent to the JFK School in Cambridge.[50]

A fourth memorial to President Kennedy, over which his widow exercised even more authority, was the Arlington gravesite. Three days after the president's funeral, Jackie, Bobby, and Jack Warnecke met at the new grave to discuss a permanent design for the 3.2 acres. After a year-long research process, Warnecke received approval from the Kennedy family for his proposal. It represented a simple yet evocative use of Cape Cod granite fieldstone on the plot, which would focus on the eternal flame, placed in the center of a five-foot circular flat granite stone at the head of the grave. Green clover and sedum were planted in the fieldstones' crevices to reflect the appearance of stones lying naturally in a Massachusetts field. Encircling the terrace leading up to the grave would be seven inscription tablets, hand-chiseled with excerpts from JFK's inaugural address. The setting of the stones occurred in the summer of 1966, supervised by master mason Billy Cleland, who was the superintendent of craftsmen completing the National Cathedral, a massive Gothic structure in northwest Washington. In March 1967 Jackie attended the dedication of the site with its new black granite stones marking the president's grave and those of their infant children, Patrick and Arabella. The former first lady now had the national shrine to her husband that she envisioned. It receives about four million visitors a year.[51]

Jackie seemed to take some comfort in the eternal flame's existence. "I care about that flame. Sometimes you drive across that bridge [to Arlington Cemetery] and see that Lee mansion all lit up, that's one of the first things Caroline learned to recognize. I wanted that flame." What she did not want was a plethora of landmarks named for her late husband. "I can't see changing the name of something like Sixth Avenue. I don't want to go out on Kennedy Driveway to a Kennedy Airport to visit a Kennedy School. . . . I'm not going around accepting plaques. I don't want medals for Jack. . . . I don't want to be seen by crowds."[52]

But the world ignored the widow's wishes, assuaging its own grief with a spate of memorials to the slain president. Around the nation and the world, John F. Kennedy's name labeled public spaces from New York City's international airport to NASA's Florida head-quarters (although Cape Kennedy reverted to its original name of Canaveral in 1973) to a bridge over the Ohio River between Louis-ville, Kentucky, and New Albany, Indiana, to a square in Berlin to numerous highways, schools, and buildings. When England's Queen Elizabeth dedicated a memorial and plot of land at Runny-mede to the late president in 1965, however, Mrs. Kennedy came out of mourning to appear at the ceremony on the site of the Magna Carta's conception. With her children at her side and a text written by Arthur Schlesinger, she expressed her "deep appreciation for the honor you are doing my husband." She concluded with one of JFK's favorite quotations, from John Buchan about Raymond Asquith, killed during World War I: "He will stand to those of us who are left as an incarnation of the spirit of the land he loved. He loved his youth and his youth became eternal. Debonair, brilliant and brave, he is now part of that immortal England which knows not age or weariness or defeat."[53]

Keeping the flame of her husband's memory burning brightly also entailed maintaining as much control as possible over the inevitable flood of books that emerged from Kennedy friends and associates. In the first few years after the assassination, the president's colleagues (Ted Sorensen, Arthur Schlesinger, and Pierre Salinger), Navy friend (Red Fay), secretary (Evelyn Lincoln), and nannie (Maud Shaw) all published volumes on their associations with JFK. Mrs. Kennedy ob-jected to parts of each manuscript. She begged Schlesinger to "take me out" of the final version "whenever you can" and excise "things I think are too personal. That is the only thing that can remain private for JFK—With everyone writing books—there won't be one shred of his whole life that the whole world won't know about. But the world has no right to his private life with me—I shared all those rooms with him—not with the Book of the Month readers—I don't want them snooping through those rooms now—even the bathtub—with the children—Please take those parts out."[54]

Most of the Kennedy book authors, except for Evelyn Lincoln, made at least some of the deletions Jackie requested. Schlesinger, a renowned historian, apparently excised just one passage (an exchange between President and Mrs. Kennedy after the failed Bay of Pigs invasion). He defended the personal anecdotes that he included in his book about the late president: "This is exactly the kind of intimate detail which critics and readers would be delighted to read." Despite their differences over the manuscript, Jackie maintained her admiration and affection for Schlesinger, who had been so helpful to her in the White House. She effusively praised his Pulitzer Prize–winning book, *A Thousand Days*, on November 23, 1965, in one of her "Dearest Arthur" handwritten notes: "[Your book] takes wings—and when you read it—Jack is alive again—I think—when my children are older—your book will tell them—more than even films of him they could see—what he was like—Only you could have done that—I know all the love and pain that went into it— Now no one will ever be able to hurt Jack—because your book is a testament against them—and for all he could not finish—Thank you dear Arthur. With all my love—Jackie."[55]

Several other authors were much less fortunate. Although Fay reportedly struck about 2,000 words from his manuscript, *The Pleasure of His Company*, Jackie returned to him his $3,000 contribution to the Kennedy Library Fund because she continued to disapprove of the book. She had the same reaction to Ben Bradlee's 1975 memoir, *Conversations with Kennedy*, and never spoke to him again. Jackie's most publicized attempt to rein in the author of a Kennedy book was her effort to censor William Manchester's epic story of the assassination, *The Death of a President*. Paradoxically, she and Bobby had specifically asked the Wesleyan University professor to produce the tome. He had left his teaching position and used his life savings to support three years of toil on the 800-page story. As it neared publication (by Harper and Row) and serialization (by *Look*) in 1967, however, she and her brother-in-law requested numerous changes and deletions, particularly personal anecdotes and those passages related to President Lyndon Johnson's conflictual relationship with Bobby. Manchester was also accused of exploiting the taped interviews Mrs. Kennedy had made with him as part of the research. With much media sensationalism, the former first lady sued Manchester, his publisher, and *Look* magazine. Ultimately, the parties settled out of court, with Manchester agreeing to delete 1,600 words from the serialized product and to strike personal passages that Jackie found objectionable from the book. He also renounced some sources of income from it. Mrs. Kennedy then dropped the lawsuit.[56]

This time the former first lady had miscalculated the impact of her effort to preserve the Camelot image. Attempts to justify the censorship of a professor, whom she had commissioned, on the grounds of her right to personal privacy were unconvincing. In late 1966 the American public had chosen her, for the fifth straight year in the Gallup Poll, as their "most admired woman in the world." One month later, in the wake of the Manchester lawsuit, Lou Harris, Jack Kennedy's one-time pollster, found that 33 percent of those polled reported that they "thought less" of the former first lady because of the book battle.[57]

Eight years later she had mellowed slightly over the episode. She explained to an interviewer from the Lyndon B. Johnson Library:

> I went to court. The worst thing in my life was trying to get all those things of Mr. Manchester's out of his book. I've never read the book. I did my oral history with him in an evening and alone, and it's rather hard to stop when the floodgates open. I just talked about private things. Then the man went away, and I think he was very upset during the writing of the book. I know that afterwards there were so many things, one, about the private things, which were mostly expressions of grief of mine and Caroline's that I wanted to take out of the book. Now it doesn't seem to matter so much, but then I had such a feeling. . . .
>
> Now, in hindsight, it seems wrong to have ever done that book at that time. Don't forget, these people were in shock. Before we moved out of the White House, Jim Bishop was saying he was going to write a book, *The Day Kennedy Was Shot.* All these people were doing these things, and you thought maybe to just not have this coming up, coming up, getting more and more sensational. Choose one person, ask everybody to just speak to him, maybe what would be the right thing to do. Well, it turned out not to be.[58]

Shortly after JFK's death, Jackie had expressed despair over her fate: "Can anyone understand how it is to have lived in the White

House, and then, suddenly, to be living alone as the president's widow? There's something so final and passé about it." Yet by 1968 she appeared to be settling into her new life. When Bobby Kennedy was assassinated just after winning the California presidential primary in June, however, she was again plunged into grief and was fearful for her children's lives. Mrs. Kennedy turned for solace and protection, as she had in 1963 after Patrick's death, to longtime friend Aristotle Onassis. In fact, he had visited the White House to pay his respects after her husband was assassinated. To Jackie he represented physical and financial security for herself, Caroline, and John. He was independently wealthy and, among his numerous homes, owned an entire island, Skorpios, off the Greek coast. Nevertheless, many Americans could not accept that their admired former first lady, the queen of Camelot, married the unattractive, unscrupulous, and divorced Onassis in the fall of 1968. Years later, Lee Radziwill, who herself had a romance with the Greek shipping magnate in the early 1960s, explained her sister's second marriage: "Contrary to what people think, Jackie and Ari Onassis did have a lot in common. They both shared a great love of the sea, they both had a great knowledge and love of Greek mythology. In fact, Jackie wrote and illustrated a beautiful book for Ari on the travels of Ulysses and then she had it magnificently bound with a large, early Greek coin in the middle and it was really a treasure. So they did share a lot more than people were aware of." Lee's evidence seems rather thin, but she explained her own attraction to Onassis this way: "[I liked him] enormously. I liked him immensely. He was very magnetic and charismatic. There was something sort of fascinating about this small man who moved like a potentate and always attracted people's attention. He was very warm."[59]

The Greek ethos clearly fascinated Jackie. She wrote to Arthur Schlesinger in 1965, disputing his claim that her late husband's persona was more Roman than Greek. Jackie cited Greek actress Melina Mercouri's view of the Greek character: "[The] conflict of man with the gods is the essence of the Greek tragedy and a key to the Greek character. . . . The Greeks are mystics. This mysticism can be traced to the influence of the sea—the boundlessness and the mystery of the sea respond to the yearning of the Greeks for a supernatural rapport with divinity. . . . The Greeks are curious and it is this curiosity that inspired a search and a thirst for knowledge." Mrs. Kennedy urged Schlesinger, "See if what [Mercouri] says does not slightly remind you of [Jack]." The marriage to Ari, which tarnished her already diminished image further, was stormy, and Mrs. Onassis spent much of its later years in New York City, separated from her husband.[60]

In 1971 she received an invitation from first lady Pat Nixon to return to the White House for the unveiling of Jackie's official portrait and that of President Kennedy. Ever vigilant of JFK's image, his widow had told artist Aaron Shikler, "I don't want him done the way everybody does him—with that puffiness under his eyes and every shadow and crease magnified." So the painter portrayed President Kennedy impressionistically, almost ethereally, in a pensive pose, the kind he struck during the Cuban missile crisis. The former first lady replied to Mrs. Nixon, "As you know, the thought of returning to the White House is difficult for me. I really do not have the courage to go through an official ceremony and bring the children back to the only home they both knew with their father under such traumatic conditions. With the press and everything, things I try to avoid in their young lives, I know the experience would be hard on them and not leave them with the memories of the White House I would like them to have." The Nixons graciously arranged a private dinner for Jackie, Caroline, and John, and the trio explored the mansion they had called home for almost three years. Jackie's thank-you note to the Nixons reflects heartfelt gratitude to them for creating a magical evening for her and her children: "Can you imagine the gift you gave us? To return to the White House privately with my little ones while they are still young enough to rediscover their childhood—with you both as guides—and with your daughters [Julie and Tricia], such extraordinary young women. What a tribute to have brought them up like that in the limelight. I pray I can do half the same with my Caroline." The former first lady seemed relieved to report to the Nixons that she was so "happy to hear the children bursting with reminiscences all the way home. Before John went to sleep, I could explain the photographs of Jack and him in his room, to him. 'There you are with Daddy right where [President Nixon] was describing the great seal; there, on the path where the president accompanied us to our car.' *Your kindness made real memories of his shadowy ones.* Thank you with all my heart. A day I always dreaded turned out to be one of the most precious I have spent with my children." The happy event marked her first and last visit to the White House after her husband's presidency.[61]

Mrs. Onassis attracted considerable media coverage for her 1975 lawsuit against celebrity photographer Ron Galella. She accused him of harassing her and her children by stalking them at close range for photos. A federal judge issued a permanent injunction against the paparazzo to maintain a distance of twenty-five feet from Jackie and thirty feet from her children. Six years later she hauled him back into court for violating the judge's order. She again won her case, and the court ordered Galella to pay Mrs. Onassis a fine of $10,000 and surrender all photographic negatives and prints of her, Caroline, and John. To avoid a jail sentence of up to six years for contempt of court, Galella vowed to cease photographing his prime subjects. He told the judge he preferred to pursue Princess Grace of Monaco and her daughter, Princess Caroline.[62]

In 1975 Aristotle Onassis died in Paris after a long illness, leaving his wife independently wealthy (once she successfully contested his will against her stepdaughter Christina) and twice widowed by the age of forty-six. Many friends say the remaining nineteen years of her life were among her happiest and most fulfilling. She achieved her fundamental goal of seeing her children grow responsibly to maturity (without many of the problems that plagued their Kennedy cousins). They both earned law degrees and embarked on their own careers. Caroline married museum exhibit designer Edwin Schlossberg in 1986 and presented her mother with three grandchildren (including a son called Jack), on whom Jackie doted. Unpredictably, the former first lady became a literary editor for Viking and then Doubleday, traveled, and contributed her name and talents to historic preservation in New York City. One of her most successful battles was to save Grand Central Station. For what she considered to be such important causes, she was willing to break her self-imposed exile from the public arena. In 1984 she appeared before the New York State Legislature to lobby against a bill that would exempt some religious institutions from landmark preservation laws, and she recorded radio announcements promoting conservation of historic sites.

By the early 1980s Jackie also began the last, and apparently most gratifying, romantic relationship of her life, with Maurice Templesman, a wealthy and sophisticated diamond merchant, who had provided her with astute financial advice over the years. Married and unable to obtain a divorce from his Orthodox Jewish wife, he became Jackie's devoted longtime companion, sharing her Fifth Avenue home and summer house on Martha's Vineyard. He was by her side, along with Caroline and John, on May 19, 1994, when she died of lymphoma at age sixty-four. The nation mourned her loss, and, in a fit of nostalgia, seemed to forgive what it had previously considered her post-Camelot transgressions. She was buried next to President Kennedy and their deceased infants at Arlington National Cemetery.

The former first lady's passing garnered banner headlines, and homage, from around the world. The *New York Times* succinctly summarized the plethora of tributes paid to her: "Since she died. . . , Mrs. Onassis has been praised by politicians, historians, and news commentators for her style, her taste, her bravery in the face of crushing tragedy, her devotion as a mother and her stubborn insistence on living by her own lights." Her brother-in-law, Senator Edward Kennedy, delivered the official eulogy, as part of the funeral mass celebrated at her childhood parish in Manhattan. He eloquently encapsulated her hold on the American imagination:

> No one else looked like her, spoke like her, wrote like her, or was so original in the way she did things. . . . And then during those four endless days in 1963, she held us together as a family and a country. In large part because of her, we could grieve and then go on. She lifted us up, and in the doubt and darkness, she gave her fellow citizens back their pride as Americans. . . . She never wanted public notice—in part, I think, because it brought back painful memories of an unbearable sorrow, endured in the glare of a million lights. In all the years since then, her genuineness and depth of character continued to shine through the privacy and reach people everywhere. . . . She made a rare and noble contribution to the American spirit. . . . She graced our history.[63]

Courage. Style. Dignity. Spirit. Grace. Important, but immeasurable, intangibles. What of Jacqueline Kennedy Onassis's substantive

Arlington Cemetery gravesite where Jacqueline Kennedy Onassis
was buried in May 1994 with President Kennedy and their
two deceased infants. (Photo by Barbara A. Perry)

contributions? While first lady, she established the infrastructure for maintaining and promoting the White House and its furnishings, spotlighted art and culture, saved Lafayette Square from destruction and encouraged historic preservation, and served as an effective goodwill ambassador for her country during a time of extreme international tensions. Her work to make the White House central to the iconography of the modern presidency has clearly survived — indeed, has been strengthened — during the image-conscious post-Kennedy era. In the television age, presidents have persistently linked themselves to this American symbol. They speak on camera from the Oval Office (especially during times of crisis), hold East Room press conferences, appear at state dinners (where C-SPAN covers the receiving line), greet guests in the Rose Garden (whose revitalization President Kennedy supervised), helicopter to and from the White House lawn, and, in the second Bush administration, stage Little League T-ball games there. Even cynical Hollywood sometimes embraces the image. The 1997 film, *The American*

President, commenced with footage of the Executive Mansion's front facade sparkling at night in floodlit splendor. Americans were appalled to learn in the wake of the September 11, 2001, terrorist attacks that their national symbol, the White House, may well have been targeted for destruction by conspirators who ultimately crashed passenger airliners into the World Trade Center, the Pentagon, and a rural Pennsylvania field.

The projects the former first lady supported as memorials to President Kennedy have been generally successful. The John F. Kennedy Center for the Performing Arts, with its three main stages and smaller theaters, hosts 3,200 performances annually, attended by two million people. Another three million visitors tour the facility each year. It awards annual honors to five performing artists, who receive their medals at the White House from the incumbent president, and then attend a gala tribute at the Kennedy Center. The performances are taped for subsequent broadcast on network television. The center also maintains an Education Resource Center, which provides displays, workshops, lectures, discussions, seminars, and classes about the performing arts for teachers and the general public. Some critics complained about the quality/variety of programming and the physical/architectural limitations of the building in the aftermath of its thirtieth anniversary. The center's president, Michael M. Kaiser, is guiding an ambitious ten-year plan to create a culture "campus" around the original edifice, with proposed plans to add two more buildings for rehearsal, administrative, and education space and to link the site to the city and its other monuments. A new Jazz Club, added to the center's offerings in 2003, was hailed as at least a small attempt to diversify its programs.[64]

The Kennedy Library and Museum serves the mission established for it by the late president's family. In the nearly quarter century since its opening, it has welcomed more than five million visitors from around the world. Each year it attracts over 2,100 researchers who use the extensive archives. JFK's personal, congressional, and presidential papers comprise over 8.4 million pages. The library also houses Robert Kennedy's papers, as well as those of more than 300 individuals associated with the Kennedy Administration or mid-twentieth-century America. The latter includes Nobel Prize–winning author Ernest Hemingway, whose manuscripts and correspondence are part of the library's collection. The archives encompass 180,000 photographs, 5,000 audio recordings, 70,000 volumes, and 8 million feet of film. In addition, the Kennedy Library supports programming for teachers, students, senior citizens, and the general public on a host of policy and history topics. C-SPAN broadcasts many of its forums. The library also recognizes with an annual award outstanding elected officials who are "profiles in courage." Stephen Ambrose, the late popular historian, observed that the common purpose of all presidential libraries (there are now twelve) is "triumphalism, not just for the president, but for the country." The Kennedy Library skillfully memorializes JFK "by wielding what Camelot itself used so adeptly: photos, film, and television." Historian and Kennedy biographer Robert Dallek admits, "The [library's] images are so powerful, so compelling—it's hard even for me to be objective."[65]

As first lady, Jacqueline Kennedy, via a memo from Tish Baldrige, asked that her colleagues preserve "all notes and memoranda you receive from [Mrs. Kennedy]—in fact any written communications from her on any matters pertaining to the White House" so that they eventually could be collected in "her files and her library at the end of the Administration." Unfortunately, her papers are still unavailable to scholars. They are simply not yet organized, according to one of the library's archivists. The Kennedy Library has a permanent exhibit devoted to Jacqueline Kennedy, and it mounted the special show on her White House years, focusing on her fashions, which appeared in Boston, New York, and Washington. The Washington exhibit alone drew over 270,000 people, and the lecture series on Mrs. Kennedy that ran simultaneously was standing room only in the 200-seat Corcoran Art Gallery auditorium.[66]

Harvard's tribute to President Kennedy, which fulfills his family's desire to narrow the gap between the academic study of government and real-world politics, offers master's degrees in public administration and public policy. Its newest degree program, the MPA in International Development, trains leaders for the world of twenty-first century globalism. The JFK School now includes ten research centers and institutes, more than twelve executive and degree programs, and an enrollment in excess of 800 students.[67]

Jacqueline Kennedy Onassis's 1994 death spared her the unbearable tragedy of her son's demise, along with his wife, Carolyn Bessette, and her sister, in a plane crash off Martha's Vineyard in 1999. John, an enthusiastic but inexperienced pilot, apparently became disoriented in a thick offshore haze and lost control of his high-performance aircraft. At the time of the fatal accident he was the founding editor of *George*, a magazine that sought to explore the intersection of politics and entertainment. It folded in 2001. Since her brother's death, Caroline Kennedy has assumed a more active public role as the family's standard-bearer and keeper of her parents' images. She has made herself available to the mass media with interviews on *Larry King Live* and in *Good Housekeeping*, and a cover story she penned for *USA Weekend* on her edited book, *Profiles in Courage for Our Time*. She also published a compendium of patriotic documents and a collection of Jacqueline Kennedy's favorite poetry. Sorting through her mother's papers and effects, Caroline was inspired to organize the special JFK Library traveling exhibit on the first lady's White House years.[68]

President Kennedy once declared, "First Ladies are not public officials. Their responsibility to their family is the same as any other woman's—efforts on behalf of charity, trips abroad, or special projects are extra. It is up to her to do what she can, within her own limitations." The context in which he spoke about the first lady's role has markedly shifted. Intervening factors, such as the women's movement, changes in how the media cover the president's wife, and the "Hillary factor," have complicated the position. Thus far, television has failed to find another first couple that so enchants it, as the Kennedys clearly did. Moreover, the goal of contemporary investigative journalism is to reveal our chief executive's feet of clay and the potential artifice of public displays of affection between presidents and their spouses. Mrs. Kennedy may well have been the last first lady to exercise some control over when and how to appear in public with her husband. Her childbearing and -rearing issues also gave her legitimate reasons (and sometimes excuses) to limit official activities. The media and the public now expect spouses of incumbents and candidates to campaign as a team, and in this era of family values, candidates are only too happy to oblige. Moreover, reality TV and America's confession-based entertainment (from *Dr. Phil* to *The Jerry Springer Show*) have obliterated the boundary between public and private spheres. Even Laura Bush, who in some manner reflects Mrs. Kennedy's more reticent public persona, speaks openly about her personal relationship with her husband. In its February 2003 edition *Good Housekeeping* queried Mrs. Bush, "Since we are coming up on Valentine's Day, I [the reporter] wanted to talk a bit about romance. I know you and the President are about to celebrate your 25th anniversary. Is he still romantic? Do you still get to do romantic things together?" She responded, "He's pretty romantic. We like to go for rides at our ranch, before dinner. . . . And it's really the only time we're alone like that, in a car. That's fun!" Although the magazine billed the interview as "an intimate conversation" with Laura Bush, the first lady hardly revealed any salacious details about her marriage. Yet Jacqueline Kennedy would never have submitted to such questioning before or after her White House tenure. "[I]n a public sea she steered a private course; . . . in the age of confession, she kept her own counsel," the *New York Times* wrote admiringly at her death.[69]

Coincidentally, Betty Friedan's *The Feminine Mystique*, challenging post–World War II assumptions about women's roles in families and society, appeared in the last year of the Kennedy administration. The 1963 book questioned the dutiful housewife/mother niche in which many women felt stifled. By the new expectations fostered during the modern women's movement, Jacqueline Kennedy's style seems quaint and outmoded. Starting with her immediate successor, Lady Bird Johnson, most first ladies have been more openly activist in advocating public policies. The repudiation of Hillary Clinton's leadership in the 1993–94 health care policy debate, however, may indicate that Americans were not ready for first ladies to play such a central part in their husbands' administrations.

Tipper Gore and Laura Bush represented an "un-Hillary" hybrid in their husbands' 2000 presidential campaigns. Playing prominent, yet largely nonpolicy, roles at the Republican and Democratic Conventions, they introduced their husbands and displayed deep affection for them (presumably in contrast to the scandal-ridden Clinton marriage). Although Jacqueline Kennedy would have balked at such public demonstrations of familial relations, she might have appreciated the updated version of creative imagery.

During her 1971 visit to the White House, Jackie told President Nixon, "I always live in a dream world." In her 1,032 days as first lady, she shared her world of fancy and imagination with the public. When her reverie ended in a nightmare, she bore the tragedy by weaving an ideal vision of her husband's presidency and her role in it. She thus fulfilled Robert Frost's 1962 prophesy of her place in history. The poet observed, "There have been some great wives in the White House—like Abigail Adams and Dolley Madison—so great that you can't think of their husbands, presidents, without thinking of *them.*"[70]

NOTES

SETTING THE STAGE

1. Richard M. Nixon, *RM: The Memoirs of Richard Nixon* (New York: Grosset and Dunlap, 1978), p. 252.

2. The wife of the foreign service officer was Audrey L. Rosselot of Bethesda, Maryland, who sat with me at a dinner for Sweet Briar College alumnae in Washington, D.C., June 2, 2003.

3. Lewis L. Gould, "First Ladies," *American Scholar* 55 (autumn 1986): 528–35, explains the celebrity status of twentieth-century first ladies, including Mrs. Kennedy. W. J. Rorabaugh, in *Kennedy and the Promise of the Sixties* (Cambridge: Cambridge University Press, 2002), chap. 1, describes JFK's use of television to create a celebrity aura around his campaign and presidency. Gould's most recent book, *The Modern American Presidency* (Lawrence: University Press of Kansas, 2003), examines the negative impact that celebrity has had on U.S. presidents.

4. William Norwich, "Her Majesty: A New Biography of Jackie O. Proves Once Again that She Will Never Be Out of Fashion," *New York Times Book Review,* December 17, 2000, p. 6 (first quotation); Daniel J. Boorstin, *The Image: A Guide to Pseudo-Events in America,* 25th anniversary edition (New York: Vintage, 1992), pp. vii–viii (second quotation); Wayne Koestenbaum, *Jackie Under My Skin: Interpreting an Icon* (New York: Farrar, Strauss, and Giroux, 1995).

5. David Halberstam, *The Fifties* (New York: Villard Books, 1993), pp. 456–86.

6. Gary Giddins, *Bing Crosby: A Pocketful of Dreams, The Early Years, 1903–1940* (Boston: Little, Brown, 2001), pp. 6–9.

7. Karen O'Connor and Larry J. Sabato, *Essentials of American Government: Continuity and Change* (New York: Longman, 2002), p. 328; for analyses of television's role in creating public personas, see Boorstin, *The Image;* and Richard Schickel, *Intimate Strangers: The Culture of Celebrity* (Garden City, NY: Doubleday, 1985).

8. Rorabaugh, *Kennedy and the Promise of the Sixties,* p. 130; "The First Lady: Her Unfair Fanfare," *Newsweek,* December 17, 1962, p. 46 (quotations); Koestenbaum, *Jackie Under My Skin,* pp. 66–82. Kennedy biographer Robert Dallek

reports that "some ultra-right-wing papers and what one historian called the 'underground market' were swamped with exposés about JFK's hidden, illicit romances. But the mainstream press resisted such scandal mongering." Dallek, *An Unfinished Life: John F. Kennedy, 1917–1963* (Boston: Little, Brown, 2003), p. 375.

9. Theodore H. White, *The Making of the President 1960* (New York: Signet, 1961); Irving Bernstein, *Promises Kept: John F. Kennedy's New Frontier* (New York: Oxford University Press, 1991), chap. 1; Rorabaugh, *Kennedy and the Promise of the Sixties*, p. 15 (quotation).

10. Kenneth Walsh, *Air Force One: A History of the Presidents and Their Planes* (New York: Hyperion, 2003), p. 60.

11. August Heckscher, "The Quality of American Culture," in *Goals for Americans: The Report of the President's Commission on National Goals* (New York: Prentice-Hall, 1960), p. 142.

12. Fletcher Knebel, "Pulitzer Prize Entry: John F. Kennedy," in *Candidates 1960: Behind the Headlines in the Presidential Race,* ed. Eric Sevareid (New York: Basic Books, 1959), n.p. (quotation).

13. Hamish Bowles, Arthur Schlesinger Jr., and Rachel Lambert Mellon, *Jacqueline Kennedy: The White House Years—Selections from the John F. Kennedy Library and Museum* (Boston: Bullfinch Press/Little Brown, 2001), p. 170 (first and second quotations).

14. Robert P. Watson, *The Presidents' Wives: Reassessing the Office of First Lady* (Boulder, CO: Lynne Rienner, 2000), table 7.1, "First Ladies' Age Profile," pp. 174–75.

15. Stephanie Coontz, *The Way We Never Were: American Families and the Nostalgia Trip* (New York: Basic Books, 1992), p. 24; Bernstein, *Promises Kept*, p. 11; William Henry Chafe, *The American Woman: Her Changing Social, Economic, and Political Roles, 1920–1970* (New York: Oxford University Press, 1972), p. 217.

16. Bernstein, *Promises Kept*, p. 14; Rorabaugh, *Kennedy and the Promise of the Sixties*, p. 131; Coontz, *The Way We Never Were*, pp. 24–25; *Newsweek*, January 1, 1962, p. 31 (quotation); Michael R. Beschloss, *The Crisis Years: Kennedy and Khrushchev, 1960–1963* (New York: Burlingame Books, 1991), p. 474.

17. Watson, *Presidents' Wives*, pp. 48–57.

18. Donnie Radcliffe, "The Generation: We Still Need Her at Any Age," *Washington Post*, May 21, 1994, p. H1; Chafe, *American Woman*, pp. 218–25.

19. Halberstam, *The Fifties*, pp. 508–20; Sara M. Evans, *Born for Liberty: A History of Women in America* (New York: Free Press, 1989), p. 246.

20. Orlando Suero and Anne Garside, *Camelot at Dawn: Jacqueline and John Kennedy in Georgetown, May 1954* (Baltimore: Johns Hopkins University Press, 2001), pp. 44–49, 56–60.

21. Halberstam, *The Fifties,* pp. 199–200 (first quotation); William Walton, Oral History, October 5, 1993, p. 211 (second quotation); Leonard Bernstein, Oral History, July 21, 1965, p. 6 (third quotation).

22. Bill Adler, ed., *The Uncommon Wisdom of Jacqueline Kennedy Onassis: A Portrait in Her Own Words* (New York: Citadel Press, 1994), pp. 34–35 (first and second quotations); Coontz, *The Way We Never Were;* Evans, *Born for Liberty;* Glenna Matthews, *"Just a Housewife": The Rise and Fall of Domesticity in America* (New York: Oxford University Press, 1987); Miriam Horn, *Rebels in White Gloves: Coming of Age with Hillary's Class—Wellesley '69* (New York: Anchor Books, 2000), p. 24 (third quotation).

23. Watson, *Presidents' Wives,* p. 56 (quotation).

24. *Newsweek,* January 1, 1962, p. 31 (first quotation); Robert Pierpoint, Oral History, November 18, 1982, pp. 22–23 (second quotation); Walter Bagehot, *The English Constitution* (New York: Appleton, 1877), n.p. (third quotation).

25. Hillary Rodham Clinton, *Living History* (New York: Simon and Schuster, 2003), pp. 466, 471 (quotation).

26. Dallek, *Unfinished Life,* p. 477.

27. Barbara Hinckley, *The Symbolic Presidency: How Presidents Portray Themselves* (New York: Routledge, 1990), p. 7 (first quotation; emphasis added); Thomas S. Langston, *With Reverence and Contempt: How Americans Think About Their President* (Baltimore: Johns Hopkins University Press, 1995), p. 1 (second quotation); for analyses of President Kennedy's image, see Thomas Brown, *JFK: History of an Image* (Bloomington: Indiana University Press, 1988); John Hellmann, *The Kennedy Obsession: The American Myth of JFK* (New York: Columbia University Press, 1997); Paul R. Henggeler, *The Kennedy Persuasion: The Politics of Style Since JFK* (Chicago: Ivan R. Dee, 1995); Vito N. Silvestri, *Becoming JFK: A Profile in Communication* (Westport, CT: Praeger, 2000); and Gary Wills, *The Kennedy Imprisonment: A Meditation on Power* (Boston: Little, Brown, 1981).

28. Richard Neustadt, *Presidential Power: The Politics of Leadership* (New York: Wiley, 1959), pp. vii–viii (first, second, and third quotations; emphasis added), p. 34 (fourth quotation; emphasis added).

29. Watson, *Presidents' Wives,* p. 179.

BECOMING JACKIE

1. Mary Van Rensselaer Thayer, *Jacqueline Bouvier Kennedy* (New York: Doubleday, 1961), p. 12 (quotation).

2. John H. Davis, *Jacqueline Bouvier: An Intimate Memoir* (New York: Wiley, 1996), p. 23; Carl Sferrazza Anthony, *As We Remember Her: Jacqueline*

Kennedy Onassis in the Words of Her Family and Friends (New York: Harper Collins, 1997), p. 27.

3. Thayer, *Jacqueline Bouvier Kennedy,* p. 37; verbatim excerpts from Jacqueline Bouvier's Prix de Paris application appear in Davis, *Jacqueline Bouvier,* pp. 142–51.

4. Caroline Kennedy, ed., *The Best-Loved Poems of Jacqueline Kennedy Onassis* (New York: Hyperion, 2001), pp. xi–xii. For examples of young Jacqueline's illustrated poems, see Thayer, *Jacqueline Bouvier Kennedy,* pp. 26, 33.

5. Anthony, *As We Remember Her,* p. 17 (first, second, and third quotations); Richard M. Nixon, *RN: The Memoirs of Richard Nixon* (New York: Grossett and Dunlap, 1978), pp. 254–55 (fourth quotation).

6. Donald Spoto, *Jacqueline Bouvier Kennedy Onassis: A Life* (New York: St. Martin's Press, 2000), pp. 27–28; Sarah Bradford, *America's Queen: The Life of Jacqueline Kennedy Onassis* (New York: Viking, 2000), pp. 3–4.

7. Jan Pottker, *Janet and Jackie: The Story of a Mother and Her Daughter, Jacqueline Kennedy Onassis* (New York: St. Martin's Press, 2001), p. 75. The book also contains the *Daily News* photograph.

8. For lengthy passages from the divorce proceedings, see John H. Davis, *The Kennedys: Dynasty and Disaster, 1848–1983* (New York: McGraw-Hill, 1984), pp. 180–86. Radziwill described her parents' divorce in an interview on CNN's *Larry King Live,* 2001.

9. Anthony, *As We Remember Her,* p. 23.

10. Anthony, *As We Remember Her,* pp. 28–29.

11. Thayer, *Jacqueline Bouvier Kennedy,* p. 61.

12. Spoto, *Jacqueline Bouvier Kennedy Onassis,* pp. 51–52; Letitia Baldrige, *A Lady, First: My Life in the Kennedy White House and the American Embassies of Paris and Rome* (New York: Viking, 2001), pp. 22–23; Baldrige made her comments on Jackie's accent in her article, "Jackie's White House Years," *Corcoran Views* (spring 2002), p. 5, Corcoran Museum of Art, and after Baldrige's lecture at Washington, D.C.'s Corcoran Museum of Art, June 6, 2002.

13. Spoto, *Jacqueline Bouvier Kennedy Onassis,* pp. 53–54.

14. Anthony, *As We Remember Her,* pp. 31–34; Spoto, *Jacqueline Bouvier Kennedy Onassis,* pp. 52–54.

15. Thayer, *Jacqueline Bouvier Kennedy,* p. 67; Spoto, *Jacqueline Bouvier Kennedy Onassis,* pp. 54–56.

16. Each quotation appears in Bradford, *America's Queen,* pp. 36–37.

17. Davis, *Jacqueline Bouvier,* pp. 108, 143 (first and second quotations); Thayer, *Jacqueline Bouvier Kennedy,* p. 74 (third quotation).

18. Davis, *Jacqueline Bouvier,* pp. 107–8, 112–39; Bradford, *America's Queen,* p. 33; Pottker, *Janet and Jackie,* p. 117.

19. Thayer, *Jacqueline Bouvier Kennedy,* pp. 76–77; Anthony, *As We Remember Her,* pp. 38–40 (quotation); Bradford, *America's Queen,* p. 43.

20. Bradford, *America's Queen,* pp. 42–43; Anthony, *As We Remember Her,* p. 41 (quotation), pp. 43–44.

21. Spoto, *Jacqueline Bouvier Kennedy Onassis,* pp. 70–71.

22. Anthony, *As We Remember Her,* pp. 48–49.

23. Spoto, *Jacqueline Bouvier Kennedy Onassis,* pp. 74–75.

24. Davis, *Jacqueline Bouvier,* pp. 142–51.

25. See Davis, *Jacqueline Bouvier,* p. 45, for a reprint of the photo that *Vogue* published of the Prix de Paris winner. Sources for the possible reasons that Jackie declined the award include, in order, Davis, *Jacqueline Bouvier,* pp. 151–52; Spoto, *Jacqueline Bouvier Kennedy Onassis,* p. 74; Pottker, *Janet and Jackie,* p. 121 (quotation); Bradford, *America's Queen,* 47–49; and Thayer, *Jacqueline Bouvier Kennedy,* p. 83.

26. Anthony, *As We Remember Her,* p. 56; Charles Bartlett, Oral History, January 6, 1965, p. 22 (quotation).

27. Spoto, *Jacqueline Bouvier Kennedy Onassis,* pp. 76–77.

28. Davis, *Jacqueline Bouvier,* pp. 151–52; Anthony, *As We Remember Her,* pp. 58–59 (quotation).

29. Thayer, *Jacqueline Bouvier Kennedy,* p. 86.

30. Bradford, *America's Queen,* p. 57 (quotation); sources for the suggested reasons that Jackie broke off her engagement with Husted include, in order, Davis, *Jacqueline Bouvier,* p. 114, and Pottker, *Janet and Jackie,* p. 123; Spoto, *Jacqueline Bouvier Kennedy Onassis,* p. 82; Anthony, *As We Remember Her,* p. 69; and Bradford, *America's Queen,* p. 58.

31. Robert Dallek, *An Unfinished Life: John F. Kennedy, 1917–1963* (Boston: Little, Brown, 2003), pp. 105, 156; see Philip B. Kunhardt Jr., ed., *Life in Camelot: The Kennedy Years* (Boston: Little, Brown, 1988), pp. 34–37, for *Life* magazine photographs of JFK on the congressional campaign trail; Thayer, *Jacqueline Bouvier Kennedy,* p. 95 (quotation from the *Saturday Evening Post*).

32. Ralph G. Martin, *A Hero for Our Time: An Intimate Story of the Kennedy Years* (New York: Macmillan, 1983), pp. 80–81; Bradford, *America's Queen,* pp. 55–56 (quotation).

33. Thayer, *Jacqueline Bouvier Kennedy,* p. 95.

34. Thayer, *Jacqueline Bouvier Kennedy,* pp. 88–89; Bill Adler, ed., *The Uncommon Wisdom of Jacqueline Kennedy Onassis: A Portrait in Her Own Words*

(New York: Citadel Press, 1994), p. 15 (first quotation); Anthony, *As We Remember Him*, p. 71 (second quotation).

35. Bouvier's "Inquiring Camera Girl" questions are quoted in Anthony, *As We Remember Her*, p. 74; Herbert S. Parmet, *Jack: The Struggles of John F. Kennedy* (New York: Dial Press, 1980), p. 260 (quotation).

36. Anthony, *As We Remember Her*, p. 76 (first quotation); Spoto, *Jacqueline Bouvier Kennedy Onassis*, p. 98 (second quotation).

37. Kunhardt, *Life in Camelot*, pp. 38–47.

38. Bradford, *America's Queen*, p. 70; Kunhardt, *Life in Camelot*, p. 51; Pottker, *Janet and Jackie*, pp. 133–36; "Special Exhibit Celebrates 50th Anniversary of the Wedding of Jacqueline Bouvier and John F. Kennedy," John F. Kennedy Library and Museum, April 23, 2003, available at: http://www.cs.umb.edu/jfklibrary/.

39. For a detailed account of Black Jack's sad experience on his daughter's wedding day, see Davis, *Kennedys*, pp. 217–22; for Janet Auchincloss's side of the story, see Pottker, *Janet and Jackie*, pp. 138–43.

40. Caroline Kennedy, *Best-Loved Poems*, pp. 172–73.

41. Orlando Suero and Anne Garside, *Camelot at Dawn: Jacqueline and John Kennedy in Georgetown, May 1954* (Baltimore: Johns Hopkins University Press, 2001), pp. 13, 24.

42. Spoto, *Jacqueline Bouvier Kennedy Onassis*, pp. 106–7; Christopher Anderson, *Jack and Jackie: Portrait of an American Marriage* (New York: Avon Books, 1996), pp. 139–40; Bradford, *America's Queen*, p. 99; Thayer, *Jacqueline Bouvier Kennedy*, p. 113 (quotations).

43. Suzanne Bauman, *Jackie: Behind the Myth* (Burbank, CA: Warner Home Video; Thirteen/WNET New York and Behind the Myth, Inc., 1999; film biography).

44. Parmet, *Jack*, p. 298; Spoto, *Jacqueline Bouvier Kennedy Onassis*, p. 106.

45. Martin, *A Hero for Our Time*, p. 103; and Anthony, *As We Remember Her*, p. 92 (quotation).

46. Anthony, *As We Remember Her*, pp. 90, 93 (first and second quotations).

47. Anderson, *Jack and Jackie*, p. 137 (first quotation); Katharine Graham, *Personal History* (New York: Vintage, 1998), p. 290 (second quotation).

48. Suero and Garside, *Camelot at Dawn*, p. 16.

49. Suero and Garside, *Camelot at Dawn*, pp. 8–11, 44–48, 56–60; Pottker, *Janet and Jackie*, p. 150.

50. Suero and Garside, *Camelot at Dawn*, pp. 37–38; Parmet, *Jack*, p. 299.

51. Suero and Garside, *Camelot at Dawn*, p. 67.

52. Geoffrey Perret, *Jack: A Life Like No Other* (New York: Random House, 2001), pp. 210–11; Dallek, *Unfinished Life*, pp. 195–97.

53. Perret, *Jack*, pp. 211–13; Spoto, *Jacqueline Bouvier Kennedy Onassis*, pp. 109–10.

54. Suero and Garside, *Camelot at Dawn*, pp. 44–45; Spoto, *Jacqueline Bouvier Kennedy Onassis*, pp. 110–12; Dallek, *Unfinished Life*, pp. 197–99; Parmet, *Jack*, 320–33; Perret, *Jack*, pp. 212–16; Doris Kearns Goodwin, *The Fitzgeralds and the Kennedys: An American Saga* (New York: St. Martin's Press, 1987), p. 898; John F. Kennedy, *Profiles in Courage* (New York: Pocket Books, 1957), p. xx (quotation).

55. Thayer, *Jacqueline Bouvier Kennedy*, p. 107 (quotation); Spoto, *Jacqueline Bouvier Kennedy Onassis*, pp. 115–17; Bradford, *America's Queen*, 103–4; Parmet, *Jack*, p. 335. In 1997 a Swedish woman, Gunilla von Post, claimed to have a spent a romantic week with JFK in a Swedish resort during the summer of 1955. Gunilla von Post with Carl Johnes, *Love, Jack* (New York: Crown Publishers, 1997), p. 103.

56. Bradford, *America's Queen*, p. 102; Anthony, *As We Remember Her*, p. 98; Pottker, *Janet and Jackie*, pp. 153–54; Anderson, *Jack and Jackie*, photo (#16) of Jackie on crutches with foot in cast; Spoto, *Jacqueline Bouvier Kennedy Onassis*, p. 118.

57. Anthony, *As We Remember Her*, p. 102; Pottker, *Janet and Jackie*, p. 155.

58. Goodwin, *The Fitzgeralds and the Kennedys*, pp. 903–7 (quotation, p. 904); Martin, *A Hero for Our Time*, 105–21; Parmet, *Jack*, 365–83; Perret, *Jack*, pp. 220–23.

59. Anthony, *As We Remember Her*, pp. 99–100; Kunhardt, *Life in Camelot*, pp. 64–65; Jacqueline Kennedy Onassis, Oral History, January 11, 1974, p. 11 (quotation).

60. Anderson, *Jack and Jackie*, pp. 171–74; Anthony, *As We Remember Her*, pp. 100–14; Bradford, *America's Queen*, pp. 107–8; Pottker, *Janet and Jackie*, pp. 155–58; Spoto, *Jacqueline Bouvier Kennedy Onassis*, pp. 21–25.

61. Spoto, *Jacqueline Bouvier Kennedy Onassis*, pp. 125–27; Anthony, *As We Remember Her*, p. 107.

62. Janet Lee Bouvier Auchincloss, Oral History, September 5, 1964, p. 9 (first quotation); Goodwin, *The Fitzgeralds and the Kennedys*, pp. 915–16 (second quotation).

63. Pottker, *Janet and Jackie*, pp. 163–65; Thayer, *Jacqueline Bouvier Kennedy*, p. 116; Auchincloss, Oral History, p. 12 (quotation); Kunhardt, *Life in Camelot*, pp. 76–83.

64. "Kennedy Team Hard to Beat: Jackie Aids Senate Fight," Boston *Evening American,* October 8, 1958, p. 4 (first and third quotations); Anthony, *As We Remember Her,* pp. 109–10 (second and fourth quotations).

65. Bauman, *Jackie,* 1960 interview with Mrs. Kennedy on video. Anthony, *As We Remember Her,* pp. 110–11 (first quotation); Bauman, *Jackie,* interview with John Kenneth Galbraith on video.

BEING FIRST LADY

1. Joe McCarthy, "His Religion May Elect Him," *Look,* November 10, 1959, pp. 102–4.

2. Papers of President Kennedy, Pre-Presidential Papers, 1960 Campaign, West Virginia, Box 969, Trips October 10, 1959–January 1, 1960, John F. Kennedy Library (JFKL).

3. Relman Morin, "Kennedy in New Hampshire Stresses Value of Primaries," *Washington Post,* January 26, 1960, p. A2.

4. Papers of President Kennedy, Pre-Presidential Papers, 1960 Campaign, Wisconsin, Box 975, Wisconsin Trips, November 12, 1959–June 11, 1960, JFKL; Kenneth P. O'Donnell and David F. Powers with Joe McCarthy, *"Johnny, We Hardly Knew Ye": Memories of John Fitzgerald Kennedy* (New York: Pocket Books, 1973), pp. 178–79 (quotation).

5. John Kenneth Galbraith, *Name-Dropping: From FDR On* (Boston: Houghton Mifflin, 1999), p. 127 (quotation).

6. Robert Drew, *Primary,* Drew Associates (producers), 1960.

7. Drew, *Primary* (quotation); O'Donnell and Powers, *Johnny, We Hardly Knew Ye,* p. 183.

8. Robert Dallek, *An Unfinished Life: John F. Kennedy, 1917–1963* (Boston: Little, Brown, 2003), p. 253 (quotation); O'Donnell and Powers, *Johnny, We Hardly Knew Ye,* pp. 188–89; Papers of John F. Kennedy, Presidential Papers, Papers of Pierre E. G. Salinger, Press Releases, White House press release, May 20, 1961, announcing arrival of "major order of glassware from the Morgantown Glassware Guild, Inc., of West Virginia. . . . Mrs. Kennedy who ordered the glassware out of gratitude and affection for West Virginia, knew of the Guild's work because of her visits to the State during last Spring's primary campaign."

9. Doris Kearns Goodwin, *The Fitzgeralds and the Kennedys: An American Saga* (New York: St. Martin's Press, 1987), pp. 922–23; John H. Davis, *The Kennedys: Dynasty and Disaster 1848–1983* (New York: McGraw-Hill, 1984), p. 236; Benjamin C. Bradlee, *Conversations with Kennedy* (New York: Norton, 1975), p. 28.

10. Stephen J. Wayne, *The Road to the White House 2004: The Politics of Presidential Elections* (Belmont, CA: Thomson/Wadsworth, 2004), p. 12. For the most detailed account of Kennedy's primary election campaign strategy, see Theodore C. Sorensen, *Kennedy* (New York: Harper and Row, 1965), chap. 5.

11. Nancy E. McGlen et al., *Women, Politics, and American Society*, 3rd ed. (New York: Longman, 2002), pp. 156–63; Betty Boyd Caroli, *First Ladies*, expanded edition (New York: Oxford University Press, 1995), p. 221; Carl Sferrazza Anthony, *First Ladies: The Saga of the Presidents' Wives and Their Power 1789–1961* (New York: Quill/William Morrow, 1990), p. 591; and "Complete 1960 Convention Guide," *Look*, July 19, 1960, p. 62 (quotation).

12. Suzanne Bauman, *Jackie: Behind the Myth* (Burbank, CA: Warner Home Video; Thirteen/WNET New York and Behind the Myth, Inc., 1999; film biography; first and second quotations); Letitia Baldrige, *A Lady, First: My Life in the Kennedy White House and the American Embassies of Paris and Rome* (New York: Viking, 2001), p. 164 (third quotation).

13. Sorensen, *Kennedy*, p. 178 (first and second quotations); Jacqueline Kennedy, "Campaign Wife," September 16, 1960 (third quotation). I am grateful to the staff of the JFKL for providing me with copies of the "Campaign Wife" columns from their files.

14. Hamish Bowles, Arthur Schlesinger Jr., and Rachel Lambert Mellon, *Jacqueline Kennedy: The White House Years—Selections from the John F. Kennedy Library and Museum* (Boston: Bullfinch Press/Little, Brown, 2001), p. 27 (quotations).

15. Collections of the Manuscript Division, Library of Congress, Anna Roosevelt to Arthur M. Schlesinger Jr., n.d. (quotation); Collections of the Manuscript Division, Library of Congress, Papers of Bess Furman Armstrong, letter from Armstrong to Jacqueline Bouvier, November 18, 1952; letter from Bouvier to Armstrong, November 24, 1952.

16. Bess Furman, "Mrs. Kennedy Will Address Italian Voters," *New York Times*, September 20, 1960, n.p.

17. Carl Sferrazza Anthony, *As We Remember Her: Jacqueline Kennedy Onassis in the Words of Her Friends and Family* (New York: Harper Collins, 1997), p. 118 (quotation).

18. "Campaign Wife," September 16, 1960 (quotations).

19. "Campaign Wife," September 29, 1960 (quotation).

20. "Campaign Wife," October 13, 1960 (first quotation); Marie Smith, "Conversation Goes 13-Ways," *Washington Post*, October 18, 1960 (second quotation); "Campaign Wife," November 1, 1960 (third and fourth quotations).

21. "Campaign Wife," October 13, 1960; Maxine Cheshire, "Jackie Has News for Jack—About Women," *Washington Post,* October 12, 1960, p. C2; "Campaign Wife," October 27, 1960 (quotation).

22. "Campaign Wife," October 27, 1960 (quotation); "Million Cheer Kennedy in N.Y." *Washington Post,* October 20, 1960, p. A22.

23. Mary Van Rensselaer Thayer, "Jackie Drops No Cliches, Lifts No Eyebrows," *Washington Post,* October 25, 1960, p. B7 (quotations).

24. "Campaign Wife," November 1, 1960 (quotation).

25. Theodore H. White, *The Making of the President 1960* (New York: Signet, 1961), p. 390 (first quotation); Maud Shaw, *White House Nannie: My Years with Caroline and John Kennedy, Jr.* (New York: New American Library, 1966), pp. 70–71 (second quotation); Sarah Bradford, *America's Queen: The Life of Jacqueline Kennedy Onassis* (New York: Viking, 2000), p. 140 (third quotation).

26. Donald Spoto, *Jacqueline Bouvier Kennedy Onassis: A Life* (New York: St. Martin's Press, 2000), pp. 147–49; Baldrige, *A Lady, First* (quotation), p. 168.

27. Oleg Cassini, *A Thousand Days of Magic: Dressing Jacqueline Kennedy for the White House* (New York: Rizzoli, 1995), pp. 15–30 (quotations).

28. Mary Van Rensselaer Thayer, *Jacqueline Kennedy: The White House Years* (Boston: Little, Brown, 1967), p. 23 (quotation).

29. Bowles, Schlesinger, and Mellon, *Jacqueline Kennedy,* pp. 56–59 (quotation); Cassini, *Thousand Days,* pp. 36–38.

30. Cassini, *Thousand Days,* p. 38 (first quotation); Thayer, *Jacqueline Kennedy,* p. 75 (second quotation).

31. Bowles, Schlesinger, and Mellon, *Jacqueline Kennedy,* pp. 64–67; Thayer, *Jacqueline Kennedy,* pp. 26–27.

32. Various photographs from (Louisville) *Courier-Journal,* January 20–21, 1961, on file with author, originally collected by her grandmother, Alberta Perry; Marie Smith, "Proud, Poised First Lady Sees Husband Take Oath," *Washington Post,* January 21, 1961, p. B9 (first quotation); "First Lady Sets the Fashion," *Washington Post,* January 21, 1961, p. B9 (second quotation); Mary Van Rensselaer Thayer, "New First Ladies First Years," *Washington Post,* January 20, 1961, p. B12; Thayer, "A New Chapter Begins for Jacqueline Kennedy," *Washington Post,* January 21, 1961, p. B10; *Ladies' Home Journal* ad, *Washington Post,* January 20, 1961, p. A9; Hecht's ad, *Washington Post,* January 20, 1961, p. A22 (third quotation); "Fit for the First Lady," *Newsweek,* January 30, 1961, p. 60 (fourth quotation).

33. Shaw, *White House Nannie;* Bradlee, *Conversations with Kennedy.*

34. Paul B. Fay Jr., *The Pleasure of His Company* (New York: Popular Library, 1966); Bauman, *Jackie* (quotation).

35. J. B. West with Mary Lynn Kotz, *Upstairs at the White House: My Life with the First Ladies* (New York: Coward, McCann and Geoghegan, 1973), pp. 202–3.

36. "The Presidency," *Time*, April 21, 1961, p. 16 (quotation); Carl Sferrazza Anthony, *The Kennedy White House: Family Life and Pictures, 1961–1963* (New York: Simon and Schuster, 2001), pp. 175–79; memo to Alice Grimes from JBK, April 11, 1963, Social Files, 947—Nursery School, Car Pool.

37. Letter from Ada C. Rose to JBK, September 14, 1961, Social Files, White House Nursery School, Integration (first and second quotations); letter from Letitia Baldrige to Wellborn Jack, July 27, 1961, Social Files, White House Nursery School, Integration (third quotation); letter from Letitia Baldrige to Emmett L. Irwin, September 20, 1961, Social Files, White House Nursery School, Integration (fourth quotation); "The White House School," press release, September 19, 1962, Papers of John F. Kennedy, Papers of Pierre E. G. Salinger, JFKL; letter from Nancy Tuckerman to Sallie M. Davis, June 28, 1963, White House Nursery School (fifth quotation).

38. Bauman, *Jackie* (quotation).

39. Letter from Stanley Tretick to JFK, June 26, 1962, displayed in the exhibit Stanley Tretick: The Kennedy Years, at the Corcoran Gallery, Washington, D.C., July 1–October 7, 2002 (first quotation); Tretick, Oral History, September 15, 1964, pp. 46–47 (second quotation).

40. Linda Hales, "Historical Value: White House Keepsakes Go Under the Gavel," *Washington Post*, November 16, 2002, p. C1.

41. Helen Thomas, "First Lady Says Family Life Is Overpublicized," *Washington Post*, January 21, 1963, n.p. (quotation).

42. Mrs. Kennedy's handwritten response to Helen Thomas's typed questions to her, n.d., displayed in the exhibit Jacqueline Kennedy: The White House Years, selections from the John F. Kennedy Library and Museum, at the Corcoran Museum, Washington, D.C., April 6–September 30, 2002 (quotation); David McCullough, *Truman* (New York: Simon and Schuster, 1992).

43. "Virginia: Notes from Glen Ora," *Time*, March 24, 1961, p. 17; Baldrige, *A Lady, First*, p. 183 (quotation); Lewis L. Gould, *Lady Bird Johnson: Our Environmental First Lady* (Lawrence: University Press of Kansas, 1999), pp. 19–20; James N. Giglio, *The Presidency of John F. Kennedy* (Lawrence: University Press of Kansas, 1991), p. 271; Rudy Abramson, "Presidential Poignancy: Jackie Kennedy Letter in LBJ Exhibit Reflects Warm Relationship," *Houston Chronicle*, May 29, 1982, n.p. (quotation).

44. Delores Phillips and Lewis H. Lapham, "The Favored Sport of Jacqueline," *Saturday Evening Post*, February 23, 1963, p. 28.

45. JBK's responses to Thomas's questions (first quotation); Thomas, "First Lady Says Family Life Is Overpublicized," n.p.; Furman, "Mrs. Kennedy Will Address Italian Voters," (second quotation).

46. Michael R. Beschloss, *The Crisis Years: Kennedy and Khrushchev, 1960–1963* (New York: Burlingame Books, 1991), p. 474.

47. Lloyd Grove, "Keeping Mum on 'JFK's Monica,'" *Washington Post,* May 15, 2003, p. C3; Grove, "This Just In. . . ," *Washington Post,* May 16, 2003, p. C3. Barbara Leaming, *Mrs. Kennedy: The Missing History of the Kennedy Years* (New York: Free Press, 2001); Giglio, *Presidency,* pp. 267–70.

48. Thomas, "First Lady Says Family Life Is Overpublicized," n.p.

49. "Mrs. Kennedy's Engagements and Official White House Social Schedule—1961, 1962," press releases, Papers of John F. Kennedy, Presidential Papers, Papers of Pierre E. G. Salinger, "Press Releases JFK/Final Copies, Social Functions," JFKL; Carroll Kilpatrick, "Kennedys Expect Their Third Child in August," *Washington Post,* April 16, 1963, p. A1; Cheshire, "Date in August Clears Calendar," *Washington Post,* April 16, 1963, p. B7.

50. Baldrige, "The Political and Social Uses of the Rose Garden," lecture sponsored by the White House Historical Society, November 12, 2002, Ronald Reagan Building, Washington, D.C., broadcast on C-SPAN, November 28, 2002 (first quotation); Baldrige, *A Lady, First,* pp. 172, 180; Baldrige, Oral History, April 24, 1964, pp. 44–45, JFKL.

51. Baldrige, *A Lady, First,* pp. 168–74; Peter Lisagor, "First Lady to the First Lady," *McCall's,* June 1961, p. 96; Papers of John F. Kennedy, Presidential Papers, White House Staff Files, Papers of Sanford Fox, "Scope and Content Note," JFKL.

52. Memo from JBK to Turnure, as printed in full by Thayer, *Jacqueline Kennedy,* pp. 33–34. Turnure reportedly was one of JFK's many paramours: Bradford, *America's Queen,* pp. 154–55.

53. "The Presidency," *Time,* April 21, 1961, pp. 16–17.

54. Maxine Cheshire, with John Greenya, *Maxine Cheshire, Reporter* (Boston: Houghton Mifflin, 1978), pp. 54, 59 (quotation).

55. Robert Pierpoint, Oral History, November 18, 1982, p. 23.

56. Baldrige, "Demystifying Jacqueline Kennedy," lecture sponsored by the Corcoran Gallery, June 6, 2002, Washington, D.C. (quotations); Ann Gerhart and Roxanne Roberts, "A Night for Polish Pride: State Dinner Honors 'Steadfast' Ally," *Washington Post,* July 18, 2002, pp. C1, 4.

57. Baldrige, *A Lady, First,* p. 186; Baldrige, Oral History, p. 49 (first quotation); Marion Cannon Schlesinger, Oral History, July 25, 1980, pp. 10, 12.

58. "How Jackie Restyled the White House," *Saturday Evening Post,* October 26, 1963, p. 50 (first quotation); Laura Berquist, "Jacqueline Kennedy: What You Don't Know About Our First Lady," *Look,* July 4, 1961, p. 64 (second quotation); "Frontier Fun," *Newsweek,* August 7, 1961, p. 72 (third quotation); Cheshire, *Maxine Cheshire,* p. 40 (fourth quotation).

59. Hamish Bowles, "Jacqueline Kennedy: Defining Style as a First Lady—An Evening with Hamish Bowles," lecture sponsored by the Corcoran Gallery, July 18, 2002 (first quotation); Bernadine Morriss, "What in your view was Jacqueline Kennedy's most important fashion legacy during her White House years?" interview, Fashion Group International, April 24, 2002, available at: http://www.fgi.org (second quotation); Bowles, Schlesinger, and Mellon, *Jacqueline Kennedy,* p. 103 (third quotation).

60. Cassini, *Thousand Days,* pp. 78–79 (first quotation); Thayer, *Jacqueline Kennedy,* pp. 201–8 (second quotation).

61. Bowles, Schlesinger, and Mellon, *Jacqueline Kennedy,* p. 94 (quotations [original emphasis] and photograph).

62. Marie Smith, "Ottawa Welcome Is French-Accented Opener of Visit," *Washington Post,* May 17, 1961, p. D1 (first quotation); "Canadian Public Cheers Mrs. Kennedy," *Washington Post,* May 18, 1961, p. D1 (second and third quotations); Bowles, Schlesinger, and Mellon, *Jacqueline Kennedy,* pp. 116–17 (fourth quotation); although Oleg Cassini was Mrs. Kennedy's official designer for her White House years, she wore clothing that she had purchased previously from other couturiers. She first appeared in the Cardin suit, for example, on a 1957 television program that chronicled "a day in the life of a U.S. Senator's wife." Yet Pierre Salinger labeled as "rot" *Women's Wear Daily* reports that the first lady was receiving *new* fashions from Paris designers: "Pierre Labels Report 'Rot,'" *Washington Post,* May 19, 1961, p. C1; *Life,* The Kennedys in Canada, May 26, 1961, cover; Chalmers M. Roberts, "Word Is Expected on Kennedy-K Talks," *Washington Post,* May 19, 1961, p. A2 (fifth quotation).

63. "*La Présidente,*" *Time,* June 9, 1961, p. 13 (first and second quotations); Bowles, Schlesinger, and Mellon, *Jacqueline Kennedy,* p. 121 (third quotation); Cassini, *Thousand Days,* pp. 68–74; Gwen Gibson, "'Jacqui' Enchants Parisians,'" *Washington Post,* June 1, 1961, p. C18; Thayer, "Elegance Reigns in Elysee Palace," *Washington Post,* June 1, 1961, p. C18; Thayer, "'La Presidente Jacqui' Sees Ballets in Louis XV Theater," *Washington Post,* June 2, 1962, p. C1.

64. Richard Reeves, *President Kennedy: Profile of Power* (New York: Simon and Schuster, 1993), pp. 159–71; Cassini, *Thousand Days,* p. 75 (first quotation); Eddy Gilmore, "Jacqueline Charms All Vienna—Especially K.; Nina Cheered

for Accepting Plea to Husband," *Washington Post,* June 4, 1961, p. A8 (second quotation); Galbraith, *Name-Dropping,* pp. 129–30 (third quotation); Perry interview with Tish Baldrige, May 17, 2002.

65. Schlesinger, recorded comment for oral tour of Jacqueline Kennedy: The White House Years, Selections from the John F. Kennedy Library and Museum, at the Corcoran Gallery, Washington, D.C., April 6, 2002–September 30, 2002 (first quotation); "First Lady Wows 'Em in Spanish," *Washington Post,* December 17, 1961, p. F21 (second and third quotations).

66. "U.S. First Lady in Audience with Pope," *Washington Post,* March 12, 1962, p. A1; "Nehru, Daughter Greet Mrs. JFK," *Washington Post,* March 12, 1962, p. B4; Philip Warden, "Mrs. Kennedy to Star in $45,000 Movies," *Washington Post,* March 21, 1962, p. C3; John Kenneth Galbraith, *Name-Dropping: From FDR On* (Boston: Houghton Mifflin, 1999), p. 129 (quotation).

67. Cable from JFK to JBK, March 16, 1962, Papers of John F. Kennedy, Executive File, "Jacqueline Kennedy," JFKL (quotation).

68. Joan Braden, "An Exclusive Chat with Jackie Kennedy," *Saturday Evening Post,* May 12, 1962, p. 85 (first quotation); Sue Cronk, "First Lady Wings In," *Washington Post,* March 30, 1962, p. C1 (second quotation).

69. "Strings Serenaded Dining First Lady," *Washington Post,* August 14, 1962, p. B2; "It's Madness, Paper Tells First Lady," *Washington Post,* August 27, 1965, p. B5 (first quotation); "Italians Pay 32c to See Kennedys," *Washington Post,* August 22, 1962, n.p.; Daniel Williams, "Fiat's Giovanni Agnelli, the Italian Prince," *Washington Post,* January 25, 2003, p. C1; Bradford, *America's Queen,* p. 231 (second quotation); "Minister Criticizes Swim Suits," *Washington* Post, August 26, 1962, n.p. (third quotation); "John Junior Takes a Plunge," *Washington Post,* August 27, 1962, p. B5.

70. Anthony, *Kennedy White House,* p. 192; Spoto, *Jacqueline Bouvier Kennedy Onassis,* pp. 192–93; Beschloss, *Crisis Years,* p. 476.

RESTORING THE WHITE HOUSE

1. James A. Abbott and Elaine M. Rice's *Designing Camelot: The Kennedy White House Restoration* (New York: Van Nostrand Reinhold, 1998) is the definitive work on Mrs. Kennedy's project. See their chap. 6 description of the Red Room's redecoration, and p. 86 for the photograph described above.

2. Letitia Baldrige, *A Lady, First: My Life in the Kennedy White House and the American Embassies of Paris and Rome* (New York: Viking, 2001), p. 166 (first quotation); Mrs. Kennedy's quotation originated in her handwritten responses to Associated Press reporter Frances Levine's questions to her in a letter of

March 8, 1963, displayed in the exhibit Jacqueline Kennedy: The White House Years, Selections from the John F. Kennedy Library and Museum, at the Corcoran Gallery, Washington, D.C., April 6, 2002–September 30, 2002.

3. Betty Monkman, *The White House: Its Historic Furnishings and First Families* (Washington, DC: White House Historical Association, and New York: Abbeville Press, 2000), p. 13; Alan Fern, "Visual Documents: Symbolic and Real Images of the White House," *White House History* 9 (spring 2001): 17; Robert V. Remini, "Becoming a National Symbol: The White House in the Early Nineteenth Century," in Frank Freidel and William Pencak, eds., *The White House: The First Two Hundred Years* (Boston: Northeastern University Press, 1994), pp. 26, 28 (first and second quotations); William Seale, *The White House: The History of an American Idea* (Washington, DC: The White House Historical Association, 2001), p. ix (third quotation).

4. Richard Norton Smith, "America's Home: The Bully Pulpit on Pennsylvania Avenue," in Freidel and Pencak, *White House*, p. 33; Seale, *White House*, p. 201 (quotation); Edwin M. Yoder Jr., "Using the White House to Further Political Agendas," in Freidel and Pencak, *White House*, pp. 156, 158. See also Daniel J. Boorstin, "Roles of the President's House," in Freidel and Pencak, *White House*, pp. 3–15, for the role that public architecture plays in American democracy.

5. From JBK's responses to Lewine's questions.

6. From JBK's responses to Lewine's questions.

7. Seale, *White House*, p. x.

8. Holly Cowan Shulman, "Dolley Payne Todd Madison," in *American First Ladies: Their Lives and Their Legacy*, ed. Lewis L. Gould, 2nd ed. (New York: Routledge, 2001), p. 27.

9. Monkman, *White House*, pp. 53, 93 (quotation).

10. Jean H. Baker, "Mary Ann Todd Lincoln," in Gould, *American First Ladies*, pp. 117–18; Monkman, *White House*, p. 123; David Herbert Donald, "'This Damned Old House': The Lincolns in the White House," in Freidel and Pencak, *White House*, pp. 61–63.

11. John Y. Simon, "Julia Dent Grant," in Gould, *American First Ladies*, pp. 137–38; Monkman, *White House*, pp. 135, 147, 292; Seale, *White House*, pp. 122–24.

12. Seale, *White House*, pp. 129, 135–36; Monkman, *White House*, pp. 164, 294.

13. Charles W. Calhoun, "Caroline Lavinia Scott Harrison," in Gould, *American First Ladies*, pp. 177–79; Monkman, *White House*, pp. 14, 172.

14. Stacy A. Cordery, "Edith Kermit Carow Roosevelt," in Gould, *American First Ladies*, p. 205 (quotation); Seale, *White House*, p. 167.

15. Lewis L. Gould, "First Ladies," *American Scholar* 55 (autumn 1986): 530; Monkman, *White House,* pp. 204–8; Seale, *White House,* p. 212.

16. Monkman, *White House,* pp. 208–10.

17. Monkman, *White House,* pp. 214; Seale, *White House,* 223, 230.

18. Monkman, *White House,* pp. 220–22; Seale, *White House,* pp. 240–81, 279 (quotation).

19. From JBK's responses to Lewine's questions.

20. "Jacqueline Kennedy," *Time,* January 20, 1961, p. 26.

21. JBK's letter to Henry Du Pont, September 20, 1963, displayed in the exhibit Jacqueline Kennedy: The White House Years; Hugh Sidey, "The First Lady Brings History and Beauty to the White House," *Life,* September 1, 1961, p. 62 (quotation, emphasis added).

22. Monkman, recorded comment for oral tour of Jacqueline Kennedy: The White House Years exhibit.

23. Schlesinger, recorded comment for oral tour of Jacqueline Kennedy: The White House Years exhibit.

24. Binder of White House photographs, annotated by JBK, in Jacqueline Kennedy: The White House Years exhibit (quotation); J. B. West, *Upstairs at the White House: My Life with the First Ladies* (New York: Coward, McCann and Geoghegan, 1973), p. 200.

25. From JBK's responses to Lewine's questions.

26. Press release, Office of the White House Press Secretary, February 23, 1961, Papers of President Kennedy, National Security Files, Departments and Agencies, Box 290A, "White House Renovation," John F. Kennedy Library (JFKL; first and second quotations).

27. Press release, February 23, 1961; "Authentic Furniture of 1802 Era Will Be Restored to White House: First Lady Announces Plans," *Washington Post,* p. A1.

28. Abbott and Rice, *Designing Camelot,* p. 22; "The First Lady and the White House," *Newsweek,* September 17, 1962, p. 71 (quotations).

29. Letter from JBK to Adlai Stevenson, n.d. (all but last quotation); letter from Stevenson to JBK, August 7, 1961 (last quotation), both contained in the Adlai Stevenson Collection, Box 47, Folder 2 "Jacqueline Kennedy," Seeley G. Mudd Manuscript Library, Princeton University.

30. Katzenbach to JBK, Papers of Arthur M. Schlesinger Jr., White House Files, Box W-H 24, "White House Museum," JFKL.

31. Maxine Cheshire, with John Greenya, *Maxine Cheshire, Reporter* (Boston: Houghton Mifflin, 1978), p. 45 (quotations).

32. Abbott and Rice, *Designing Camelot*, pp. 23–24; Henry du Pont to the Commission of Fine Arts, Fine Arts Committee for the White House, Advisors to the Fine Arts Committee for the White House, May 3, 1961, cover memo for Julian Boyd and Lyman Butterfield's "The White House as a Symbol," April 24, 1961, Papers of President Kennedy, National Security Files, Departments and Agencies, Box 290A, "White House Restoration," JFKL (first and second quotations; original emphasis).

33. Abbott and Rice's *Designing Camelot* superbly captures the "palace intrigues" resulting from the three primary decorators' attempts to govern Mrs. Kennedy's restoration decisions. *Washington Post* correspondent Maxine Cheshire caught wind of the desk scandal and reported on it and other questionable elements of the restoration in a series of articles in late summer 1962. See Abbott and Rice, *Designing Camelot*, p. 37. White House Curator William Elder had to explain the facts of the desk case to a displeased President Kennedy. (JFK's typed questions to Elder and the latter's responses are in White House Central Subject File, WH3, "Buildings and Grounds," Box 1005, JFKL.) Congressman Steven B. Derounian (R.-N.Y.) tried to make political hay out of the wallpaper caper by entering newspaper stories on the embarrassing episode into the *Congressional Record*, October 17, 1961, p. A8414. Cheshire's article on the wallpaper, and other White House decorating controversies, is "The Green Room Carpet Magically Comes and Goes," *Washington Post*, September 12, 1962, p. C1. Even so, Cheshire could not accuse the first lady of being profligate spender of *public* funds. Quite oppositely, Cheshire wrote, "[W]ith antiques dealers . . . Mrs. Kennedy has gotten the reputation for being 'a terrible tightwad' with taxpayers' money. 'She never asks how much something will cost if it is for her self,' says one Washington dealer. 'She trusts us, she has done business with us for years. She knows we will be fair. But if it is for the White House, she says in a sad little voice, "It won't be too much, will it, we don't have very much money"'" (p. C1). "The First Lady and the White House," *Newsweek*, September 17, 1962, p. 77 (quotation).

34. Letter from JBK to du Pont, September 20, 1963, displayed in the Jacqueline Kennedy: The White House Years exhibit (all quotations).

35. JBK quoted in Abbott and Rice, *Designing Camelot*, p. 101 (first quotation); Seale, *White House*, p. 299 (second quotation). See John Hellmann's *The Kennedy Obsession: The American Myth of JFK* (New York: Columbia, 1997), pp. 116–23, for a jargony, but fascinating, literary deconstruction of the New Frontier metaphor.

36. Letter from JBK to du Pont (all quotations).

37. From JBK's responses to Lewine's questions (quotation); Nash Castro, "The Association's Twentieth Year," *White House History* 1 (1983): 24–25.

38. Schlesinger, White House Files, Box W-H 24, Schlesinger to J. B. West, June 19, 1961 (JFKL); Castro, "Association's Twentieth Year," 24; Public Law 87-286, *United States Statutes at Large* 75 (September 22, 1961): 586 (quotation).

39. Public Law 87-286 (first quotation); from JBK's responses to Lewine's questions (second quotation).

40. "How Jackie Restyled the White House," *Saturday Evening Post,* October 26, 1963, p. 43; "The First Lady and the White House," *Newsweek,* September 17, 1962, p. 71 (quotation), 78; Frank Rose, *The Agency: William Morris and the Hidden History of Show Business* (New York: Harper Collins, 1995), p. 237.

41. Castro, "Association's Twentieth Year," 26; JBK's responses to Lewine's questions; Papers of John F. Kennedy, Presidential Papers of Pierre E. G. Salinger, press releases, November 3, 1962, JFKL (first and second quotations).

42. Castro, "Association's Twentieth Year," 24 (first quotation, emphasis added; second quotation); from Mrs. Kennedy's responses to Lewine's questions (third quotation).

43. Castro, "Association's Twentieth Year," 26 (quotation).

44. Schlesinger, Writings, Box W-7, Jacqueline B. Kennedy Correspondence—1962, JBK to Schlesinger, February 14, 1962, JFKL (quotations, original emphasis).

45. JBK to Schlesinger, February 14, 1962.

46. Schlesinger, Writings, Box W-7, Jacqueline B. Kennedy Correspondence-1962, JBK's handwritten edits on Pearce to JBK memo, March 5, 1962, JFKL (first quotation); JBK to Schlesinger, no date, JFKL (second and third quotations).

47. As quoted in Mary Van Rensselaer Thayer, *Jacqueline Kennedy: The White House Years* (Boston: Little, Brown, 1967), p. 297.

48. From JBK's responses to Lewine's questions (quotation).

49. White House Central Subject Files, WH3, McNally to JFK, September 6, 1961, and November 7, 1961, JFKL; JBK's responses to Lewine's questions (quotation).

50. Marie Smith, "JFK Praises a White House Editor: Her Name Is Jacqueline Kennedy," *Washington Post,* June 29, 1962, pp. D1, 4 (first quotation); Maxine Cheshire, "'One-Woman REA Electrifies America,'" *Washington Post,* June 29, 1962, pp. D1, 4 (second quotation).

51. Thayer, *Jacqueline Kennedy,* pp. 296–301.

52. Thayer, *Jacqueline Kennedy,* pp. 300–301; West, *Upstairs at the White House,* p. 223 (quotation).

53. Thayer, *Jacqueline Kennedy*, p. 300.

54. Schlesinger, Writings, Box W-7, Jacqueline B. Kennedy Correspondence-1962, Robert L. Breeden of National Geographic to West, February 12, 1962; West to JBK, February 13, 1962; JBK to Schlesinger, February 14, 1962, JFKL.

55. Schlesinger, Writings, Box W-7, Jacqueline B. Kennedy Correspondence—1962, JBK to Schlesinger, no date, JFKL (first, second, and third quotations); Schlesinger, Private Papers, Box P-6, Jacqueline Kennedy Correspondence, Schlesinger to JBK, July 17, 1962, JFKL (fourth quotation).

56. "White House Historical Association: By Mail," (Washington: White House Historical Association, 2001), p. 8; "About the White House Historical Association" insert (quotation).

57. From JBK's response to Lewine's questions (first quotation); "Toward the Ideal," *Time*, September 6, 1963, p. 60 (second quotation).

58. Abbott and Rice, *Designing Camelot*, pp. 27–28; White House Central Subject File, WH2, Box PP5, Jacqueline B. Kennedy, Baldrige to JBK, n.d., JFKL (quotation); Frances Lewine, Associated Press, "First Lady Picks Curator: To Keep Tabs on Treasures," *Washington Post*, March 30, 1961, n.p.; Monkman, *White House*, p. 236.

59. Abbot and Rice, *Designing Camelot*, pp. 35–41; Papers of President Kennedy, National Security Files, Departments and Agencies, Box 290A, White House Renovation, Pearce to JFK, November 14, 1961, JFKL (first quotation); West, *Upstairs at the White House*, pp. 250–51; Papers of John F. Kennedy, Presidential Papers, Papers of Pierre E. G. Salinger, Press Releases, August 2, 1962, JFKL (second quotation).

60. Pierre E. G. Salinger, *With Kennedy* (Garden City, NY: Doubleday, 1966), p. 379; White House Central Subject Files, WH3, Baldrige to Kenneth O'Donnell, July 25, 1961; Pearce to Salinger, July 25, 1961; Salinger to Pearce, July 26, 1961, JFKL (quotation).

61. "White House Has Antiques Windfall," *Washington Post*, July 4, 1961, n.p. The article contained a complete list of antiques donated or loaned to the White House, as well as those discovered in White House storage. Mrs. Kennedy was quoted as saying that "[w]here non-American furnishings have been acquired, it is because they have connection with American history, or are similar to furnishings used by Presidents in the past." Undoubtedly, she felt compelled to clarify the record in light of U.S. law that required furniture purchased for use in the White House "be, as far as practicable, of domestic manufacture." Title 3 United States Code, Sec. 110, cited in a memo from Henry du Pont (Papers of President John F. Kennedy, National Security Files, Departments and

Agencies, Box 290A, White House Renovation, May 18, 1961, JFKL); Marie Smith, "Red Room Reigns in Empire: Rules White House in Decor," *Washington Post,* January 18, 1962, n.p. (quotation).

62. Smith, "New Blue Room Goes on View: Green Room, Too," *Washington Post,* January 22, 1963, p. B5 (first quotation); White House Central Subject File, WH3, Box 1005, memo for Salinger (no author listed), September 7, 1962, JFKL (second quotation).

63. Dorothy McCardle, "Dinner Guests View New Rooms," *Washington Post,* January 22, 1963, p. B5 (first quotation); Monkman, *White House,* p. 249.

64. "How Jackie Restyled the White House," *Saturday Evening Post,* October 26, 1963, pp. 42–57; Sidey, *Life,* pp. 54–65, 22–29; Laura Berquist, "Life on the New Frontier," *Look,* January 2, 1962, pp. 16–29; "New Look in the White House," *Look,* January 2, 1962, p. 23 (first quotation); "Toward the Ideal," *Time,* September 6, 1963, p. 60 (second quotation).

65. "The First Lady and the White House," *Newsweek,* September 17, 1962, pp. 71, 72, 78 (quotations).

66. "Jacqueline Kennedy White House Tour: Lincoln Bedroom," online transcript.

67. "Jacqueline Kennedy White House Tour: Interview of Pres. Kennedy," online transcript; Maxine Cheshire, "JFK Gets Last Word on White House Tour," *Washington Post,* February 15, 1962, p. C1.

68. "Jacqueline Kennedy White House Tour: Letter from Frank Phoneme," online (first quotation); "Jackie, Igor, and Pierre," *Time,* January 26, 1962, p. 17 (second quotation); Collingwood, written comment, Jacqueline Kennedy: The White House Years exhibit (third quotation) .

69. Karen O'Connor and Larry J. Sabato, *Essentials of American Government: Continuity and Change* (New York: Longman, 2002), p. 328.

70. Carl Sferrazza Anthony, "Thelma Catherine (Patricia) Ryan Nixon," in Gould, *American First Ladies,* p. 356; Hillary Rodham Clinton, *Living History* (New York: Simon and Schuster, 2003), p. 449.

PROMOTING THE ARTS AND CULTURE

1. Mary Van Rensselaer Thayer, *Jacqueline Kennedy: The White House Years* (Boston: Little, Brown, 1967), pp. 192–99.

2. Oleg Cassini, *A Thousand Days of Magic: Dressing Jacqueline Kennedy for the White House* (New York: Rizzoli, 1995), pp. 152–58; Letitia Baldrige, *A Lady, First: My Life in the Kennedy White House and the American Embassies of Paris and Rome* (New York: Viking, 2001), p. 190 (first and second quotations); Dor-

othy McCardle, "Guests From Three Worlds Gather at the White House," *Washington Post*, May 12, 1962, p. A14.

3. Geraldine Page to JBK, letter displayed in the exhibit Jacqueline Kennedy: The White House Years, Selections from the John F. Kennedy Library and Museum, at the Corcoran Gallery, Washington, D.C., April 26, 2002–September 30, 2002 (first quotation, original emphasis); Isaac Stern to JBK, July 16, 1961, letter displayed in Corcoran exhibit (second quotation).

4. Waverly Root, "Reporter Makes Dream Come True," *Washington Post*, December 11, 1962, n.p. (first and second quotations); Frank Getlein, "Mona Lisa Due Special Care at Gallery, Kennedy Pledges," *Evening Star*, December 13, 1962, p. A2 (third quotation).

5. Press release, Office of the White House Press Secretary, January 8, 1963, Papers of John F. Kennedy, Presidential Papers, White House Staff Files, August Heckscher, Box 13, "Fine Arts: Mona Lisa," John F. Kennedy Library (JFKL; quotation).

6. Cassini, *A Thousand Days of Magic*, pp. 177–79; Hamish Bowles, Arthur M. Schlesinger Jr., and Rachel Lambert Mellon, *Jacqueline Kennedy: The White House Years—Selections from the John F. Kennedy Library and Museum* (Boston: Bullfinch Press/Little, Brown, 2001), pp. 112–13 (first quotation); "Mona Will Smile on TV Today," *Washington Post*, January 9, 1963, p. A1; postcard in author's files (second quotation).

7. "Report on Inaugural Committee Project," June 1961, White House Papers, Heckscher, Box 40, "Presidential Recognition Awards," "Artists and Intellectuals: Inauguration," JFKL (first and second quotations); Frost's poetry and Caroline's comment about her mother may be found in Caroline Kennedy's *The Best-Loved Poems of Jacqueline Kennedy Onassis* (New York: Hyperion, 2001), pp. 5, 9–12.

8. Memo from Barbara Donald to August Heckscher, November 21, 1962, Presidential Papers, "Conversation with Mrs. Kennedy," Heckscher, Box 5, Correspondence, "White House Memos," JFKL; memo to files from Nancy Newhouse, January 3, 1963, "Literary Prize Dinner by the White House," Heckscher, Box 5 (first quotation); letter from Schlesinger to JBK, January 9, 1963, Papers of Arthur M. Schlesinger Jr., White House Files, Box WH 24, "White House Library," JFKL (second quotation); "Presentation of the Presidential Medals of Freedom," program, December 6, 1963, Papers of Arthur M. Schlesinger Jr., Writings, Box W-3, "The Arts: Misc.," JFKL.

9. Marianne Means, *The Woman in the White House: The Lives, Times, and Influence of Twelve Notable First Ladies* (New York: Random House, 1963),

p. 274 (first quotation); Carl Sferrazza Anthony, *First Ladies: The Saga of the Presidents' Wives and Their Power, 1961–1990,* vol. 2 (New York: William Morrow, 1991), p. 37 (second quotation); Baldrige, *A Lady, First,* p. 188.

10. Elise K. Kirk, "Music at the White House: Legacy of American Romanticism," in Frank Freidel and William Pencak, eds., *The White House: The First Two Hundred Years* (Boston: Northeastern University Press, 1994), pp. 186–200.

11. Marie Smith and Maxine Cheshire, "2 Presidents Cruise to Mt. Vernon, Dine in Shadow of Nation's History," *Washington Post,* July 12, 1961, p. A1 (quotation).

12. Chesire, "Curtain Call Outrings that Dinner Bell," *Washington Post,* October 5, 1961, n.p. (quotation); Richard. E. Coe, "Global Event Brings Bard to East Room," *Washington Post,* October 5, 1961, p. C22.

13. David McCullough, *Truman* (New York: Simon and Schuster, 1992), p. 975.

14. "White House Bows to Immortal Casals," *Washington Post,* November 14, 1961, p. B7 (quotations); Dorothy McCardle, "Casals' Triumph Is Encore After Half Century," *Washington Post,* November 14, 1961, p. B7.

15. McCardle, "49 Nobel Guests at a Notable Evening," *Washington Post,* April 30, 1962, p. B5 (quotation).

16. McCardle, "Guests From Three Worlds Gather at the White House," *Washington Post,* May 12, 1962, p. A14 (quotation).

17. Baldrige, Oral History, April 24, 1964, pp. 122–23 (quotation).

18. Caroline Kennedy, *Best-Loved Poems,* p. 117 (quotation).

19. "A Triumph Starts Nancy on Her Way," *Washington Post,* June 4, 1963, p. A27 (first quotation); Baldrige, *A Lady, First,* p. 206 (second quotation).

20. Thayer, *Jacqueline Kennedy,* pp. 208–9 (quotation).

21. Smith, "JFK Follows an Open Door Policy on Music," *Washington Post,* August 23, 1961, p. C1 (quotation).

22. Baldrige, Oral History, pp. 98–99.

23. William McPherson, "President Kennedy Praises Bolshoi Dancers," *Washington Post,* November 16, 1962, p. D1 (first quotation); John H. Davis, *Jacqueline Bouvier: An Intimate Memoir* (New York: Wiley, 1996), p. 151 (second quotation).

24. Public Law 85-874, September 2, 1958; Smithsonian Report for 1963, *Report on the National Cultural Center: For the Period April 1959 Through June 30, 1963* (Washington, DC: U.S. Government Printing Office, 1964), pp. 234–35; "Downtown Site for Cultural Center, Not Foggy Bottom, Urged by Builders," *Washington Post,* February 22, 1962, p. A4.

25. Smithsonian Report, p. 236.

26. Dorothy McCardle, "Cultural Center Model Is Unveiled," *Washington Post*, September 12, 1962, p. C3 (quotations); Jan Pottker, *Janet and Jackie: The Story of a Mother and Her Daughter, Jacqueline Kennedy Onassis* (New York: St. Martin's Press, 2001), pp. 186–88.

27. Richard L. Coe, "Time Is Now on the Center," *Washington Post*, November 18, 1962, p. G1 (quotation).

28. Press release, Office of the White House Press Secretary, White House Papers, Heckscher, Box 40, President Kennedy and the Arts, General, "Remarks of the President and Mrs. John F. Kennedy at a Closed-Circuit Television Broadcast on Behalf of the National Cultural Center," JFKL (quotations).

29. "Remarks of the President and Mrs. Kennedy at Closed-Circuit Television Broadcast" (quotations).

30. "Remarks of the President and Mrs. Kennedy at Closed-Circuit Television Broadcast" (quotations); Pottker, *Janet and Jackie*, p. 188.

31. Smithsonian Report, pp. 235–38.

32. Press release, Office of the Press Secretary to Mrs. Kennedy, September 11, 1963, Presidential Papers, Papers of Pierre E. G. Salinger, "Press Releases," JFKL; "The Christmas Paintings of Jacqueline Kennedy: 'The Journey of the Magi' and 'Glad Tidings,'" *McCall's*, December 1963, pp. 98–99.

33. Press release, Office of Carroll D. Kearns, February 7, 1961, Heckscher, Box 36, JFKL (quotations).

34. Letter from JBK to Kearns, February 8, 1961, Heckscher, Box 36, JFKL (quotations).

35. Letter from Heckscher to JBK, October 10, 1962, Presidential Papers, Heckscher, "Mrs. Kennedy: Meetings, Memos," JFKL (quotation).

36. Memo from Donald to Heckscher, November 21, 1962, "Meeting with Mrs. Kennedy," Presidential Papers, Heckscher, "Mrs. Kennedy: Meetings, Memos," JFKL (quotation, original emphasis).

37. Memo from Donald to Heckscher, November 21, 1962 (first and second quotations, original emphasis).

38. Memo from Donald to Heckscher, November 21, 1962, "Conversation with Mrs. Kennedy," Presidential Papers, Heckscher, "Mrs. Kennedy: Meetings, Memos," JFKL (first and second quotations); McCardle, "Lawn Party and Egg Roll on Bill," *Washington Post*, March 1, 1963, p. C3.

39. August Heckscher, Oral History, December 10, 1965, p. 51 (original emphasis).

40. See Chapter 6 for JBK's June 1962 note to Walton; note from Baldrige to Heckscher, n.d., Presidential Papers, Heckscher, "Mrs. Kennedy: Meetings,

Memos," JFKL (first quotation); Means, *Woman in the White House,* pp. 269, 272 (second and third quotations).

41. Heckscher, "The Arts and the National Government," May 28, 1963, Papers of Richard Goodwin, Box 2,"President's Advisory Council on the Arts, Background Materials," JFKL; John F. Kennedy, Executive Order #11112, "Establishing the President's Advisory Council on the Arts," June 12, 1963.

42. Henry Rayment, "Richard N. Goodwin May Be Next Arts Adviser," *New York Times,* August 3, 1963, n.p. (quotation).

43. Sarah Booth Conroy, "The Lady of the Manor," *Washington Post,* Washington Home, May 26, 1994, p. 18 (first quotation); McCardle, "The Kennedys Drum Up a Dinner," *Washington Post,* May 4, 1961, p. D1 (second quotation).

44. "First Lady Selects Art for the White House," *Washington Post,* April 7, 1961, p. D3 (quotation).

45. Marie Smith, "A Big Ben Strikes Decor Note," *Washington Post,* May 3, 1961, p. C1; "White House Has Antiques Windfall," *Washington Post,* July 4, 1961, n.p.

46. Thayer, *Jacqueline Kennedy,* p. 289; "Letters from Jacqueline Kennedy to James W. Fosburgh, 1961," online (quotations); press release, Office of the Assistant Social Secretary for the Press, November 21, 1961, Salinger papers, "Press Releases," JFKL.

47. "Toward the Ideal," *Time,* September 6, 1963, p. 60; press release, Office of the Assistant Social Secretary for the Press, February 13, 1962, Salinger papers, "Press Releases," JFKL (quotation).

48. Press releases, Office of the Press Secretary to Mrs. Kennedy, December 8, 1962, December 10, 1962, January 21, 1963, Salinger papers, "Press Releases," JFKL; "How Jackie Restyled the White House," *Saturday Evening Post,* October 26, 1963, p. 46; Clark Clifford with Richard Holbrooke, *Counsel to the President: A Memoir* (New York: Random House, 1991), p. 365 (first quotation); "Toward the Ideal," *Time,* pp. 60, 67 (second and third quotations).

49. James A. Abbott and Elaine M. Rice, *Designing Camelot: The Kennedy White House Restoration* (New York: Van Nostrand Reinhold, 1998), pp. 122–27; press release, Office of the Assistant Social Secretary for the Press, June 21, 1962, Salinger papers, "Press Releases," JFKL.

50. McCardle, "This Library Plans to 'Work,'" *Washington Post,* June 22, 1961, p. B1 (first quotation); American Book Sellers Association, "The 1957 Presentation to the Home Library of the White House: A Quadrennial Gift from the Booksellers of America" (New York: American Booksellers Association, 1957) (second quotation).

51. Letter from Julian P. Boyd to JBK, October 26, 1961, Papers of Arthur M. Schlesinger Jr., White House Files, Box WH 14, "White House Library," JFKL (first and second quotations); letter from Lyman H. Butterfield to JBK, January 23, 1962, Schlesinger papers, Box WH 24, "White House Library," JFKL; letter from JBK to Butterfield, February 1, 1962 (third quotation) and memo from Baldrige to Schlesinger, February 1, 1962, Schlesinger papers, Box WH 24, "White House Library," JFKL.

52. Nan Robertson, "Books Selected for White House," *New York Times*, August 16, 1963, n.p.; letter from Schlesinger to Paul Buck, May 1, 1962, Schlesinger papers, Box WH 24, "White House Library," JFKL (quotation).

53. Handwritten notes by JBK on letter from Schlesinger to JBK, July 17, 1962, Schlesinger, Box WH 24, "White House Library," JFKL (quotation).

54. Letter from JBK to Schlesinger, January 4, 1963, Schlesinger papers, Box WH 24, "White House Library," JFKL (first and second quotation); letter from Schlesinger to JBK, January 9, 1963, Schlesinger papers, Box WH 24, "White House Library," JFKL (third quotation).

55. Letter from Babb to JBK, April 23, 1963 (first quotation), and letter from JBK to Babb, April 30, 1963 (second quotation), Schlesinger papers, Box WH 24, "White House Library," JFKL.

56. Letter from Schlesinger to JBK, May 9, 1963, Schlesinger papers, Box WH 24, "White House Library," JFKL; Robertson, "Books Selected for White House," n.p.; Felix Blair Jr., "Johnson Presses Kennedy Plan for Library at the White House," *New York Times*, February 22, 1964, n.p.; letter from Schlesinger to Babb, February 29, 1964, Schlesinger papers (quotation).

57. William V. Shannon, "A Mutual Friend," *New York Post*, n.d., n.p. (quotation).

58. Letter from JBK to William Walton, June 8, 1962, Personal Papers of William Walton, Box 1, "Letters from Kennedys," JFKL (quotations).

59. Robert J. Lewis, "President Appoints 5 to Fine Arts Group," *Washington Evening Star*, June 21, 1963, p. A1; Karel Yasko, Oral History, December 14, 1966, p. 49; letters from JBK to Walton, July 29, 1963, August 27, 1963, Walton papers, Box 1, "Letters from Kennedys," JFKL (quotations).

60. William Seale, "The Design of Lafayette Park," in *White House History* 2 (June 1997): 14–19 (quotation, 15).

61. William Walton, "An Intimate Friend Tells of JFK's Concern for Lafayette Square and Even Trash Baskets," article in Schlesinger papers, JFKL (quotations).

62. Extensive excerpts from Mrs. Kennedy's March 6, 1962, letter to Boutin, a copy of which is in John Carl Warnecke's files, appeared in Sarah Booth

Conroy, "Preserving Lafayette Square," *Washington Post,* Washington Home, May 26, 1994, pp. 16, 21.

63. Conroy, "Preserving Lafayette Square," p. 21 (quotation).

64. Conroy, "Preserving Lafayette Square," p. 21 (quotation).

65. Warnecke, Lecture, "Saving Lafayette Square: A Conversation with John Carl Warnecke," National Building Museum, July 16, 2002; phone conversation with Perry, July 31, 2002; letter from JBK to Finley, April 18, 1962, Jacqueline Kennedy exhibit, Corcoran Gallery, April 2002–September 2002 (first quotation); Bernard Boutin, Oral History, June 3, 1964, p. 24 (second and third quotations).

66. Letter from JBK to Finley (quotations).

67. Letter from JBK to Finley (quotations).

68. Paul A. Schuette, "Mrs. Kennedy Previews New Lafayette Sq.," *Washington Post,* September 27, 1962, p. D1 (first quotation); "Lafayette Sq. May Keep Its Historic Aura," *Washington Post,* October 18, 1962, p. A1 (second quotation).

69. Letter from Warnecke to JFK, October 15, 1962, Schlesinger papers, Writings, Box W-2, "The Arts: Correspondence," JFKL; Warnecke lecture; Seale, "Design of Lafayette Park," 18; Conroy, "Preserving Lafayette Square," p. 21.

70. Letter from Warnecke to Lyndon Johnson, January 24, 1964, Schlesinger papers, Writings, Box W-2, "The Arts: Correspondence," JFKL; JCWA News Clips, "Lafayette Square," spring 1965, Schlesinger papers, Writings, Box W-3, "The Arts: Correspondence," JFKL; Warnecke lecture (first quotation); Seale, "Design of Lafayette Park," p. 19 (second quotation).

71. Memo in Thayer, *Jacqueline Kennedy,* pp. 143–44.

72. Lewis L. Gould, *Lady Bird Johnson: Our Environmental First Lady* (Lawrence: University Press of Kansas, 1999), pp. 46–47 (quotations).

KEEPING THE FLAME

1. Oleg Cassini, *A Thousand Days of Magic: Dressing Jacqueline Kennedy for the White House* (New York: Rizzoli, 1995), pp. 190–91.

2. Letitia Baldrige, *A Lady, First: My Life in the Kennedy White House and the American Embassies of Paris and Rome* (New York: Viking, 2001), pp. 186, 201, 205 (first, second, and third quotations); Personal Papers of William Walton, Box 1, Letters from Kennedys 1960–64, John F. Kennedy Library (JFKL; fourth quotation).

3. J. B. West with Mary Lynn Kotz, *Upstairs at the White House: My Life with the First Ladies* (New York: Coward, McCann, and Geoghegan, 1973), pp. 264–65 (first and second quotations); "A Triumph Starts Nancy on Her Way," *Washington Post,* June 4, 1963, p. A27.

4. West, *Upstairs at the White House,* pp. 270–71 (quotations).

5. Mary Van Rensselaer Thayer, *Jacqueline Kennedy: The White House Years* (Boston: Little, Brown, 1967), pp. 208–12.

6. "Kennedy Baby Gains in Air Chamber," Edward T. Folliard, "New Device Aids Child's Breathing," *Washington Post,* August 9, 1963, p. A1; Janet Lee Bouvier Auchincloss, Oral History, September 5, 1964, p. 25 (quotation).

7. Folliard, "Kennedy Baby Dies; Private Rites Today," *Washington Post,* August 10, 1963, p. A1; John Barbour, "Baby Disease Baffling in Cause and Effects," *Washington Post* August 10, 1963, p. A6.

8. "World Grieves with Kennedys," *Washington Post,* August 10, 1963, p. A6.

9. Benjamin C. Bradlee, *Conversations with Kennedy* (New York: Norton, 1975), p. 206 (first quotation); Auchincloss, Oral History, pp. 27–28 (second quotation); Robert Pierpoint, Oral History, November 18, 1982, p. 22 (third quotation); Lloyd Grove, "Keeping Mum on 'JFK's Monica,'" *Washington Post,* May 15, 2003; Grove, *Washington Post,* May 16, 2003, p. C3 (fourth quotation); Barbara Leaming, *Mrs. Kennedy: The Missing History of the Kennedy Years* (New York: Free Press, 2001), pp. 323–27.

10. "Grecian Holiday," *Time,* October 11, 1963, p. 27 (quotations).

11. Alice Mosby, "'Captain' Kennedy Cruises," *Washington Post,* October 5, 1963, p. A10 (quotations).

12. Sarah Bradford, *America's Queen: Jacqueline Kennedy Onassis* (New York: Viking, 2000), p. 258.

13. "The Presidency: The Arabian Nights," *Time,* October 25, 1963, pp. 24–25.

14. Dorothy McCardle, "First Lady Is Back Home," *Washington Post,* October 18, 1963, p. C1.

15. McCardle, "Highland Fling Is Flung at Home of Clan Kennedy," *Washington Post,* November 14, 1963, pp. E1, E3 (quotation).

16. See Hugh Sidey, Chester V. Clifton, and Cecil Stoughton, *JFK: The Memories* (New York: Norton, 1973) for photographs of the Kennedy family's last weekend together; Jackie Kennedy's biographer, Barbara Leaming, reports that despite the seeming closeness of the family in the aftermath of Patrick's death, the president continued his womanizing in the weeks before November 22, 1963. Leaming bases this conclusion on her analysis of Secret Service logs; Leaming, *Mrs. Kennedy,* pp. 313–27. James N. Giglio offers a balanced appraisal of the Kennedys' marriage in *The Presidency of John F. Kennedy* (Lawrence: University Press of Kansas, 1991), pp. 267–71.

17. McCardle, "None Was Left Hanging on the Line," *Washington Post,* November 21, 1963, p. C1; "Chancellor Erhard Is Next," *Washington Post,* November

21, 1963, p. C1; Bradlee, *Conversations with Kennedy*, pp. 218–20 (first through fifth quotations); Baldrige, *A Lady, First*, p. 208 (sixth quotation); "Jacqueline Kennedy Onassis," *Headliners and Legends*, MS-NBC, 2001 (seventh quotation).

18. Pierpoint, Oral History, p. 22.

19. William Manchester, *The Death of a President: November 20–November 25, 1963* (New York: Harper and Row, 1967), p. 11 (quotation).

20. "First Lady on Election Trail," *Washington Post*, November 22, 1963, p. C1 (quotation); Edward T. Folliard, "Texas Democrats Spat as JFK Begins Tour," *Washington Post*, November 22, 1963, p. A2; *Four Days in November*, documentary of the assassination and its immediate aftermath, David L. Wolper (producer) 1964.

21. Kenneth P. O'Donnell and David F. Powers, with Joe McCarthy, *"Johnny, We Hardly Knew Ye": Memories of John Fitzgerald Kennedy* (New York: Pocket Books, 1973), p. 24 (first quotation); Pierpoint, Oral History, p. 22 (second quotation); *Four Days in November*, Wolper (third, fourth, and fifth quotations).

22. Conover Hunt, *JFK for a New Generation* (Dallas: The Sixth Floor Museum and Southern Methodist University Press, 1996), p. 2.

23. Nellie Connally, *Larry King Live*, CNN, July 2002 (first quotation); Nellie Connally and Mikey Herskowitz, *From Love Field: Our Final Hours with President John F. Kennedy* (New York: Rugged Land, 2003), pp. 7–8 (second quotation); Mrs. Kennedy's testimony to the Warren Commission, as quoted in Bradford, *America's Queen*, p. 268 (third quotation); Mrs. Kennedy had no recollection of climbing on the limousine's trunk; for a sequence of the assassination, see photos (some of which never before published) made from Abraham Zapruder's famous home-movie film in David R. Wrone's superb book, *The Zapruder Film: Reframing JFK's Assassination* (Lawrence: University Press of Kansas, 2003).

24. Papers of Theodore White, Box 4, Camelot Papers, White's December 19, 1963, typed transcription of notes from his November 29, 1963, interview with JBK, p. 1, JFKL (first quotation); Manchester, *Death of a President*, p. 248 (second quotation).

25. Manchester, *Death of a President*, pp. 333–34; and White, typed transcription of notes from his November 29, 1963, interview with JBK, p. 2 (quotation).

26. Chuck Lindell, "For Austinites, 'She Captured Our Hearts,'" *Austin American-Statesman*, May 20, 1994, p. A13 (first quotation); Jack Valenti, "One Day's Passage of Power," *Washington Post*, November 21, 1993, p. C7 (second quotation).

27. Edward T. Folliard, "President Kennedy Shot Dead; Lyndon B. Johnson Is Sworn In," *Washington Post*, November 23, 1963, pp. A1, A9; Maxine Cheshire, "Stoicism Made Grief Poignant," *Washington Post*, November 23, 1963, p. C1.

28. Manchester, *Death of a President*, pp. 465, 467 (first and second quotations); U.S. Supreme Court Chief Justice Earl Warren would head a special commission to investigate President Kennedy's assassination. The Warren Commission determined that Oswald, who himself was murdered two days after the assassination by a Dallas nightclub owner, Jack Ruby, acted alone. Conspiracy theorists have challenged the commission's final report, from its release to the present.

29. Manchester, *Death of a President*, p. 499 (quotation).

30. McCardle, "Mrs. Kennedy Leads Nation in Sorrow," *Washington Post*, November 25, 1963, p. C16; *Four Days in November*, Wolper.

31. Dorothy McCardle, "Each Step Was Planned Toward His Immorality," *Washington Post*, November 26, 1963, p. D1.

32. Manchester, *Death of a President*, p. 681 (quotation).

33. Manchester, *Death of a President*, p. 682 (quotation); Ellen Key Blunt, "Small Son Salutes Like a Real Soldier," *Washington Post*, November 26, 1963, p. D3.

34. Manchester, *Death of a President*, pp. 566–72.

35. Manchester, *Death of a President*, pp. 635–38; "Mrs. Kennedy Pays Night Visit to Grave," *Washington Post*, November 26, 1963, p. A1.

36. Dora Jane Hamblin, "Saying Goodbye," *Life*, December 6, 1963, in Philip B. Kunhardt Jr., ed., *Life in Camelot: The Kennedy Years* (Boston: Little, Brown, 1988), pp. 300–5; Theodore H. White, "An Epilogue," *Life*, December 9, 1963, in Kunhardt, *Life in Camelot*, pp. 314–15 (quotation); Theodore H. White, *In Search of History: A Personal Adventure* (New York: Harper and Row, 1978), pp. 517–25; Joyce Hoffmann, "How 'Camelot' Lived Happily Ever After," *Washington Post*, May 21, 1995, p. C1; Joyce Hoffman, *Theodore H. White and Journalism as Illusion* (Columbia: University of Missouri Press, 1995); Mrs. Kennedy related to White intimate details of her last hours with JFK and her reaction to his death, some of which White did not include in his *Life* essay, particularly because she edited his drafts. See Edward Klein, *Just Jackie: Her Private Years* (New York: Ballantine Books, 1998), pp. 5–21.

37. William Walton, Oral History, October 5, 1993, p. 214 (first quotation); Personal Papers of William Walton, Box 1, Letters from Kennedys 1960–64, JFKL (second quotation); Caitlin Flanagan, "Costumes from Camelot," *Atlantic Monthly*, December 2001, p. 148 (third quotation).

38. Connally and Herskowitz, *From Love Field*, p. 95 (quotation).

39. Jacqueline Kennedy Onassis, Oral History, January 11, 1974, pp. 7–8 (first quotation); Rudy Abramson, "Presidential Library: Jackie Kennedy Letter in LBJ Exhibit Reflects Warm Relationship," *Houston Chronicle*, May 29, 1982, n.p. (second quotation); White, "An Epilogue," p. 315 (third quotation); "The Capital," *Time*, December 13, 1963, pp. 25–26; "The Capital," *Time*, December 20, 1963, p. 12; Maud Shaw, *White House Nannie: My Years with Caroline and John F. Kennedy, Jr.* (New York: New American Library, 1966), pp. 163–76.

40. Donald Spoto, *Jacqueline Bouvier Kennedy Onassis* (New York: St. Martin's Press, 2000), p. 218 (first quotation); Richard M. Nixon, *RN: The Memoirs of Richard Nixon* (New York: Grosset and Dunlap, 1978), pp. 254–55 (second quotation); "Jacqueline Kennedy Onassis," *Headliners and Legends*, MSNBC, 2001; Benjamin C. Bradlee, *A Good Life: Newspapering and Other Adventures* (New York: Simon and Schuster, 1995), p. 262 (third quotation).

41. Caryle Murphy, "Jackie Kennedy's Spiritual Crisis: Diary of Priest Reveals Widow's Thoughts of Suicide," *Washington Post*, November 13, 2003, p. C1.

42. Bradford, *America's Queen*, p. 304 (quotation).

43. Letter from Stevenson to JBK, May 30, 1964, and letter from JBK to Stevenson, June 15, 1964 (first quotation): both letters are contained in the Adlai Stevenson Papers, Box 47, Folder 2 "Jacqueline Kennedy," Seeley G. Mudd Manuscript Library, Princeton University; Billy Baldwin, "Jacqueline Kennedy Onassis: A Memoir," *McCall's*, December 1974, p. 26 (second quotation); Evan Thomas, *Robert Kennedy: His Life* (New York: Touchstone, 2000), p. 285.

44. Note from Stevenson to JBK, September 16, 1964 (first quotation); note from JBK to Stevenson, April 1965 (second quotation): both are contained, along with the newspaper clipping from an unknown French newspaper, in the Stevenson Papers, Box 47, Folder 2 "Jacqueline Kennedy."

45. "Center May Be Named for President Kennedy," *Washington Post*, November 26, 1963, p. D2 (quotation); "Ground-Breaking Ceremony on the Site of the John F. Kennedy Center for the Performing Arts," Program, Papers of Arthur M. Schlesinger Jr., Private Files, Box P-4, Kennedy Center for the Performing Arts: Correspondence—Hecksher-Kennedy; Box P-5, Tuckerman-Wisner, JFKL; "John F. Kennedy Center for the Performing Arts," Friends of the Kennedy Center, n.d.; "The John F. Kennedy Center for the Performing Arts," brochure, 2002.

46. Spoto, *Jacqueline Bouvier Kennedy Onassis*, pp. 218–19 (quotation).

47. "Summary of Preliminary Meeting of Committee on Arts and Architecture for the Kennedy Library," p. 5, Personal Papers of William Walton, Box 3, JFK Library 7, JFKL (quotation; original emphasis).

48. Dan H. Fenn Jr., "Launching the John F. Kennedy Library," *American Archivist* 42 (October 1979): 429–42; John Carl Warnecke, "John F. Kennedy on Architecture: A Legacy and a Challenge," draft article, June 17, 1964, Papers of Arthur M. Schlesinger Jr., Writings, Box W-3, "The Arts: Reports," JFKL; Perry interview with Warnecke, July 31, 2002.

49. Jacqueline Kennedy Onassis, "The Bright Light of His Days," *McCall's*, November 1973, pp. 81–82 (quotation).

50. Spoto, *Jacqueline Bouvier Kennedy Onassis*, p. 220; Personal Papers of Richard Neustadt, Box 15, Harvard University Institute of Politics, JFKL; information on the Institute of Politics is available at: http://www.iop.harvard.edu/.

51. John Carl Warnecke and Associates, *News Clips*, "Kennedy Grave," spring 1965, p. 1; Perry interview with Warnecke, July 31, 2002; "Creating the Kennedy Gravesite with Master Mason Peter 'Billy' Cleland," June 13, 2002, Washington National Cathedral, brochure and lecture; R. A. Zaldivar, "She Chose the Site Years Ago," *Philadelphia Enquirer*, May 22, 1994, p. A8.

52. Papers of White, Box 4, Camelot Papers, White's December 19, 1963, typed transcription of notes from his November 29, 1963, interview with JBK, p. 4, JFKL (first and second quotations).

53. Memo from Schlesinger to JBK, n.d., Papers of Arthur M. Schlesinger Jr., Writings, Box W-7, Jacqueline B. Kennedy Correspondence, JFKL (quotation).

54. Michael R. Beschloss, *The Crisis Years: Kennedy and Khrushchev, 1960–1963* (New York: Edward Burlingame Books, 1991), p. 473 (quotations).

55. William Manchester, "William Manchester's Own Story," *Look*, April 4, 1967, pp. 62–77; Note from JBK to Schlesinger, November 23, 1965, Papers of Arthur M. Schlesinger Jr., Writings, Box W-7, Jacqueline B. Kennedy Correspondence—1965, JFKL (quotation); Jackie was not immune from books written about her by members of her own staff. J. B. West's *Upstairs at the White House* and Tish Baldrige's *Of Diamonds and Diplomats* (New York: Ballantine, 1968) were generally positive reflections on working with Mrs. Kennedy. Baldrige was slightly more critical of the first lady in her updated memoir, *A Lady, First*, but she published it seven years after Jackie's death. Mrs. Kennedy's personal secretary, Mary Barelli Gallagher, published the most reproachful publication on her former boss. *My Life with Jacqueline Kennedy* (New York: Paperback Library, 1970) portrayed Jackie as an imperious, selfish spendthrift.

56. Manchester, "William Manchester's Own Story," pp. 62–77; Bradlee, *Good Life*, p. 400.

57. Bradford, *America's Queen*, p. 320.

58. Onassis, Oral History, pp. 16–17 (quotations); Hugh Sidey, "Jackie Onassis' Memory Fragments on Tape," *Time*, April 24, 1978, p. 30.

59. Baldwin, "Jacqueline Kennedy Onassis," p. 26 (first quotation); Cheshire, "Mrs. Kennedy Weds on Rainy Greek Isle," *Washington Post*, October 21, 1968, p. A1; Lee Radziwill, *Larry King Live*, CNN, 2001 (second and third quotations).

60. Note from JBK to Schlesinger, May 28, 1965, Papers of Arthur M. Schlesinger Jr., Writings, Box W-7, Jacqueline B. Kennedy Correspondence—1965, JFKL (quotations).

61. Aaron Shikler, "The Painting of a Legend," *McCall's*, March 1971, p. 127 (first quotation); Christopher Matthews, *Kennedy and Nixon: The Rivalry that Shaped Post-War America* (New York: Simon and Schuster, 1996), pp. 292–95 (second, third, and fourth quotations; original emphasis).

62. "Galella Promises to Avoid Onassis," *Austin American-Statesman*, March 25, 1982, p. A2.

63. R. W. Apple Jr., "Last Farewell to Jacqueline Kennedy Onassis," *New York Times*, May 24, 1994, p. A1 (first quotation); Edward M. Kennedy, "The Texts of Personal Tributes and Poems at the Services for Mrs. Onassis," *New York Times*, May 24, 1994, p. 10 (second quotation).

64. Tim Page, "At 30, Kennedy Center Is Ready to Grow Up," *Washington Post*, September 8, 2001, p. C4; Jacqueline Trescott, "Kennedy Center Picks Architect for Expansion," *Washington Post*, January 23, 2003, p. C1; Benjamin Forgey, "A Welcome Sign: Design Plan Would Give the Kennedy Center New Connections," *Washington Post*, January 23, 2003, p. C1; Marc Fisher, "At Kennedy, a Little Jazz Music," *Washington Post*, January 30, 2003, p. B 1; Kennedy Center informational film, narrated by Caroline Kennedy, 2002 (Kaiser quotation).

65. "The John F. Kennedy Library and Museum," brochure; "Kennedy Library Programs," brochure, fall 1998; Paula Span, "Monumental Ambition," *Washington Post Magazine*, February 17, 2002, pp. 29–30 (first, second, and third quotations).

66. Memo from Baldrige to Arthur Schlesinger, General Ted Clifton, General Godfrey McHugh, Captain Taz Shepherd, J. B. West, Evelyn Lincoln, Bill Elder's staff, and Anne Lincoln, May 29, 1963, Papers of Arthur M. Schlesinger Jr., Private Papers, Box P-6, Jacqueline Kennedy Correspondence, JFKL (quotations); Corcoran Art Gallery attendance figures provided by the gallery's Press Office, July 2003.

67. Harvard University John F. Kennedy School of Government, available at: http://www.ksg.harvard.edu/.

68. "John Fitzgerald Kennedy, Jr., 1960–1999," *Time* Commemorative Issue, July 26, 1999; "Charmed Life, Tragic Death, John F. Kennedy, Jr. 1960–1999, Carolyn Bessette Kennedy, 1966–1999," *People,* August 2, 1999; *George* farewell issue, vol. 6, no. 1, March 2001; Edward Klein, *The Kennedy Curse: Why Tragedy Has Haunted America's First Family for 150 Years* (New York: St. Martin's Press, 2003); Elizabeth Kastor, "'You Just Keep Going,'" *Good Housekeeping,* October 2001, pp. 148–51, 182–84; Caroline Kennedy, "The Courage Within," *USA Weekend,* June 7–9, 2002, pp. 5–8; Caroline Kennedy, ed., *Profiles in Courage for Our Time* (New York: Hyperion, 2002); Caroline Kennedy, ed., *A Patriot's Handbook: Poems, Stories, and Speeches Celebrating the Land We Love* (New York: Warner Books, 2003); Caroline Kennedy, ed., *The Best-Loved Poems of Jacqueline Kennedy Onassis* (New York: Hyperion, 2001).

69. Marianne Means, *The Woman in the White House: The Lives, Times, and Influence of Twelve Notable First Ladies* (New York: Random House, 1963), p. 268 (first quotation); Ellen Levine, "Laura Bush: An Intimate Conversation," *Good Housekeeping,* February 2003, pp. 92, 94 (second and third quotations); "Jacqueline Kennedy Onassis," *New York Times,* May 21, 1994, p. 12 (fourth quotation).

70. Nixon, *RN,* p. 503 (first quotation); *Newsweek,* January 1, 1962, p. 35 (second quotation).

BIBLIOGRAPHIC ESSAY

MANUSCRIPTS

Jacqueline Kennedy's papers and oral history at the John F. Kennedy Library in Boston are closed. Apparently, the papers are not embargoed but simply have not been organized for use at the JFKL. The oral history will remain unopened for fifty years after Mrs. Kennedy's 1994 death or until her last surviving child (Caroline Kennedy) dies. Collecting documentary information on Mrs. Kennedy, therefore, necessitates a systematic search through other collections at the JFKL. Very few files marked "Jacqueline Kennedy" exist, so researchers must painstakingly sort through other people's papers to unearth correspondence from or references to the first lady. The library's Web site (http://www.cs.umb.cdu/jfklibrary/) contains an annotated list of archival holdings.

Only partially useful are the White House Social Files, contained in the Presidential Papers of John F. Kennedy, which include a small amount of correspondence documenting Mrs. Kennedy's activities and interests as first lady. The bulk of these files, however, consists of correspondence with the general public, particularly invitations, requests for photographs and autographs, birthday greetings, sympathy cards and messages, and requests for advice about hairstyles, fashions, etc. Security concerns in the aftermath of the September 11, 2001, terrorist attacks have necessitated closing material related to restoration of the White House in the White House Central Files. The papers of Clark Clifford, advisor to President and Mrs. Kennedy, opened recently but were unavailable for research because the library did not have more than one copy of the microfilm reel that contains Clifford's correspondence with the first lady.

The papers (official and personal) of White House staffers during the Kennedy administration are currently the richest sources of material on Jacqueline Kennedy. White House Press Secretary Pierre Salinger's files contain all press releases for the Kennedy administration, including those under the heading of the assistant social secretary for the press. Pamela Turnure served in that position, whose title changed to press secretary for the first lady in 1963. Unfortunately, the JFKL has no Turnure papers, and her oral history, with Nancy Tuckerman, Mrs. Kennedy's second social secretary, is closed. The Salinger papers also contain lists of Mrs. Kennedy's scheduled official (and occasionally unofficial) activities for 1961, 1962, and the first four months of 1963 (after which the first lady stopped most official appearances because of her pregnancy). The press releases are an excellent source of information on Mrs. Kennedy's White House restoration and state entertaining.

Without doubt, Arthur Schlesinger Jr.'s papers (Writings and White House Staff Files) offer a gold mine of material on his work with Mrs. Kennedy. True to his academic and history pedigrees, Professor Schlesinger, a special assistant to President Kennedy, maintained comprehensive files, meticulously labeled and carefully organized. They are indispensable for piecing together the story of his and the first lady's contributions to the White House guidebook, the White House library, the arts, the National Cultural Center, and the Kennedy Library. In addition, he maintained a warm relationship with Jacqueline Kennedy, and she seemed comfortable revealing her private thoughts and impish sense of humor to him. Another helpful collection is that of August Heckscher, President Kennedy's special consultant on the arts. Although his files contain no direct correspondence from Mrs. Kennedy, he kept detailed memos and letters regarding arts policy during the Kennedy Administration. The comprehensive report that he prepared on arts in the United States is a superb resource. The papers of Richard Goodwin, who was to succeed Heckscher as special consultant to the president, a succession truncated by JFK's assassination, provide some material on the arts. The papers of Sanford Fox, chief of the White House Social Entertainments Office, offer scrupulously compiled files of White House entertaining, complete with guest lists and programs of entertainment. Bernard Boutin, administrator of the General Services Administration, corresponded with Mrs. Kennedy on the Lafayette Square project; unfortunately, the microfilm on which this material is contained is another victim of 9/11—it has been removed from public circulation for security reasons. Bill Walton, a mutual friend of the Kennedys, their informal arts consultant, and, eventually, chair of the Fine Arts Commission, kept less systematic but fascinating files, particularly correspondence from the first lady. Her handwritten letters and notes to him are the most personally revealing of any available. Journalist Theodore White's papers contain handwritten notes and a typed script of his interview with Mrs. Kennedy one week after the assassination. Forty years beyond November 1963 they are still poignant and shocking in their vivid detail. Professor Richard Neustadt's papers provide enlightening information on the establishment of the Kennedy Institute of Politics and the Kennedy School of Government at Harvard.

A number of oral histories at the JFKL, available through interlibrary loan, offer fascinating accounts of Jackie Kennedy's life, as well as the Kennedy administration and Mrs. Kennedy's role in it. Among the most revealing are those by Janet Auchincloss, Tish Baldrige, Charles Bartlett, Bernard Boutin, Angier Biddle Duke, August Heckscher, Jacqueline Kennedy Onassis (1974 interview conducted by the Lyndon B. Johnson Library), Robert Pierpoint, Marion Cannon Schlesinger, Stanley Tretick, William Walton, J. B. West, and Karel Yasko. The Kennedy Library's Web site contains a complete list of its oral histories.

Archival materials on Mrs. Kennedy's participation in the her husband's 1960 presidential campaign are disappointingly few. Although the future first lady's campaign activities were limited because of her pregnancy with John Jr., she did participate in a variety of ways. The JFKL staff maintains a file of her "Campaign Wife" columns, published in newspapers on a syndicated basis by the Democratic National Committee. The Prepresidential Papers of JFK include correspondence on his state-by-state political activities; some letters refer to his wife's appearances with him. Newspaper stories about Jackie's work for her husband are the best sources for determining what she did on a daily basis. Robert Drew's documentary, *Primary,* a 1960 film about the Wisconsin presidential primary election, offers rare video footage of Mrs. Kennedy campaigning for JFK in the Dairy State.

A small but delightful collection of Mrs. Kennedy's and Adlai Stevenson's correspondence is available in the latter's papers at the Seeley G. Mudd Manuscript Library at Princeton University.

BIOGRAPHIES AND SECONDARY WORKS

Because Jacqueline Kennedy penned neither an autobiography nor a personal memoir, two authorized books about her take on special worth. Mary Van Rensselaer Thayer, a journalist, received cooperation from Mrs. Kennedy on the book, *Jacqueline Bouvier Kennedy* (New

York: Doubleday, 1961). Reportedly, Jackie turned over scrapbooks and other biographical documentation to Thayer and even edited her drafts of the book. Thus, while the slim volume is not an objective account, it represents how Jacqueline Kennedy wanted the world to view her life up to the time she entered the White House. The *Ladies Home Journal* and the *Washington Post* serialized the book in early 1961. After her husband's death, the widowed first lady gave Thayer access to her official papers. The book that resulted in 1971, *Jacqueline Kennedy: The White House Years* (Boston: Little, Brown, 1967), while by no means a critical assessment of her first ladyship, provides numerous verbatim re-creations of Mrs. Kennedy's correspondence, most of which is still unavailable to researchers. A compilation of quotations by and about Jacqueline Kennedy, along with biographical narrative, constitute Carl Sferrazza Anthony's 1997 tribute, *As We Remember Her: Jacqueline Kennedy Onassis in the Words of Her Friends and Family* (New York: Harper Collins, 1997). The most recent comprehensive and balanced biography of the former first lady is *America's Queen: The Life of Jacqueline Kennedy Onassis* (New York: Viking, 2000), by Sarah Bradford, which contains voluminous material from her interviews with Kennedy family, friends, and associates. Donald Spoto's *Jacqueline Bouvier Kennedy Onassis: A Life* (New York: St. Martin's Press, 2000) is another popular recent biography.

Jackie's cousin, John H. Davis, includes a wealth of Bouvier family history in *The Bouviers: Portrait of an American Family* (New York: Farrar, Strauss, and Giroux, 1969; revised 1993). His *Jacqueline Bouvier: An Intimate Memoir* (New York: Wiley, 1996) describes stories of Jackie's childhood and early adulthood to which only a family member would be privy. C. David Heymann was among the first to interview a wide assortment of Kennedy associates for his biography, *A Woman Named Jackie* (New York: Birch Lane Press, 1995, revised edition). Jan Pottker's *Janet and Jackie: The Story of a Mother and Her Daughter, Jacqueline Kennedy Onassis* (New York: St. Martin's Press, 2001) focuses on Jackie's relationship with her mother Janet Auchincloss. Several books dissect the Kennedys' marriage. An intriguing photo essay of a very young Jack and Jackie during the first year of their marriage can be found in *Camelot at Dawn: Jacqueline and John Kennedy in Georgetown, May 1954* (Baltimore: Johns Hopkins University Press, 2001). *Jack and Jackie: Portrait of an American Marriage* (New York: Avon Books, 1996), by Christopher

Anderson, presents a sensationalized account of the troubled union. Edward Klein, a self-described friend of the former first lady, wrote *Just Jackie: Her Private Years* (New York: Ballantine Books, 1998) about her personal and professional life after the White House. Film biographies include *Jackie: Behind the Myth,* produced by Suzanne Bauman for PBS, and A&E's *Jacqueline Kennedy Onassis.* Caroline Kennedy's *The Best-Loved Poems of Jacqueline Kennedy Onassis* (New York: Hyperion, 2001) is a touching collection of her mother's favorite poetry, with remembrances by the first lady's daughter.

Jacqueline Kennedy's life with JFK is revealed in biographies of him, or histories of his presidency, by Michael R. Beschloss, *The Crisis Years: Kennedy and Khrushchev, 1960–1963* (New York: Burlingame Books, 1991); Robert Dallek, *An Unfinished Life: John F. Kennedy, 1971–1963* (Boston: Little, Brown, 2003); James N. Giglio, *The Presidency of John F. Kennedy* (Lawrence: University Press of Kansas, 1991); Doris Kearns Goodwin, *The Fitzgeralds and the Kennedys: An American Saga* (New York: St. Martin's Press, 1987); Ralph G. Martin, *A Hero for Our Time: An Intimate Story of the Kennedy Years* (New York: Macmillan, 1983); Herbert S. Parmet, *Jack: The Struggles of John F. Kennedy* (New York: Dial Press, 1980); Geoffrey Perret, *Jack: A Life Like No Other* (New York: Random House, 2001); and Richard Reeves, *President Kennedy: Profile of Power* (New York: Simon and Schuster, 1993).

Volumes of books on the 1950s and 1960s are available for placing Jacqueline Kennedy's life into historical, political, and social contexts. David Halberstam's *The Fifties* (New York: Villard Books, 1993) is a popular narrative of that decade. Several histories connect the Kennedy administration to its era. Scholarly works include Irving Bernstein's *Promises Kept: John F. Kennedy's New Frontier* (New York: Oxford University Press, 1991) and W. J. Rorabaugh, *Kennedy and the Promise of the Sixties* (New York: Cambridge University Press, 2002). Journalistic accounts include Theodore White's *The Making of the President 1960* (New York: Signet, 1961) and Christopher Matthews' *Kennedy and Nixon: The Rivalry that Shaped Post-War America* (New York: Simon and Schuster, 1996). Robert MacNeil's coffee-table book, *The Way We Were: 1963, the Year Kennedy Was Shot* (New York: Carroll and Graf, 1988), provides a pictorial essay of American culture in that watershed year. Interesting studies of women's and family history are Stephanie Coontz, *The Way We Never Were: American Families and the Nostalgia*

Trap (New York: Basic Books, 1992); Nan Enstad, *Ladies of Labor, Girls of Adventure: Working Women, Popular Culture, and Labor Politics at the Turn of the Twentieth Century* (New York: Columbia University Press, 1999); Sara M. Evans, *Born for Liberty: A History of Women in America* (New York: Free Press, 1989); Miriam Horn, *Rebels in White Gloves: Coming of Age with Hillary's Class—Wellesley '69* (New York: Anchor Books, 2000); and Glenna Matthews, *"Just a Housewife": The Rise and Fall of Domesticity in America* (New York: Oxford University Press, 1987). A host of books intriguingly examines the role of image, symbolism, and celebrity in American culture and politics: Daniel J. Boorstin, *The Image: A Guide to Pseudo-Events in America* (New York: Vintage Books, 1992); Leo Braudy, *The Frenzy of Renown: Fame and Its History* (New York: Oxford University Press, 1986); Lewis L. Gould, *The Modern American Presidency* (Lawrence: University Press of Kansas, 2003); Barbara Hinkley, *The Symbolic Presidency: How Presidents Portray Themselves* (New York: Routledge, 1990); Joyce Hoffman, *Theodore H. White and Journalism as Illusion* (Columbia: University of Missouri Press, 1995); Thomas S. Langston, *With Reverence and Contempt: How Americans Think About Their President* (Baltimore: Johns Hopkins University Press, 1995); Bruce Miroff, *Icons of Democracy: American Leaders as Heroes, Aristocrats, Dissenters, and Democrats* (Lawrence: University Press of Kansas, 1993, 2000); and Richard Schickel, *Intimate Strangers: The Culture of Celebrity* (Garden City, NY: Doubleday, 1985). Other studies specifically focus on the Kennedy image: Thomas Brown, *JFK: History of an Image* (Bloomington: Indiana University Press, 1988); John Hellmann, *The Kennedy Obsession: The American Myth of JFK* (New York: Columbia University Press, 1997); Paul R. Henggeler, *The Kennedy Persuasion: The Politics of Style Since JFK* (Chicago: Ivan R. Dee, 1995); Wayne Koestenbaum, *Jackie Under My Skin: Interpreting an Icon* (New York: Farrar, Strauss, and Giroux, 1995); Vito N. Silvestri, *Becoming JFK: A Profile in Communication* (Westport, CT: Praeger, 2000); and Gary Wills, *The Kennedy Imprisonment: A Meditation on Power* (Boston: Little, Brown, 1981).

Scholarship on first ladies includes examination of Jacqueline Kennedy's tenure in the White House, along with studies of her predecessors and successors. These works consist of Carl Sferrazza Anthony, *First Ladies: The Saga of the Presidents' Wives and Their Power 1789–1961* (New York: Quill/William Morrow, 1990); Betty Boyd Caroli, *First*

Ladies, expanded edition (New York: Oxford University Press, 1995); Lewis L. Gould, ed., *American First Ladies: Their Lives and Their Legacy*, 2nd ed. (New York: Routledge, 2001); Edith P. Mayo and Denise D. Meringolo, *First Ladies: Political Role and Public Image* (Washington, DC: National Museum of American History, 1994); Gil Troy, *Mr. and Mrs. President: From the Trumans to the Clintons* (Lawrence: University Press of Kansas, 2000); Robert Watson, *The Presidents' Wives: Reassessing the Office of First Lady* (Boulder, CO: Lynne Rienner, 2000); and Watson and Anthony J. Eksterowicz, *The Presidential Companion: Readings on the First Lady* (Columbia: University of South Carolina Press, 2003). Marianne Means's *The Woman in the White House: The Lives, Times, and Influence of Twelve Notable First Ladies* (New York: Random House, 1963) is journalistic but particularly interesting because it contains an interview with President Kennedy about his wife. Lewis L. Gould's article, "First Ladies," in *American Scholar* 55 (autumn 1986): 528–35, analyzes the celebrity status of presidential spouses.

Three memoirs by JBK's social secretary, Tish Baldrige, recall the first lady's travel, fashion, entertainment, and administrative habits: *Of Diamonds and Diplomats* (New York: Ballantine, 1968); *In the Kennedy Style* (New York: Madison Press/Doubleday, 1998); and *A Lady, First: My Life in the Kennedy White House and the American Embassies of Paris and Rome* (New York: Viking, 2001). J. B. West, head usher in the Kennedy White House, covers his working relationship with Mrs. Kennedy in his book *Upstairs at the White House: My Life with the First Ladies* (New York: Coward, McCann and Geoghegan, 1973). Two coffee-table books devoted to Jacqueline Kennedy's fashions are Hamish Bowls, Arthur Schlesinger Jr., and Rachel Lambert Mellon, *Jacqueline Kennedy: The White House Years—Selections from the John F. Kennedy Library and Museum* (Boston: Bullfinch Press/Little, Brown, 2001) and Oleg Cassini, *A Thousand Days of Magic: Dressing Jacqueline Kennedy for the White House* (New York: Rizzoli, 1995). Memoirs of Kennedy associates include Benjamin C. Bradlee's two volumes, *Conversations with Kennedy* (New York: Norton, 1975) and *A Good Life: Newspapering and Other Adventures* (New York: Simon and Schuster, 1995); Clark Clifford, with Richard Holbrooke, *Counsel to the President: A Memoir* (New York: Random House, 1991); Mary Barelli Gallagher, *My Life with Jacqueline Kennedy* (New York: Paperback Library, 1970); Kenneth P. O'Donnell and David F. Powers with Joe McCarthy, *"Johnny, We*

Hardly Knew Ye": Memories of John Fitzgerald Kennedy (New York: Pocket Books, 1973); Pierre E. G. Salinger, *With Kennedy* (Garden City, NY: Doubleday, 1966); Maud Shaw, *White House Nannie: My Years with Caroline and John Kennedy, Jr.* (New York: New American Library, 1966); and Arthur M. Schlesinger Jr., *A Thousand Days: John F. Kennedy in the White House* (New York: Fawcett Crest Book, 1965). A recent study of Mrs. Kennedy's years in the White House is Barbara Leaming's *Mrs. Kennedy: The Missing History of the Kennedy Years* (New York: Free Press, 2001). A pictorial retrospective on the Kennedy White House can be found in Philip B. Kunhardt Jr., ed., *Life in Camelot: The Kennedy Years* (Boston: Little, Brown, 1988). Journalist Maxine Cheshire's memoir, *Maxine Cheshire, Reporter,* with John Greenya (Boston: Houghton Mifflin, 1978), describes how the Washington press corps covered the Kennedys.

Several recent works on the White House provide informative histories of the Executive Mansion: Frank Freidel and William Pencak, eds., *The White House: The First Two Hundred Years* (Boston: Northeastern University Press, 1994); Betty C. Monkman, *The White House: Its Historic Furnishings and First Families* (Washington, DC: White House Historical Association, and New York: Abbeville Press, 2000); and William Seale, *The White House: The History of an American Idea* (Washington, DC: White House Historical Association, 2001). *White House History,* the journal of the White House Historical Association, publishes scholarly articles on the president's home and surroundings, including Lafayette Square. The definitive history of Mrs. Kennedy's redecoration of the White House is *Designing Camelot: The Kennedy White House Restoration* (New York: Van Nostrand Reinhold, 1998) by James A. Abbott and Elaine M. Rice.

Jacqueline Kennedy's reaction to her husband's assassination is chronicled at length in William Manchester's epic, *The Death of a President: November 20–November 25, 1963* (New York: Harper and Row, 1967), and briefly in Theodore H. White's *In Search of History: A Personal Adventure* (New York: Harper and Row, 1978). *JFK for a New Generation* (Dallas: The Sixth Floor Museum and Southern Methodist University Press, 1996), by Conover Hunt, explains the Kennedy assassination for readers who have no personal memories of it. David L. Wolper's contemporary documentary of the assassination and its immediate aftermath, *Four Days in November* (1964), is a stunning black-and-white film. The most recent study of JFK's murder is *The Zapruder Film: Reframing JFK's Assassination* (Lawrence: University Press of Kansas, 2003) by David R. Wrone. Nellie Connally's gripping eyewitness account of the assassination from the last surviving passenger in the presidental limousine is presented in her book (coauthored with Mickey Herskowitz) *From Love Field: Our Final Hours with President John F. Kennedy* (New York: Rugged Land, 2003).

INDEX